One Writer's Journey

A TIME TO LEARN

A MEMOIR

CANDICE GIBBONS

Book #3 in the *Times* series

A Time to Learn

Copyright © 2024 by Candice Gibbons

Published by Writing Momentum LLC

Print and ebook formatting by Writing Momentum LLC

Cover photography by Allison Gibbons

Cover design by Lauren Short

All rights reserved.

Printed in the United States of America. All rights reserved under the International Copyright Law. Contents and/or cover may not be reproduced in whole or in part in any form without the expressed written consent of the author.

Scripture quotations marked (NLT) are taken from the *Holy Bible, New Living Translation*, Copyright © 1996, 2004, 2015 by Tyndale House Foundation. Used by permission of Tyndale House Publishers, Inc., Carol Stream, Illinois 60188. All rights reserved.

Scripture quotations marked (NIV) are taken from the *Holy Bible, New International Version®*, NIV® Copyright ©1973, 1978, 1984, 2011 by Biblica, Inc.® Used by permission. All rights reserved worldwide.

Scripture quotations marked (ESV) are taken from *The Holy Bible, English Standard Version*. ESV® Text Edition: 2016. Copyright © 2001 by Crossway Bibles, a publishing ministry of Good News Publishers.

Scripture quotations marked (NCV) are taken from *The Holy Bible, New Century Version®*. Copyright © 2005 by Thomas Nelson, Inc.

WHAT GIRLS ARE SAYING ABOUT THE TIMES SERIES

Reading *A Time to Trust* was so refreshing. I loved how relatable the book was, as well as the spiritual aspects included.

—Brooklyn, age 16

I loved *A Time to Stand*! It helped me see that having blues about moving doesn't just happen to me, and that even in times of seemingly endless stress, God always shows a way through. It's an amazing book!

—Shylah, age 13

These books have taught me so, so much as I've read them, especially how to trust the Lord even if His plans for you aren't exactly what you were expecting, and how to be firm in your faith, even when situations become overwhelming.

—Aylie, age 14

I love Candice's books! They challenge me to trust the Lord even when life feels impossible! Reading her words about her life experiences makes me feel like I know her on a deeper level. I can hardly wait for the next thing she writes!

—Raegan, age 16

I absolutely loved *A Time to Trust* and *A Time to Stand* because of the trueness and authenticity that is shared. It makes the books super relatable and emotionally intriguing.

—Hannah, age 19

CONTENTS

Author's Note — xi

Previously in the Times Series — 1

PART ONE
COGITO, ERGO SUM

1. Feux d'Artifice — 9
2. Dancing in the Fire — 23
3. Blue-Collar Job — 41
4. The Consequence of Ideas — 55
5. Explicitly Childhood — 71
6. The Making of Candiceyland — 89

PART TWO
ACTA NON VERBA

7. Jo Writes — 111
8. Rebel Intro — 121
9. Lockdown — 129
10. An English Summer — 133
11. It's Just Entertainment! — 147
12. The Executive Office — 173
13. News That Stays News — 195
14. Finish, Candice! — 201

PART THREE
AD MELIORA

15. Michaelmas Begins — 213
16. A Modern Poet — 221
17. You Think Like a Camera — 233
18. The London Stage — 243
19. You're Like a Journalist, Candice — 261
20. Surprised by Riley — 277
21. Run Club — 289
22. Look Up, the Sky Lies Open — 305

Acknowledgments	311
About the Author	313
End Notes	315

for the girl who's ready to become

The realm of becoming is the realm of change.
—*RC Sproul*

AUTHOR'S NOTE

It is with great pleasure I present the most true-to-life *Times* book yet to appear in the series, as most names and places have not been changed. *A Time to Learn* is a compilation of ten handwritten journals, including real dialogues and selected travel diaries. Not every life-changing moment that occurred in my life between ages 16 to 21 was included in this book, so if an era ends mysteriously, its conclusion was either uninteresting or presently too raw, hence a string to be pulled when my journals are later published. Some conversations within *A Time to Learn* are true in spirit of multiple occasions; some parts curated for optimal reading and cohesive storytelling. But as a whole, you will read real names and conversations, so I hope you enjoy the authenticity. One final note: as *A Time to Learn* encompasses five years of life, it is recommended to be read slowly, one chapter at a time.

Take note on coincidences.

Candice

PREVIOUSLY IN THE TIMES SERIES

The quiet town of Ozark in the purple state of Missouri is where I lived for my first sixteen years of life. The word *Missouri* has always been the color purple in my mind, as are most *M*-words, probably due to some chart of the alphabet I was shown as a child. Home reflected in everything from Ozark's green exit signs to the tunnel of trees leading to our happy yellow cottage up a hill in the woods. I was the oldest of six and firstborn grandchild of twenty-plus cousins, and both roles afforded many barefoot adventures. We watched cows line the fence at breakfast and rode horses on acres of family-owned farmland. We built houses, laid sod, and carved our names in the cement of those houses, marking our legacy.

Then the foundation cracked.

Suddenly, life in Missouri was on the brink of expiring, and it was all rather unexpected. Everything hurried to a climax. One set of cousins moved away. A faithful oak tree snapped. Close friendships ended. Lights literally began flickering in our always-warm cottage, and water flooded beneath its squeaky floorboards. A finale loomed over everything normal, predictable, and safe. But the invisible signs scared us the most.

Prophecies were spoken over our family by four different people, two being a visiting electrician and a lady from out of state we barely knew. The common message was change was coming—change I interpreted as moving away. *Moving* became the dreaded *M*-word of my freshman summer.

More personally alarming, I dreamed that I was sent to a school with a checkered-floor hallway. I saw an image of me running on a track. Not only did this sound impossible for a homeschooler with five screws in her feet, it was rather scary, far too cinematic for real life. Everything about it seemed artificial—red dye spilling on my organic childhood. We weren't the kind of family that moved—not houses across town, and certainly not to different states. People told us that moving would demonstrate our obedience to follow God and we would be blessed. To a fifteen-year-old not yet interested in leaving for college, I was more than skeptical. I was horrified. How would our family's act of obedience to an invisible God lead to blessings? What kind of blessings would they be? Were they even worth it?

Then the prophecies came true.

My father told us to pack up. My father, who loved Missouri's memories—*his* home, *his* family—stuck a FOR SALE sign in the very sod he laid. My logical father, whom I deeply trusted and viewed as exceptionally wise, told me to trust God even more than my own perspective. He accepted a job offer in Oklahoma.

I, Candice, was accepted into a private school. It had a checkered-floor hallway. I immediately joined track and field.

As shocking as it was to witness a dream come true (good or otherwise), fear set in like the first tip of my foot into an icy, moonlit lake.

Moving was like losing a friend. Lots of friends. I did not think I would cry over Ozark banks, pharmacies, and gas station chains, the ease of smooth gray-blue roads or the coolness of grass between toes, but I missed everything. Some people in my family never looked back; I couldn't look forward.

I could not look forward to making new friends; I didn't want any.

I could not look forward to a new school; I was too scared.

I could not see myself feeling comfortable … ever.

But I moved, and I trusted God.

It took six months to realize it was because God loved us that my family had to leave the violet state of Missouri for red dirt Oklahoma. I didn't have to like it, and I certainly didn't need to understand it. Once you learn to trust God, you realize He will never leave you.

Being a 'light' may sound abstract, but it became quite tangible to me, bringing choices like breaking cliques and befriending students from alternative crowds at my intimidating new private school, even running circles around a track with searing foot pain. I wasn't liked. I wasn't having fun. But I was in the right place. That was what the dream meant. That was why I was sent to private school: to become awake to myself, alive to the feelings of others, and active in the work of God. By the end of my first semester at private school, I was making friends, winning awards, and finally feeling comfortable being myself. My fear of suffering, fear of sacrificing, diminished. But as the harsh spring softened to a healing summer, I felt the door to private school was closing to me.

Why would God suddenly change everything again?

It was the same chill of Missouri expiring. In January leaving private school would have sounded like an escape. By May it felt like loss. Why would I not stay and finally savor high school, become a cheerleader, and do all the things I had persevered to enjoy? Would I now simply return home and dig my heels into books? How would I make friends or even date?

These are all serious questions for a soon-to-be junior, especially one who doesn't know what she wants to do with her life.

But I cannot follow what is expected of me during high school. What I traded my newly thriving life at private school for I have no idea, but once I decided to wholeheartedly follow God, I could not pretend to turn deaf when I felt like He told me to leave.

Sometimes it is easier gripping onto what you have rather than admitting there is a time for everything, and the end may come sooner than you think. Sometimes it is easier to think what was granted to you for a season is yours for a lifetime, but that isn't true. So here we launch into my junior year of high school with no friends or really anything, except I am bringing my spiritual history with me, trusting the pattern of *obedience leading to sacrifice, which will lead to great blessings.*

PART ONE
COGITO, ERGO SUM
(I THINK, THEREFORE I AM)

*What fun is there in isolated dedication
to study and growth???*
—Journal #4, 16 years old

CHAPTER 1
FEUX D'ARTIFICE

10th grade summer, Ozark, Missouri

I accept all challenges!!!
—*Journal #4, 16 years old*

Four months post-private school I have black hair and a tan. That first one was an accident.

The drama of having artificially colored hair officially began three months ago in June, right after my sophomore year ended at private school, which is rather comical considering it was in June of last year the winds of change swept in and six months later I was packing cardboard boxes and shipping my life to Oklahoma. Sometimes I really wonder if life is a movie.

Everyone said my hair was fine. I was even fine with it; I just wanted it a shade darker. A *shade*. Burnt-toast Candice quickly realized how drastic her attempt to boost her appearance backfired, and unfortunately, the consequences were not easily reversible.

Contrast this to last summer: I was a freckled fifteen-year-old, slightly less self-conscious, and my only worries were moving to Oklahoma and making friends at school (of course those things were big, but appearance is *everything*). This wasn't my grandmother-the-dyer's fault; this was me; thinking I could artificially rise to a stronger level of maturity or magnetism without calculating how the dye may interact with my natural hair color. Mentally, having a darker shade of brown hair represented deeper wisdom and discernment, beauty and influence, height and refinement, and perhaps even a romantic boost.

None of those things happened.

In fact, it reversed every good and humble aspect that elucidated natural charm.

Betrayal of oneself is subtle. I thought it was an improvement, but it was another *I*-word: *invasion*. When it was time for the exciting dye, I played double-crosser to the real Candice. I had never attempted something so daring, so drastic!

How fun it is being a teenager! I had thought. *I've got nothing to lose!*

But as the formula was poured and my head fell backward, my heart raced and skin itched. I felt so dirty and wrong, pushing for the unnatural. And at the hair reveal, I realized my toast wasn't just burnt, it was in flames.

This is called taking blessings into your own hands.

Was trying to alter my God-given appearance an external communication to the world I didn't like who I was, validation that I really wasn't good enough?

Or perhaps this was simply a milestone in my journey of 'becoming,' one that inevitably required risk and consequence? Was this necessarily a bad thing?

I thought about this while staring at the disaster in the mirror, realizing that, unlike some fortunate girls, I was not one on which black hair fit well.

Invisible headlines appeared in my mind:

CANDICE GIBBONS GOES REBELLIOUS AND DYES HAIR BLACK. REPUTATION RUINED.

[Interlude for how shunned Candice felt at this time.]

The tan came later. I certainly didn't mind that change. Tanning was gradual, and unlike my hair, it wasn't artificial. But paired together, I felt so un-Candicey. My family is fair-skinned and mirrors the characters and storyline of the classic book *Little Women*, add two additional Amy and Laurie characters, and none of us five girls had ever done such a thing as *dyeing their hair* apart from my mother's bleaching treatments. This wasn't some unspoken family illegality, but it certainly made me, the firstborn rule follower, not only feel but look darkly incriminated. Not that dying my hair was bad, but my attempt to 'find myself'' felt more like I was losing the real me.

I, Candice Marie Gibbons, am the girl who tucks the corners of her sheets and who is endeared to Mozart concertos. I am not merely a rule follower; I make the rules. Every child who has come after me in this eight-person family has looked up to this brown-haired ISFJ with won respect.[1] *What would they think now?* I thought guiltily.

Ashamedly, I don't recall asking for permission. When I realized that I must call my parents, a rare combination of Enneagram Ones, the same generous parents who paid for my personalized bath towel and continue paying for me to eat spinach frittatas every morning, the flames of self-reproach rose into a furnace of hot-cheek embarrassment.[2] Appealing to parental pathos did nothing. I could see them laughing and thinking back to their southern childhoods skating in the streets. Back in that day, you never showed your bruises. Just be home by dark …

No, this is my consequence. They won't fund any hair repair expense.

My heart sunk lower as the phone rang.

How low can one's heart sink? Surely it would stop somewhere. I thought. But somehow it kept falling further and further, reminding me of my spirit's void of self-worth and purpose. How did I know my parents would not support the Clear Candice's Guilt campaign? We may be a notably visible family, slightly exemplary and quite literally pastoral, but we are not pharisaic. This was my fault, and I would have to endure looking like a rebel as long as it took.

After an unsuccessful call with my parents, I escaped my grandmother's house where it all went down to run the neighborhood trail and cry, a common coping mechanism. Actually, I didn't cry aloud. It takes a lot for that. My emotions tend to spread inverse wings in inopportune settings, like laughing during funerals. The good cries happen most frequently during movies, ones that aren't always sad but more directly impactful. Otherwise, Candice has very unfitting crying moments, like in elementary schools or empty auditoriums.

No, this particular run heard an inward cry: *Candice, you just ruined your life.*

Running has become more than a coping mechanism; in one sense, it saved my life.

I had situational depression while I was at private school. Never heard of it before, prior to moving. Two U-hauls later, and I was the one crying in the counselor's office pouring out things from my childhood, which was, overall, a pleasant one. Until last year, life was spent inside a warm, yellow cottage as the third head in a household of eight built on freedom's cornerstone, which basically meant popsicles and prairie dresses and *Anne of Green Gables*. All of that is distant ash. We now live in a gray rental house in Oklahoma; no one is the same.

When we moved and I joined private school, I also signed up for track and field. Not because I was good at running—I had five screws in my feet—but because I needed to run. Isolated running against the wind toward a distant sewer plant smell trained me to recognize that through purposed steps of sacrificing comfort, you find your greatest confidence. You don't have to see the blessings; you just need to put one foot in front of the other and trust God through the process. This mindset was difficult for an idealist, someone who heavily relied on her friendships for security, her home for comfort. But we had already moved, and I had already decided to give God every part of my life. I learned there is one thing that fulfills: having a relationship with Jesus—a personal, ongoing relationship, not propped on any religion—and this continues to completely anchor and fulfill me. So while I can still slip into melodramatics whether with black hair or a self-inflicted lack of wisdom in general, I recognize God is in control of the world, and He really cares about the details of my life. And He is already blessing us for moving to Oklahoma. We are building a house! My parents decided on blue as the exterior color instead of the gold stucco chosen for our old cottage. I don't mind because blue represents grief, and I also sense it entails loyalty. I hope it will be steady ground to start a new life, but my main assurance is that what I have done by leaving private school is no accident.

If you follow God, you can expect obedience and sacrifice on your part, followed by a blessing on God's part. And so I know more blessings are ahead.

That is, if I don't ruin them by my own foolishness.

It is August before my junior year of high school, and I am in Orlando, Florida, still with slightly black hair but mostly over the guilt. Celebration certainly feels due after the scars of moving, renting, and private schooling. To leave Oklahoma City behind, where sirens wail and traffic sears, is complete bliss.

I arrived in the land of sunshine by road tripping with my younger sister Kelly Grace, our cousin Weston, and our grandparents—the ones who live on Riverview Ranch, where we grow tomatoes and such—whom we call Gigi and Poppy. We drove through Mississippi and Georgia on our way to Poppy's business-related conference and a student fine arts competition held at the same convention center. We have enjoyed this tradition bi-annually since I was twelve. Traditions stabilize.

It has been a lovely barefoot vacation. We visited both beach and mountain, tipping to a sky-view of Georgia in a gondola lift, riding around in an open train and car, splashing in foamy waves, and forgetting where we're going down light-extinguished streets. We savored Krystal burger eating contests, midnight Krispy Kreme stops, and arguments over which gas stations are safe, followed by crime news-watching that somehow makes it into your dreams. Apart from being scared to go to the bathroom at night, even that has been fun.

We enjoyed staying everywhere from the elegant Gaylord Resort to the Evergreen Hotel overlooking pines and water. Kelly Grace, whom I call Kelly or even Kel, is my best friend, and we are within one month of being considered Irish twins. She is an ethereal songbird and ecclesiastical scholar. Kelly, like the delicacy of the double *L*s in her name, has long, naturally silky blond hair (and we all know what I have). After we enjoyed kayaking alone in mountain silence, we met Pensacola's ombre sky for beach-view breakfasts where we drank in orange juice and sunshine and then retreated to our very own hotel room—such luxury!—where Kelly read and I wrote. She tells me to be a writer I must read. I tell her I don't like books.

Teen writers from across the United States now surround me hopeful for the Award of Merit title granted to the best writing entry at the National Fine Arts Festival. The nervousness I have over scoring well amuses me. I always feel a bit inferior competing, not being a reader or academic student, but here I am, looking official with a lanyard and participant badge while standing at a table draped in black, dotted with white papers of contest entries. One of them has my name on it.

I started participating in writing competitions at thirteen. I recall my first taste of criticism from a judge commenting about my book chapter being 'not what girls talk like,' which would have been fair, given it wasn't historical fiction. Whether it was my own neglect of research or them missing the point, I eventually tried my hand at First Person Essay, which brought me to Nationals this year, and they can't say my essay isn't what teenagers experience because it is literally my life.

As a writer, especially being a writer about my own life, I know I need to get over insecurities quickly. Making my life an open book is not my personality type, but because my life has felt like a movie the last year, I thought, *why not let others enjoy it?* Memoir is my genre, or life-writing, as it is called. Writing about moving to Oklahoma was something that started in my journals, and now, someone is reading my Oklahoma Award of Merit-winning essay titled *Obedience, Sacrifice, and Blessings.* It won the top score in the state-level competition.

I can't watch.

What am I doing being a memoirist! Here is my life story—plopped down on the table, my low and embarrassing moments explicit. It's a relief to see it stapled. It already feels rather *exposing* looking at the cover page.

As I casually walk away from the writer's section in the exhibit hall so as to allude I am completely unrelated to the author, my mind wanders down the checkered-floor halls of the private school I was locked inside for five months, mere days after shipping my grand sixteen years of life to Oklahoma.

When you first attend private school, it does not take long to learn whose family is wealthy and who is just lucky to just be there, which was me. I say *family* because of course the kids did not make millions. The school had an all-access digital directory which allowed you to look up everyone's houses, and so you quickly learned who had money and eventually found out why. One annoyingly attractive kid I sat by in World History had a dad who was a dentist. As haunts the nightmares of most sixteen-year-old girls, his dad became my dentist, and with a salient grin he talked about how he made his empire the entirety of the time it took to extract my molar.

"Dad, are we rich?" The boy asked.

"I'm rich; you're not," the dentist told his son, choking down a laugh.

That may very well be true, and it should have comforted me, but for those of us who walked around with other kids wearing their parents' money, this truth did not debase invisible hierarchies. Parental affluency, along with high academic expectations, fell on the student body just like the splash of Valentino met you in the locker room littered with Lulus. Yes, even if you were a reject from the popular crowd due to lack of social or personal awareness, you at least had your parents' credit card to treat you and your average friends to a round of Starbucks every morning, Ventis and all.

Student high hopes were even expressed verbally with such a degree of self-airs it made you wish you had the talent, or at least the confidence, to announce at the lunch table as one average sophomore so casually did, of plans to attend Pepperdine. Some wore Harvard sweatshirts. That bold act would have scared me unless I had been accepted into the empire itself. Thankfully *we* were never one of those families. Mom and Dad have *never* put pressure on me to be a straight-A student, which is good, because otherwise I'd be a failure. I am barely surviving math—as in barely surviving the math that I am a grade behind in.

At this thought I circle back to the writers' table where, again, I don't feel like I belong. It is true I don't read. It is true I don't like books or academics. I am not so keen on going back to Missouri to attend my dream university in my parents' footsteps. I sort of assumed a position to go there since I wore their maroon cheerleader's uniform as a preschooler, proudly attending tailgate parties in middle school, pretending as though I was 'beyond' high school football games. Last year I met their English professor as well as another tall, brown-haired writer who agreed we were destined to be roommates. It all seemed so perfect, so expected. I am not saying I am against the idea, but considering everything upside down that occurred in the last year and two months, I have no lean towards a particular school. Oklahoma has me friendless with no future expectations to uphold, but unfortunately, any relishing feeling those words should bring isn't there.

A girl approaches me with tears in her eyes. She tells me that she is in her season of sacrifice, that reading my essay gave her hope she'll make it through it.

Yes, she will, if she relies on God. I think, listening to her share.

Could I really encourage someone with my simple story of moving?

It may very well be a book someday, but for now, I just want to get back to my room. I am tired of the noise, the attention, the explaining. I should be honored and others-focused. I have been, I promise. I am also just an introverted sophomore.

It's one thing to write about your story, but another thing to defend yourself verbally on the spot. It's weird when people question the validity of your personal experience. To a degree, it's like, "Well, I can tell you it happened, but I can't explain why." And you hope they don't think you're crazy. But when you follow God, you won't always be understood. I guess that will be true for the rest of my life. As long as He is happy with me, I have no guilt from anything or obligations to anyone. Tomorrow we go to Disney World, and I find out my final placement and score for my essay, announced at a ceremony called the Celebration Service—a very fitting name for the winners, very unfitting for losers. *Le suspense!*

My family and I just toured Southeastern University in Lakeland, Florida. It was on my parents' list for me to explore. I went with eyes wide open, feeling like a real junior with all the airs of a private school student. But then we met with the admissions office, and all airs left me the moment they asked for my embarrassing ACT score. As we toured the campus, all I could think about was how it was so serenely fitting for someone else. Palm trees proportionally planted. Buildings cream and blocky, golden from the eastern sun. The food court even has a convenient Chick-fil-A and their workout room has cushioned floor and mirrored walls.

My parents ask, "Do you think you'll go to college here?" and I don't know. It is a wonderful school, I just don't know if I am a good fit. Being an idealist, I guess I will never like any option completely, and between you and me, I don't even know if I could get in anywhere. But all of this is not for me to discern ... not in one day, at least.

Oh Lord, I can't base any of this off my own thoughts or perceptions.

In the harsh world of driving, dentistry, and ACTs, holding a gold medal in sensitivity is not an asset. I really don't care about the scholarship prize allotted to the first-place winner of the National Fine Arts Festival because, again, I don't know if I will go to college. I am one of those people who just likes the certificate with 'Superior' on it. It is probably a pride issue or an identity deficiency—or both.

Speaking of identities, now that the rest of my immediate family has flown to Florida for a little family vacation, I don't know why I am surprised that staying together in this random orange Airbnb feels more natural than living in Oklahoma. Perhaps this is because I have escaped the confusion of wondering where my life was going. I'm just here to have fun! All I really, really, want is to feel good—to be myself again, but better. And I feel like I'm on the brink of finding out how.

I received my rudimentary results for my First Person Essay—three straight 39s! This means there is a high percentage I will have one of the top scores in the nation! There is always the possibility others who scored Superior made a perfect score of all 40s. But can you believe that! To be entering the phase of blessing, which I think that is what is coming next, is so exciting I can hardly wait to see what is about to happen.

Oh no.

I hear a yell downstairs. "Bria is in the hospital!"

Tiny dramatic footsteps pound up the stairs to hunt me down. "Candice, come help, we have all these groceries and Mom's not here."

I fling myself off the bed and throw my journal in a pile of clothes. Journaling time is consistently interrupted, but this appears to be a worthy cause. "Don't worry; I'm coming." I run down, still thanking the Lord for three 39s!

The rest of the night I clean, cook, and lead the four children left behind as my parents take action on the health crisis.

I am not sure why I am surprised that someone in our family is ill, but why now? I guess I thought summer magically had a way of making people healthy again. Why can't we have a normal vacation? Everything, and I mean everything, under the category of health has been continuously under attack.

Oftentimes people don't connect the physical and the spiritual, but when you follow God, you join sides with light and darkness becomes your adversary, waiting to shoot you at your weakest point. This year alone, Dad was in the hospital—I almost thought he was going to die. In addition to severely debilitating back pain, his heart continued palpitating, and he developed shingles from stress. Mom is still depressed in a far deeper sense than the situational depression I had in the spring; Kelly has had fainting spells and nose bleeds; and then Allison, my fourth sister, has had terrible flu-like reactions to stress caused by a rare autoimmune disorder.

Now we are here in Florida, supposedly the happiest place on earth. Bria, whom I call Brother, is the rock of our sisterhood, and always willingly volunteered to play the boy when we played make believe as sisters. I used to call her the 'brother we never had' (although this is technically no longer accurate after we were made into a six-kid family). Contrastingly, Bria is the most stunning Gibbons girl, and could easily pass as a famous glamorous actress. Now she has been admitted into a hospital with the norovirus. Poor Mom, who's had a crazy year herself, is at the ER with Bria. And poor us ... No, I shouldn't think like that. I was going to say the trip could take a total detour. We could spend the rest of vacation in the hospital. We might not make it to the Celebration Service. But really, how disoriented Brother must feel in a humid, white-walled room amidst tropical wall décor. *Lord, help her.*

These days of dense heat and mist have a way of submerging one into selfishness, and I kind of accept it. Clad in a Mickey Mouse shirt that unattractively shrunk in the wash, I have been wandering around by myself, looking for myself, in the Disney sunset for what feels like years, or maybe just since last June. I watch girls link arms with friends, taking pictures that will be shared and liked. I think, *At least you have family, Candice,* but it hardly consoles. I don't have friends, or social media, or really anything but this melting mango drink in my hand.

Upon boarding with my family in our orange condo, my parents have been in and out of the hospital with Bria, still intensely sick. Yet even they prioritized today to be something necessary for the half of us, something to serve like a statement to our continuously fragmented family. Mom, who isn't well herself, has been caring for the unwell, and is now here, pretending to be well. Mom, who wants Missouri back more than any of us, is walking around with Minnie Mouse ears, pointing and smiling at a man with a handful of balloons. Fake joy.

No. That kid over there likes it. Maybe there is value in plastic. Some things you just have to blow into to make special. Some outings you go on—like Mom—for the well kids looking for a stable parent. Even when all the air has been puffed out of you. Even when you've been hit unconscious. I marvel at her and despair at myself in one sigh. It's like we're held in mid-air, breath sucked in.

Who am I? Why am I here? Where am I going?

"Can you sketch my profile?" This is the only question-mark thought I say aloud to the lady who draws your silhouette for a price. Who pays for a sketch of their profile? Me! Is it worth it? Who cares!

This is the tipping point of my summer: sitting up straight with my nose tilted in the air like a cartoon rat, hot and adrenalized and unarmed. I am surprised and deflated at how much the sketch resembles me—not the me I imagine myself to be, but the real me.

I guess it's better to be disappointed in the real Candice than horrified at an artificial one.

I am hopeful of the me I am becoming, the me that can now at least compare itself to this sketch of my sixteen-year-old self and have a starting point for this project.

Some girls are aware of what they look like before they are allowed to wear makeup. Then there are girls past that age who are still vague about the idea of who they are, and that is me. It isn't as though I had never seen a picture of myself, but I really don't *know* what I look like. Having been on the other end of vanity growing up, I need to be more self-aware. Girls my age are either becoming sophisticated or purposely unrefined. I know at some point I will have to choose how to dress and talk, but perhaps not today. This is primarily because I have no role model. Deep down, I desire to have beauty and elegance, but I am afraid of what that actually means for Candice per the black hair incident. Do I even have the capacity to be refined? Private school may have enhanced me, but how much of 'you' can really change, anyway?

The same bronzed legs that ran 400-meter sprints in the spring now make their way back to my family. I take hold of my darling Angel's hand, eight years old, so delicate and unaware of all I learned at private school. I remember her despondent face when I announced I was going to private school. I remember returning home from track practice to homework and noise at a table sprinkled with crumbs, fighting with a heavy math textbook before plates were passed and dinner commenced. Those were such painful attempts of normalcy as a family. The nights we didn't feel like family at all. The times I wondered who these people even *were*.

Angel and I approach our discombobulated family as they eat ice cream. Now there is a delicious childhood expression of Candice. I *was* an ice cream cone. Peppermint and birthday cake were my flavors, double-scooped, just as rollercoasters and escalators and ziplines were associated with my face. Anything that was in some way adventurous or unconventional was mine. Anyone would have been lucky to have been invited to one of my wild birthday parties to eat off a donut tower or a flaming bowl of swirly cotton candy. Worm hospitals after storms, makeshift elevator shafts, secret hideouts, and strategic pranks were all on the list of pastimes if you were one of my many chosen friends in elementary school. Like being the oldest of five girls for my first twelve years, all of my friendships fell under a sort of dynastic order. I led, they followed. I was the one who insisted on being Queen Candice at dress up time, not interested in being any of the pre-existing princesses. If it was October 31 and we were all to dress as pretty princesses in plastic heels with a cartoon face in the center, I wanted no part in it. No, I wanted a *real* queen outfit in royal blue and gold. Further revealing of my divided self, if boy cousins came over and offered an adventure involving mud and a dog, I left the girl games entirely.

Are all of these mirrors really distant ash? Or perhaps this image of an artificial princess face really does reveal what has never been and will never be my aim: *of course* I won't go to college or do anything conventional. *Of course* I will struggle at defining adult Candice because she will always be rediscovering childhood.

I don't even know if worms live in Oklahoma, or if I will ever find friends. But the ground is bare for new life all the same. Though it may only be meant for the cacti that can survive without water.

We made it to the Celebration Service just in time for the award ceremony. I feel absolutely electric standing in the dark auditorium to the left of the concert stage wearing a lanyard, jumper, and a ribbon in my hair taken from the belt of a dress.

Oddly untangled, exceptionally free.

Unfortunately, Brother is feeling worse. (Rumor has it, out of exhaustion, Mom crawled in her hospital bed and cut off her intravenous cord, and machines started beeping and the room filled with nurses.) But instead of acting sullen and feeling medically obligated to intervene, which I still feel, I try to enjoy the night.

Dad drops me off and tells me to be a carefree teenager. To have parents who care about such things is a blessing I neither deserve nor fully appreciate. But here we are.

Southeastern University's songwriters open tonight's ceremony by singing their new release, "Fire in My Bones." I try to not think of it as a sign that I should attend their university just because they're here in front of me, although the song is making a mark on this trip.

"And the top three scores for First Person Essay are …"

"Candice! Look—it's your name on the screen!" Kelly points.

I can't believe it! I place top three in the nation for First Person Essay!

Fire in my bones—that is it. A new rekindling and reconciliation of my former self—that ten-year-old Candice who really did think anything was possible. Even if it is small, I feel it.

I trusted God by moving to Oklahoma.

I endured the loneliness of private school.

And here I am—winning top three in the nation for the very story that broke me.

I go to an uncrowded section left of the stage and sink down to my knees, giving God full permission to use my talents. I would gladly give up anything 'Candice' to have Him by my side—yes, even non-Candicey things that may sound cool due to being 'different' from me. I don't want anything artificial or temporary or distracting from the real me. Even if I don't know who that is yet, I can reject what I know is *not* for me, if I will continue asking God to give me wisdom. In the bumps on my arms, I feel God's peace and joy as if He is saying, "I am here." That is better than making top three.

Whatever is ahead will be big and bright and dark like tonight—like fireworks, *feux d'artifice*, I can feel it. I surrendered my life to God no matter the cost. I am only sixteen. The adventure is just beginning. Who *knows* what is to come!

CHAPTER 2
DANCING IN THE FIRE

11th grade fall, Edmond, Oklahoma

I can't take this passively.
—*Tedashii*

There is no escape to the luxury of living the unexamined life—not when you are sixteen and friendless and your mom is in a hard season. In this case, the unexamined life is living without struggle or forethought, strategy or mantle, a life I thought would be merited to these last two months of my very eventful sixteenth year. Basically, more blessings. Merely a week ago I was barefoot and lying on the beach, lazing on the highs of placing top three in the nation, ready to sit back and reel in the blessings. It was a feeling of success I had not really felt since running sunburnt in April. Even that high was more like a blurry, overdue reward post-pain, a whirling color wheel of track meets and finals and parties with cheerleaders as I spun out of loneliness and into what many high schoolers get to enjoy without sweating. Yet I knew *that* much was over once I said to the school, "Sorry, I won't be coming to the cheerleaders' bonfire or attending the Junior-Senior brunch next fall," which is such a bummer. I can't even keep the friends I was making at private school. Do you know how awkward it was when I had to explain why

I was leaving private school after only five months? My parents weren't making me leave. I even got my math grades up. Did I make a mistake?

No, it was time to leave—time in the God-timing sense. Time in the *Candice doesn't want it to be time but knows it is time* sense. If only people understood you can't make this up!

Driving home through the Arkansas hills, I set my mind on how I could redeem that season of sacrifice through some sort of, I don't know, documentary or something. I believed I was out of the eye of the storm, given I wasn't depressed or disillusioned about life. My identity was returning, even if it was as slow as the reappearance of my natural hair color. *Yes, I am very stable.* I thought, curling my legs under the blanket in the car. Rope bracelets, ginger soda, and word searches made up that drive. Basically, nothing important.

Should I write a book? How does one even *do* that?

I figured it would all come to me as soon as the trip ended. I half-expected a surprise to be waiting in a package at our rental house door, perhaps a sign saying WELCOME HOME, GIBBONS FAMILY with the keys to leave my gray shared room and enter a land of colors and space and light … alone. Maybe I couldn't go back to private school, but I could enjoy the promise of getting out of this rental house and having my own room, or even some other unexpected blessing. I'm up for surprises—I'll take anything at this point!

It must've had a shipping delay. What waited on me instead was the news that I shouldn't get too comfortable because I must apply for my first job. *How do you do that?*

As if finding a suitable source of income isn't enough pressure—one that requires the least amount of physical and social labor for an introverted sixteen-year-old—my dear mother, the one that just yesterday stormed out of the house to get away from us, also has me enrolled in three online college course classes with that cream-colored Southeastern University. I know that isn't unheard of, but considering the rocky season I am in, why would she do this to me?

Maybe this is the perfect time …

No. It can't be. I don't need nine credits. I need *friends*.

We stand in the master bedroom as she relates the news. Online boredom isn't the issue. I don't think I can *do* college. I don't even know what a credit *is*.

"There are a lot of things you don't know that you'll need to learn in life," she says.

But nothing is screaming at me to become a nerd. Nothing is in logical order in this house. Contrary to our old house, we don't have a functioning library, and I don't even have a desk in my room. Learning in the off-road sense is so unattractive. If I were to really become an academic student, I'd want to look the part and have the proper setting, unlike this very room that serves as four people's bedrooms and Dad's office. In our old house, the master bedroom was ideal, perfected with a pentagonal ceiling tiered three levels and windows overlooking the cottage grounds. Mom used to spread an old quilt on the grass where bonnets would be untied and violins plucked as she read from a classic in the winds of fall …

Mom yells at five-year-old Jordan to get out of the fridge.

The refrigerator is full of artificial lunches and rainbow-colored popsicles.

"Whatever happened to healthy food?" I follow her into the kitchen.

"I've been a little busy," she says. "You're the one who needed easy food for school."

I can't argue. I actually enjoy scarfing down Lunchables on those dreary school days. It was so unlike my organic childhood. It was so unlike me, or her. But now, there is too much foreign in my life and I actually miss the days of health and order and routine. Why can't our house just hurry up and get here? On the other hand, why can't we go back to Missouri where everything was so simple and normal and happy?

"What college classes am I taking this fall?" This is the only question I say aloud.

"Literature, history, and philosophy, I think," Mom recalls.

"How do I access these classes?" I try to sound inquisitive, not lazy.

"I don't know baby," she says. "Figure it out."

Many philosophies hit me at once. First of all, Mom used to help with these kinds of things. Secondly, I have a nagging side cramp philosophy has much to do with reading and memorization. I can read, but I can't comprehend. I can write, but I can't remember. *Am I ready to be a philosophical failure?*

Even before we hit start on this program, we have a problem. Where am I going to do school in this house? To even get my high school diploma I'll certainly need a school desk, now that I am not in the American private school paradigm.

I mention to Mom this is a sensible expense I am sure we could afford as she shuffles around the kitchen. Her hands, fair and piano-elegant and sparkling with her wedding ring, are coarse. She won Miss American Teen with those fingers.

"You can work just fine at the kitchen table like you did for homework last spring." She sounds like a deflated balloon.

"Do you realize how distracting that is?"

Her eyes say: *"Figure it out."*

I get back to what has me on my tip toes. "Any updates on the house?"

"Your dad and I haven't talked about it." She snaps back.

Another bummer. My sock is wet from a neglected ice cube on the floor. My breath holds for three seconds. I start to sweat.

Back to self-preservation.

"Is there anything else life-changing I should know about?" *As if.*

"You will go to an in-person co-op one day a week like you did in Missouri. The rest of the time, you will do your college classes at home. I know it isn't fun, but it's necessary."

What's necessary is that Candice finds friends again. Here is another disappointing reminder I am no longer a popular, independent cheerleader. Technically I never committed to cheer, it was just fun having the idea thrown around. At least at school I was working on a friend circle. A homeschool co-op sounds like the reverse of anything new and exciting and progressive. Sure, it may be academically rigorous, but that's definitely not on my priority list, and it certainly doesn't make the cut on Make Candice's Life Fun list.

Did I get the equation wrong? This is supposed to be a season of blessing—not a new season of sacrifice. Haven't I spent enough time stressed and friendless?

I can't think about it. I go on a run.

This rental neighborhood is like an ant maze. Steep, short hills. Sharp corners. If you recall our old neighborhood up a hill in the woods, you can see where my mind lapses as I trudge up this first incline in the most unfitting running outfit imaginable.

I don't have anything good for running. My track shoes have the soles cut out to fit a pair of foot inserts for my poor feet, pinned together by five screws after double surgery just over two years ago. Running track in the spring was a miracle. Anything in addition, I am supposedly crazy. But crazy is *not* running when life is falling apart.

I wish I were a real runner. I wish I could run in the right shorts, run with actual friends, run without holding my phone, run without dying ... all the things real athletes enjoy. But I don't even know where to start. I don't know how to get there. I am only sixteen! I don't even have social media! How in the world will I make it in life? *Why am I even running up these hills!*

Two more months until our new home is finished. Two. Whole. Months. It isn't just a building; to me, our new house has been a castle in the sky. The walls went up. The pipes were connected. The dump trucks arrived and poured pure, brown dirt to evenly distribute the sloped surface of our lot. Dirt that smells like home. Dirt that could be our steady ground for starting a life not sucked in and held midair. It's right down the road, ten minutes east, ironically back in the direction of Missouri.

I thought surely once the stairs were added and the smell of sawdust deliciously filled the air, we were close. It has been more exciting than a countdown to Christmas!

Imagine Christmas getting moved again and again like a bad

dream. Delayed doesn't mean denied, but it also doesn't mean delivered. And a delayed delivery is concerning.

The home is in a relatively beautiful neighborhood, and I say *relative* only to our neighborhood in Missouri, an ancient, wooded castle drive. The blue English cottage is nearly a replica of our old-world European cottage in Missouri, except it will have black doors, white walls, and brown beams, in contrast to the yellow and cream of my childhood home. Someday I will get to add my future Jeep in an additional garage—a Jeep that will be earned with this new unknown job of mine. This all may sound exciting, but it also feels scary and far away. I don't even want to drive, and I couldn't care less about having my own garage. This is because we got our first offer from someone interested in buying our old house today. If only you grew up in the yellow cottage. If only you knew how much it symbolized our happy family. Thinking about how this really concludes the end of childhood, I can't celebrate our new house at all.

Besides that, other things are falling apart, too. Big Roy the Suburban broke down, and Mom exploded three times today. Bria is in hospital again with complications from the norovirus. Jordan is bursting with 5-year-old rebellion. Mom and Dad leave tomorrow for four days, which means I'll be head of the house. Dad is so overloaded with work, the house, and his back pain. Can all that be going on and I just watch?

Of course not! I run faster up the incline in the neighborhood.

Thoughts deserve action attached. If I am to spiritually fight for our family to stay focused and united, it will have to be won physically, too.

After my run, I tape sticky notes to the back of my empty bookshelf that have these main concerns written in bold: Dad, Mom, our house, the family, me. My plan is to move the sticky note down a level when I sense things are changing. I have faith to see things actually change. Sticky notes aren't permanent.

I am more mentally stable than I have ever been in life. I read the Bible in the morning and at night; I quote it and believe it and change because of it. Tonight I will pray for wisdom to know exactly what to do, how to do it, and when to find the time to do it; for college, for my job, for our house to finish; and I also just pray in general for everyone who feels like me or worse. Mom is in a worse season than me. Bria is in the hospital.

I thank God for my bed tonight and pet my dog, Charlie, to sleep. I know God hears me and that He won't leave us in this bracket of prolonged stress because He promised us blessings if we obeyed Him. And not-yet blessings don't mean non-existent blessings.

Ran again. I can't say anything is better necessarily, but at least we are closer to our new house, even if it is by a week. I have to admit how hopeful it sounds: acreage, woods, secret passageways and ziplines, perhaps … my imagination turns it into a castle. Why not!

Running gives me plenty of time to dream. I can't wait for the temperature to drop to the 70s of fall. It has always been my favorite season, perhaps because my birthday is at the prettiest peak, the third week of October. The air is warm and breezy, then cold—a sweet, humid taste of rain mixed with pumpkin spice. Fall equals a new grade and even new school sometimes, like this year. It means a fresh routine, studying late at night, football games, and, historically, Candice's birthday parties with ice cream cake …

How do I plan a birthday party without friends?

Farewell, mental image of my high school self: laughing to tears, dancing unashamedly, singing in the car with friends, sharing long bus rides, and wearing a school t-shirt to football games with popcorn in hand. This is what I traded at private school for these college classes and a real job. What makes it worse is this is one of those Friday nights I knew was coming—the first football game at my old private school—and here I am about to spend it in my room with this journal.

I had a better life in Missouri. At least I had friends who were homeschooled too. But I realize I am thinking from a sixteen-year-old girl's perspective, not like how God probably sees all of this. The Israelites complained about their captivity in Egypt, then about being hungry in the desert after God helped them escape. The fact that I haven't died in Oklahoma—the fact that God did give me a great last month at private school should be something I thank Him for.

Journaling is a very real escape—a real-time documentation of how I am going to get out of this place. I don't understand how God works, but I won't try to force any blessings as if I did not trust Him to care for me. I don't need a new home to thrive. Everything won't magically change just by moving into a new room. I embrace these rental house cabinets with no handles. I learn from the steep neighborhood hill and driveway bumps that grow increasingly annoying. There *has* to be a reason why I am homeschooled again this year. I just don't know why yet.

Thunder hints of rain outside the windows. The smell of apple cinnamon muffins fills the kitchen. It's a cloudy Sunday, a dark, humid morning, and I, the sixteen-year-old 'mother of the house,' feeling clever and poetic, have just cleaned up the last of the baking utensils. Wind wings the familiar cluster of chimes we brought from our home in Missouri. The porch overlooks nothing. *At least we have a fence.* I correct my negativity. I've got to watch myself.

My mind is on Dad today. He is never negative, condescending, or insincere by any means. I can learn from him. As a pastor, author, speaker (and secret spy for all I know), he is more than a parent but a real-life role model—a humble, selfless man with a strategist's mind. I traveled with him a lot as a child, which was exciting—flying to new states and dressing up for banquets or arena-packed conferences while other kids were in school. My world revolved around watching him lead interns and students and meet with various leaders, businessmen, and random teenagers who looked up to him. I loved seeing new cities and *chillaxing*, as Dad would say, in greenrooms before watching him from backstage hold his microphone in large auditoriums. Today I murmur a quick prayer for him, imagining him ironing his shirt in a hotel far away, preparing to speak in front of thousands of people while feeling invisible pain.

I was eleven when it hit me that he wasn't a normal father.

One spring day, Dad was home; the next he was in Minnesota, checking himself into the Mayo Clinic to enroll in their pain rehabilitation program. His job, which involved weekly airplane trips and hours of standing on stages, was physically demanding—literally impossible for someone who could say his pain prevented him from working. His doctor warned that if he didn't cut back on pain medications, he would eventually die from liver failure. We children were flown in to meet Dad halfway through the program and split into two hotel rooms—everything in our family always seems split because there are eight of us:

Dad and Mom
Candice and Kelly Grace
Bria and Allison
Angel and Jordan

I roomed with Dad and Kelly Grace, who willingly tagged along with the daddy-daughter clique between him and me, a kind forged from the deepest affection. I was intense like Dad and, though yet to figure out how to help his pain, began to *get* him; Kelly, the peacemaking problem-solver that she is, was there too, bringing calm stability. Countless doctors had increased Dad's medicine and dosage over the years trying anything to help manage his pain. By God's grace, he never became addicted, but there was no denying he had become extremely dependent on the meds to make it through each day. The experts in the Pain Management Department of the world-renown Mayo Clinic explained how those strong drugs were actually making his pain worse alongside the side effects. The goal was to get him off of the medications and learn to live life by managing chronic pain.

Cue the agony of Dad having to spend three days detoxing from his body's dependence on the opioids. Seeing him at night while his body detoxed years of toxic medications pace back and forth, back and forth, made the leaky midnight hours drag like a latent pendulum. Kelly and I were too scared to speak, too scared to interrupt his pacing. We felt so helpless for him.

Was being in ministry—doing what God wanted you to do—too hard?

Was following Christ not worth the cost?

"Muffins!" Angel walks into the kitchen in the present, and I remember I am not in Rochester, Minnesota, but in the twilight zone of Oklahoma. Why is this rental house feeling more and more like a hotel room. I can't even put a question mark at the end of that because it's really not surprising nor something I want to think about deeply. I don't have a desire to uncover hidden answers. I have no passion to be mad over inevitable realities. I don't even want to run today.

"Do you remember these muffins?" I ask Angel. "We used to make them in Missouri." I wonder if they represent home to her, or if, because she is still a child, their smell will come to represent this estranged house.

Angel rubs her eyes. "Is it raining?"

"Yeah, I love storms." I untie Mom's apron from my waist.

"That's weird," she yawns. "You're weird."

"Oh, I raised you better than that! You should love storms!" I walk to the window. "Even though it's dark and dangerous outside, here we are eating muffins safe and sound."

Seriously? I am not callous enough to avoid analyzing whether saying that is actually true. I should never deny myself the hard questions, lest an artificial layer coat my heart. I know *that* didn't turn out well for the Israelites …

Would I really be comfortable here, in Oklahoma, if we lived in this rental house forever? Would I really be at peace if we never went home to Missouri to see old friends and family? What if my parents were gone on a trip for weeks or months at a time and never returned?

What *is* real safety without God?

When the storm ends, I go on a run.

It was the vending machine snacks I stocked up on before afternoon lectures that made living in Minnesota fun during Dad's medical detox. I remember this while running in the lower section of our Oklahoma neighborhood, the part that looks like it might sink underwater if a flood were to come. It sounds grim, but my old hometown saw it after big storms multiple times.

There was no question that all patients in the pain rehabilitation program were desperate. Once patients signed up, they basically paid to feel every muscle tension more vividly, to endure every fiery-strewn nerve and tendon more excruciatingly than with pain relievers.

All patients' families were invited to be present and involved, given how extreme withdrawals could be after decades of medication. Afternoon lectures were offered to the family members coinciding with the patients' program. Mom, ten-year-old Kelly Grace, and eleven-year-old Candice were among the listeners. The lectures taught us how to live with someone who has pain that will never go away. It was like taking a lesson in caring for someone while they died.

Eleven-year-old Candice was immune. All she wanted was a blue purse in the hospital gift shop, and she schemed a way to get it while she played with her pearl earring after drawing over the lecture handout with her own sarcastic interpretations of the fill-in-the-blank acronyms.

Then she realized her earring was stuck.

"There are two types of pain," the lecturer hummed on, like someone underwater through one ear, "acute pain and chronic pain. And you are all here because your loved one is experiencing what we call chronic pain."

I fiddled with the pearl no longer connected to my earlobe. The rest of the earring had turned inward and lodged itself in backwards. But I could not interrupt Mom and her fervent cursive notes. No way—she had recently been admitted and discharged into the Mayo Clinic's emergency wing for pregnancy complications with baby number six.

I wondered if the earring would continue to slip, slip, slip away, like everything else at that time. Aside from moving to Oklahoma, that year was one of the rockiest seasons for our family. We did not know it, but we weren't halfway through the hard season as of that day at the Mayo Clinic. Mom tried to be a stabilizing figure, holding it all together as much as any mother could with five girls and a very large unborn baby.

Flinging myself into panic at a fifteen-minute break, I met Mom and Kelly Grace at the vending machine where they tried to pry the earring out. They called over a doctor and an entourage of nurses who sat me in a chair and flipped my head to the side. It came out after stares, tweezers, and embarrassment on my end not to play with unplayable things.

The ultimate sobering point, however, was more than a pearl in an ear canal, but a seasick company of suicidal patients. Why does he not only have meaning in life, but choose to stand on stages and fly on planes? The mental focus for such torturous situations terrifies me, thinking about the pain combined with adrenaline spikes after a four-hour plane ride preceding a one-hour standing session and two-hour rental car drive, only to stand in a security line and race through terminals then be held on the runway a plane for an unnecessary hour. Silent torment.

"With the levels of pain you have, you should be suicidal," they told my dad.

"Detoxing from twenty years of meds is no joke," he said, "but God has helped me."

How much more does my dad trust God than I do?

How much of his endurance can I connect to the present day—my new kind of sacrifice?

People don't realize the barstool on the stage behind him is a fire escape, a last-resort, dreaded crutch if he can no longer stand up. As if he, the college football athlete, would prefer to lean into a chair in front of thousands of people. But that's the humility of being entirely dependent on God. Dad dies daily to himself, and teaches me to do so, too.

What if my own dying-to-self is being okay with not having the fun of friendships or the escape of a football game? What if I am supposed to endure this growing up season alone on purpose? I want God to fix it, but I also prayed for Him to mature me. Maybe this is His way of answering my prayer. As Dad says, "Sometimes He heals you; sometimes He helps you."

Sometimes I wish the physical and spiritual weren't so integrated.

I haven't told anyone, but I cry aloud on my runs now.

Candice, the sixteen-year-old eldest, feels like she is literally on fire.

I just traced the vertebrae of my spine and found a sea of swelling red dots. Hives that didn't itch but made me fatigued and feverish. My hands trembled as I raced to the bathroom mirror and hopped on the counter.

Why is my body freaking out? Why am I freaking out?

Voices of siblings' arguments bled through the walls.

You can't heal Dad's pain, and you certainly can't fix you.

The room spun, and my eyes blurred from crying. I wasn't sad; I was furious. Furious that my own body was against me: the body I trained to fight *for* me, muscles that tear and repair while I sleep. An inner enemy existed that I couldn't control. How do you fight the invisible?

I opened my favorite Book.

As pressure and stress bear down on me, I find joy in your commands.[1]

It was hard to accept, but I found myself sighing calmly. I did find joy in re-reading God's promises to those who follow His will, which is ultimately for our own good:

Keep this Book of the Law always on your lips; meditate on it day and night, so that you may be careful to do everything written in it. Then you will be prosperous and successful.[2]

What surprised me was to read a command which spoke courage over my situation. I've read it numerous times. But considering it an order, it felt new:

Have I not commanded you? Be strong and courageous. Do not be afraid; do not be discouraged, for the Lord your God will be with you wherever you go.[3]

If it was law, of course I would adhere. He would be with me. I would have to recall my season of trusting God by moving to Oklahoma again, if not for the first time, and learn it in a deeper way.

Give thanks to him who led his people through the wilderness. His faithful love endures forever.[4]

The Israelites' wilderness test in the Old Testament seemed to have been a way of getting the 'Egypt' out of God's people—their sense of self-trust. Time and time again, a wilderness season showed up in the Bible like a default test. It reminded me of watching Dad detoxing in the middle of the night, ready to die. I drew in a deep breath and counted the cost.

If you fail under pressure, your strength is too small.[5]

I asked myself if I actually thought my obedience was measured by the success of my family's unity.
Do I get to decide when I pass the sacrifice test?
Is my identity in outward success at all?
No!

It's in Christ that we find out who we are and what we are living for.[6]

Yes. This was lived out in Rochester, Minnesota, as eleven-year-old Candice studied two mug shots revealing one father with a swollen, seasick face, a glaze over his eyes and a cracked, gritted smile, the other, a flushed, razor-sharp profile of a thin face with an alert gaze.

"Mr. Gibbons, you are now free from depending on pain medications." The doctor said.

All came to a climax in a boardroom. My parents sat in a final protocol evaluation at the end of the long month in Minnesota and heard the warning: "If you want to be independent from pain medications, you cannot continue your current lifestyle. You're going to need to quit your job as a traveling speaker, never lift your girls, and ration your energy."

"Actually, I don't plan to slow down." Dad sat up straight, fully aware of all pain.

"You can't humanly live like this." A nurse pressed, flipping through his file.

It would never make sense to those who didn't believe that God actually helped people.

"Here is why I can live the way I live. I can't humanly do this on my own. God supernaturally helps me."

It wasn't fun to keep traveling and speaking. It certainly didn't make sense. But it was the cost of doing what God told him to do, and after obedience—even through his daily sacrifice of comfort—Dad was blessed. Blessed with the chance to put one foot in front of the other. Blessed with one more day with his family, one more day to tell people about his peace found in Jesus, one more day to serve God with every part of his life.

The doctors sat there, stunned. And then the eight of us packed our luggage, boarded the plane with a dad free from medications, aware his pain would only increase.

Why do I trust God with this prolonged season of sacrifice?

Because that is what Dad does.

My first job interview is this Thursday at 2 p.m. I know I am not supposed to be afraid with Christ living inside of me, but I am scared out of my mind. Scared of coworkers. Scared of failing my CPR certification. Scared of even getting myself to work. Mom has me convinced I should become a childcare worker. I can't think of anything else better than playing with children (I say this half-sarcastically; I like some kids). Yes, I suppose childcare occupation is better than the food industry, depending on the children. But what if one of the kids I am watching goes crazy? What if the parents blame me for it, and I'm off to prison for animal cracker poisoning?

At least my parents trust me. Knowing I am right with God, and knowing I have my parents' approval in life is a strange but amazing feeling. It brings a heavy sense of humility and maturity. It pushes me to a greater responsibility. I am grateful of who I am becoming.

No, I will not stress. If I fail under pressure, my strength is too small.[7]

I am ready for a job. I am ready to work. I want to have an excellent attitude. I want to be trustworthy in my responsibilities. I want to have a consistent walk God. I want to be privately pure and publicly pure. I want to be a woman of integrity no matter what.

Guess what? God is answering prayers I never prayed—things I didn't even think I wanted but know will stretch me into an adult—like finding this job! I didn't *really* pray for an opportunity to come so soon; I honestly prayed against it. But God knows best.

Also, a girl just texted me about how junior high has been hard for her. I was able to tell her, "Yeah, school is so hard, but you can't give up because that's just not what you do. God will help you if you give Him your life." I am so glad I learned this through moving and running track. Track, like any sport, not only teaches you aggression (especially good for those of us who prefer *flight* when attacked, as this mindset can hinder us when it's time to face our problems), but it literally rewires your brain. I am thankful God intertwines the physical and the mental. This is my time to grow, in addition to what I have faith for is a season of feeling settled in Oklahoma. It's coming.

The job interview went well. I was professional and felt like I answered all of the questions right. I also felt young and underserving and, well, pitiful. But I tried to remember all I came from—not just the places I wish I could erase. I haven't lived a normal life.

Thankfulness is key to survival.

It's hard going against the flow. Culture isn't exactly screaming at girls to journal and pray and develop disciplined minds. Good grief, my own family and friends hardly journal! Why has God compelled me to do this? I honestly don't know.

I am thinking of the girl who sat next to me on her phone while waiting for her interview, scrolling on social media. It drained me being aware of everything she was reading and seeing. My mind felt heavy and exhausted even though I wasn't the one doing it. I hope I will succeed in relationships and academia this year, and that I become socially skilled and mentally ready for the future, college or otherwise. I want to be prepared to master work and business relationships. Although I often use bad grammar and I still have a slight southern accent that I adore, I want to sound refined and educated. I don't know why I feel this yet other than this job is my first opportunity to be an 'adult,' and I have a feeling all of these little things are connected.

We went by the new house tonight and built-in bookshelves have been put in my room! I don't know what I am going to put in them yet because I don't really read. I got to move the *Mom* sticky note down today on my current bookshelf plastered with prayer requests. After praying for her, she sat with me in the car and poured out her heart. I did my best to listen and be her friend. She isn't herself yet, but she's at least talking about some of the things that have been hard for her this year. I also moved the *Release from Worrying About Dad* sticky note down today, because I haven't worried once about his back pain or heart problems. As hard as that is, I've given him to God.

I try to keep track of the little things. They may not be new car kinds of blessings, but they are reminders that God still sees me. My youth pastor caught my attention when he said, "God gives you permission to beg Him for your requests." I thought that was very interesting.

Today is still hard. Everyone is sick in our house. I still have hives, and cry a lot, and don't really eat anymore. But soon I will be better. Trials run their course, and there is always time and a way to do what is right, even when you're in trouble. Suppose this is a prolonged season of sacrifice. Suppose I really do need to learn what a deeper layer of sacrifice feels like.

God, may I steward this season well.

CHAPTER 3
BLUE-COLLAR JOB

*This is a real place. A real job.
You're in the real world.*
—Korie

I got the job! Today I join the American work force as an eager sixteen-year-old. The preschool is located in such proximity to our neighborhood I am able to walk to work, which feels so grown-up and a bit alarming, but this girl must earn money for a car before she can drive one. My training began in a small janitorial closet watching a VCR on how we women who literally wear blue-collar shirts are to act at this technically 'pink-collar' job, and the philosophy behind this well-acclaimed daycare of electric blues and sapwood. Their methods are integrated schedules of cookie-cutter standards which I find naturally easy to adopt, and I don't plan on becoming anything less than what their staff values. I am also the only minor (somewhere I heard, technically underage).

As I cross the street and walk alongside luxury cars turning into the parking lot, I wonder what these parents are thinking of one of their children's teachers walking to work. I am certainly underqualified, but here I am, one of the blue-collared women assigned to one of the STEM-infused, rainbow block classrooms, each named after a type of biome.

The hilarious thing is, here I am, going from being an average sophomore that barely says hello to her brother, to actively choosing to sit in a children's classroom chair to talk with two infants who can't even compute what I am saying. Their names are Weldon and John.

Weldon has a man's face, deep-set brown eyes, and more hair than your average one-year-old. John is like an even older man with white, fuzzy hair and a wide, toothless smile. As soon as I kneel to their level, I feel transported into another world. Within this dim, thick-aired classroom of white-railed twin beds are minds so new to the world that it gives me a great sense of fear and awe of childhood.

Having been stripped away from any chance of getting invited to another high school party, this now becomes my social sphere. Why do I suddenly feel so young and pale and slow? At least I don't have black hair.

I smile at two rather heavy-set nursery workers in rocking chairs. "Hi, my name is Candice." They return my gesture with halfhearted eye contact.

The shorter and older one speaks up. "That's Jenny. I'm Helen."

"Nice to meet you."

Silence follows.

My presence is so awkward. "How long have you guys worked here?"

"Five years," Jenny murmurs.

"Seven," says Helen. "And I worked at another preschool ten years before this one."

"Wow." I am subconsciously waiting for a handshake, but I reach for a cloth on the counter to wipe a baby's face, trying not to look like I am waiting on someone to do something for me. "This is my first time working at a preschool." Immediately after the words slip out, I regret it. It would have been best to list my experience at home with five siblings. Instead, my mouth gets ahead of me and adds something worse. "This is my first job."

This gets Helen's attention. "How old are you?"

I naturally expect this question. I have always looked a few years older than my real age. Sixteen sounds so young right now, and Helen looks three times my age.

"I can't believe they're letting kids work here." Jenny mutters.

Helen shakes her head at my age. "You've got to be kidding. Well, welcome to Ocean."

"Thanks," I smile. I am like a sponge. A tiny, dry sponge.

This room really is like an underwater nursery, I realize as I hear whale noises on the sound machine and note seagrass paintings of algae and Nemo clownfish. It feels like time stopped as soon as I swam down here. I sense early childhood is a realm hard to overprotect, watching the hands of women hold and feed these infants. Babies are literally helpless. I have so much to learn and observe, yet it is almost underwhelming. *Oh, the bubble of childhood …*

"Why don't you change him?" Helen tests, picking up a rather chunky baby with squash on his face.

"Sure." I am ready to prove myself. But after I do it, I realize I completely forget gloves—a strict institutional policy. *Should I let Helen know or just pretend it didn't happen? Perhaps I should ask.* "Helen, are we supposed to wear gloves?"

"Of course," she says, now feeding the tiniest baby in the room. "DHS requires it."

A wave of fear hits that I am already going to be fired. Thankfully Helen seems to have other interests than turning me in to the Department of Health and Human Services. She directs me back to the snack table to supervise Weldon and John, who are clawing at angel food cake.

"They're our oldest in here," Helen yells across the room. "About to be transferred to Tropics next door with Gina," she says this last part more to Jenny, "in October."

I joke, "They look like grown men, especially with names like that!"

Helen doesn't find this funny. "Fill up their bottles and give them something to drink."

I do as I am told.

Immediately, the 'tiny men' stop smiling. In fact, Weldon even stops eating—not even attempting to get his drink—and believe it or not, looks me up and down. It sounds preposterous, but these little people actually have *looks*. John does the same thing.

I sheepishly set down their bottles. These silent seconds drag on like the last class at school. I keep tapping my watch to make sure the second hand is moving. After the longest hour, the door creaks with the arrival of my boss, a frazzled 30-something festooned in a colorful shirt that reads "It's all a MESS" in sequins paired with a headband dotted with pearls. Her face reads she is overdue on her afternoon coffee run. I hope she likes kids; I don't quite see the enthusiasm. *I guess the blue-collar shirt and khaki pant dress code doesn't apply to her ...*

"Candice, we're going to move you to Savanna."

"Alright," I stand up. *Where in the world is Savanna?*

"Savanna is the two-year-old class down the hall on the right. The walls are orange."

"Oh, okay!" I wave to Weldon and John. Helen and Jenny don't bother to glance up.

As I walk past the Tropics to Savanna, I hear kids yell and scream inside the room. In the hall window I see a 20-something tying a toddler's shoe. Before I open the door, I say a quick prayer that I don't get trampled ... by her or the kids.

"SIT ON THE CARPET, NOW!"

"Ah!" I dodge a flying shoe. "Hello!"

A voice calls from the bathroom, "Who's 'dat, Korie?"

Two boys fight over a plastic tractor. Three girls pretend to cook in a pink kitchen. One boy cries up against the wall.

The woman, whom I assume is Korie, walks to meet me. "What can I do for you?" As she approaches, all I can think is that I dare not shake her hand.

"My name is Candice. Is this Savanna? I was told to come in here. This is my first day."

"Yeah, this is Savanna. Nice to meet you. I'm Korie." She turns around and grabs a kid off the table and yells to the voice in the bathroom, "It's a new girl!"

Korie is a long-haired brunette with quick knees that bend up and down to wrangle her wild and sticky toddlers. I soon gather her mother's yell is as trademark as her khaki pants stained with juice. Her class is loud and frightfully busy with two-foot-tall energy and windows facing a playground where I plan on having a great deal of fun—as much as they will let me.

"How long have you worked here?" I ask Korie.

"Welp, that's a loaded question. I—Layton! What did I tell you about hitting Liz?"

An olive-skinned toddler moseys over to Korie's bent khaki knee.

"He knows better." She tells me, giving him a look.

I begin to understand conversations will always be fragmented, and my words start to come out in 'really' adverbs in reply to everything she teaches me. As much as I am shocked by what sounds like harshness with the children, I see she is much like a mother to them.

"William! No sir! Out of the sandbox!"

"Don't give in to Oliver. He's a crier and knows better too."

"Don't ever wear jewelry. It is against dress code."

"I love you, Jaxon. You's a sweet boy."

"Don't forget to wash Samantha's cup. Her mom's bougie and doesn't like it sticky."

"Don't ever ignore a parent when they show up at the door."

"Carter! Liz! No hitting! Get over here so I can give you a hug!"

I love the noise, the routine, the colors and shapes.

I love the graham cracker crumbs and designated seats.

I love the labeled lockers and chalkboard font of typed names.

And I especially love having an escape from the rental house.

After work, I am invited (i.e. required) to attend an early childhood education lecture by a guest speaker, well-versed in the science behind my recent encounters. Generally, science does not intrigue me, but childhood does, and secretly, I am a bit fascinated with neuroscience.

Haha, that's funny even admitting I like something science-y. I think as I take notes.

"The third part of the brain to develop in utero is the limbic system." The lecturer explains. "The amygdala registers emotions such as fear and anxiety, and this is all housed in the hippocampus. I share all this with you because it's the first thing to develop in utero."

"*I'll be in the bathroom,*" a disinterested teacher whispers to Korie.

Korie is like a mother to these young women, minus Gina and a few older women who hold their own. To me, Korie symbolizes a brown beam holding up a roof alongside a bunch of rickety sticks. No employee matches her authority. She isn't even taking notes; she's seen it all.

"Thank you everyone for your attention this evening," my boss, who in her life passivity, also seems passively favorable of me, says to us in front of the hospital-lit classroom. "Tonight's staff-wide training lecture was designed to equip all of you to take bigger steps towards cognitive growth in your own classrooms. We will hold these educational lectures weekly this fall. Each one of us plays a big role in early childhood development. Even as early as year one we are seeing children affected by lack of nurture …"

"Yes!" The lecturer interrupts excitedly. "Keep in mind that the academic parts of the brain have already been affected by lack of nurture. By as early as years one and two, we can already see some delays in learning. Isn't that astounding! So even though our children are coming from very loving families, building secure attachments at an early childhood center is still important because it helps with trustworthiness at such a young age."

"That's right." My boss nods with less enthusiasm. "We want to think about building friendships as well. This is the best time for teaching children how to work together in groups and build together, even before children have language skills. Not only does this prepare for building their language skills, but it also builds social, emotional, and memory abilities."

Korie taps the corner of my blue polo and whispers, "Note this with Coulter. He had head trauma at an early age. Watch the next time we do playtime outside; he won't join. Hermit tendencies."

Hermit tendencies? Maybe I hit my head as a baby …

"That's all, ladies. Have a good night." Our boss motions for us to stand.

Tiffany slaps the table. "Giddy up!" I have yet to speak to her, but from distant observation, she is Korie's classroom neighbor and fellow sarcasm dealer. "That was as boring as detention. Hey, what's your name, baby?"

"Candice," I smile and extend a hand, one that is being eyed warily.

Tiffany finally clops it with her sweaty palm. "Yeah, *Candice*," she drags out in a remembering sort of way. "Korie told me about you."

Overhearing, Korie smiles at me patronizingly. "You are the littlest member of the team."

"Yeah, little baby!" Tiffany snickers.

I laugh to relax myself. "It's true. I am sixteen."

"Told ya!" Korie laughs.

"Girl, and they let you work with the babies?" Tiffany shakes her head.

"I have five siblings."

"Great Aunt Jemima!" Tiffany says.

"That's cray-cray," Korie jangles her keys and slurps the last of her Sonic slushy. She can't be more than ten years older than me, but she is clearly respected—a well-trained auntie in a jungle of nurture-starved children. She's like a rough yet stable nurse. I see there are many types of nurses for many different needs. Korie fits her role and supplants this institution in her very nonchalant, young adult way.

What kind of 'nurse' am I? I breathe off the latex smell of the room and think about what kind of person I want to be to these children.

Two hefty blonds approach Korie and whisper off to the side. The blonds are known as gossipers. I know the taller woman as Morgan, the one with an immensely broad scowl who reminds me of one of those nurses that enjoy giving kids shots. The other I don't know.

Apart from immunizations, I loved visiting the doctor's office. My pediatric doctor's office had a fish tank and one long, electric-blue fish. My sisters and I named each nurse after a fruit (dependent on face and figure). 'Peach' was our favorite, and 'Apple' was borderline good, but 'Pear' was the worst. Morgan would probably be named 'Tomato,' right up there with Pear. And no, I don't consider tomatoes fruit, just as Morgan should never be handed a needle.

Hospitals are dear to my heart. Before I ever picked up a pen, I wore a little doctor's coat. I lined up my porcelain dolls and stuffed animals for haircuts or bandages. Some had legs chopped off, others needed check-ups. In early childhood, after Kelly Grace pushed her baby dolls down the slide, I picked them up and patted them until they 'stopped crying.'

Now that I think about this, maybe I didn't hit my head. I have always been a nurturer. I spent my fifth birthday touring an emergency room. I used to think it would be cool to become a brain surgeon. Then I hit high school and realized how much science would be required to be a brain surgeon. I passed.

It was a hot September workday. I should have worn shorts, but I had no alternate option to fit dress code than Mom's khaki pants. Oklahoma had a harsh fall breeze, and yellow leaves finally shaded half of the fenced yard. Yet apart from still having hives down my back and being on the clock, the day actually started off promising.

Ready to be a good nurse, I watched Coulter patiently.

Korie's khaki shorts squatted on the poured-in-place rubber playground surface. "Would you like to join Candice and Elizabeth in the playhouse?"

"Here, Coulter." I motioned him over to me and curly-headed Liz, a little doll of a girl who cries a lot. "Come play with us. We were just about to have a ... uh ... party!"

Coulter hid behind a wall of spinning tic-tac-toe blocks.

Layton and Jaxon, two troublemaker boys, waddled over to the house where Liz sat inside. I could only fit my head in and was honestly sad that I was too big.

In a burst of excitement, I clapped my hands and rounded up Oliver and Carter and Scarlett, all of whom were hard to please. "C'mon in, Layton and Jaxon. Come in and sit by Liz here, we are going to sing *Happy Birthday*."

Korie watched in amazement.

"Alright, it's someone's birthday today ..." I stalled to see if Coulter would join, also wondering where I was going with the game. Twelve eyes were captivated on my sweaty face.

My world, which had shrunk by four feet, was locked inside a plastic playhouse. My popularity boiled down to the receptiveness of six toddlers. "And this person is very special because his name starts with a … *C*." I gasped for effect.

No response.

"Whose name starts with a *C*?"

Jaxon picked his nose.

"Um, Candice," Korie yelled from the doorway, "we're only at letter *B* right now in the curriculum.". I could hear the ice crunch under her Sonic straw. Not one to leave me hanging, she added, "Try asking them who has a red truck on their shirt."

"Oh. Who can find a red truck?" I began again, the children's attention waning.

The good news was they were tracking with me. The bad news was no one in visibility had a red truck on their shirt. Elizabeth looked down at her Texas A&M maroon jacket. Oliver poked his belly in a green tractor onesie.

Losing time and credibility in the hot playhouse, I chose Ollie's green onesie. "Never mind! Surprise! It's actually Ollie's birthday! Now, on the count of three, we are going to sing *Happy Birthday* to Oliver. One, two, three …"

I sang all by myself.

Surely they had learned Happy Birthday?

Miss Korie rang the cowbell, "Snack time!" In one flat clanging tone, the party ended.

It's a lovely commute here, this road and grass. It sees me crying most afternoons. Trudging up the hill, I unbutton my blue-collared shirt and prepare for more sweat to pour as I walk home. Another day complete.

I turn seventeen next month. I can't mentally think about my birthday. I feel so undeserving, so beyond all that fuss which comes with a celebration of yourself.

This is the first year for as long as I can remember that I haven't at least had some idea of what I wanted to do for my birthday. If only my blessing could be our family not being estranged from each other, for Mom to be home and Dad to not be in pain. If only my gift could be for our house to sell, for Dad's sake, to the right people and for our new house to be finished quickly. If only I could meet friends.

I did get to visit my future room last night! It is so 'Candice'—small, with a pointy attic ceiling and slanted walls, and windows overlooking country plains to the left and Oklahoma City skyscrapers to the right. But that is far away, and I must spend my time making the 'now' better, like learning how to love little Coulter.

I am different, and I know it. I'm calmer and less opinionated than I was in the summer. My tan is going away, but my hair is brown again and growing quite long. I am really pushing myself in my workouts. I think it is tied to pushing myself with this job. I like how the mental and physical intertwine. I like having a physically active job.

I still can't believe I am an employee. I want to be respectable at work. I want to earn the favor of both Korie and Tiffany and even tomatoes like Morgan. But I also know relationships take time. I guess I am excited for something besides my new room: I get to see close friends and grandparents in Missouri for my birthday! You never fully realize how much relationships are like gifts—until they're taken away. *Thank You, God, for the little things.*

A terrible day at work. I can't believe the nerve of some people who work in childcare that don't like children. I didn't have the energy to open my mouth when I heard what I heard. It's as if some teachers took all our instructions to nurture and turned them upside down.

I was determined to try the *Happy Birthday* game.

Elizabeth knew exactly where to go. Oliver soon followed, but the others acted like they had never seen this tall, freckled teenager before in their little life.

"Jaxon! Layton! Do you want to come to the party?"

I might as well have spoken French.

"Scarlett, do you want to play with us?"

No answer from the pouter.

"Declan? Lucy?" I smiled grittily to the white-haired twins. *Of course, not*, I thought. They are among the richest of these privately schooled toddlers. It is funny how they act just as stuck up as their blond, athletic parents. It's as if they knew I felt inferior.

"Coulter ... ?" I said slowly, but to my dismay, the door swung open to the classroom.

It was Morgan the Tomato.

"Candice-Tiffany-needs-your-help-in-Rainforest." She said it all in one giant slur.

I stood reluctantly. *Where is Korie when I need her?*

"You're supposed to go now," Morgan stared at me with bored amusement, like she wanted to find a reason to pull me from our outside time, everyone's favorite hour. Nobody I have met likes Rainforest. Little Candice the Sponge was about to be dipped in the Amazon.

"Oh, okay. I will go right now." I dusted off my khaki pants and patted Ollie on the back before walking dumbly through the open door Morgan held for me.

Korie met us in the classroom with her giant water bottle and questioning eyes, but there was no time to explain.

"She's needed," Morgan said, waddling swiftly behind me.

It didn't matter. Korie was already past us, yelling at Oliver to stop hitting Scarlett.

Miss Tiffany's rainforest was more like a nighttime taiga. Everything hot and orange in Korie's adjacent room turned shadowy and cool in her territory. It smelled like an unfavorable scent of Lysol, the kind used to disinfect a cot after a kid throws up. Jackets were strewn and name tags were falling off the kid cubbies. When the lights were on, it was less of an igloo, but it was naptime, and frankly, I didn't know why I was needed at all.

By the time the door to Tropics locked, I was face-to-face with Miss Tiffany herself, who seemed just as surprised as I was to be in the room that felt so dark and bleak compared to outside.

"Help me fold these towels," she said.

And that's what I did the rest of the workday.

I really can't complain; I think the idealist inside me is just ready to win. Can I not even find favor with the two-year-olds? Why does everyone seem to be against me?

"You need to stop letting people be mean to you," Korie later told me. "I've heard how others talk to you. Stand up for yourself."

But I'm only sixteen, I thought. *Everyone else knows more than me.*

"If I were you, I would've told people like Morgan to get out of my face."

Korie probably would say that. I can't think of comeback lines on the spot! "I don't want to be rude or mean." I admitted.

"This is a real place. A real job. You're in the real world." She said dryly.

I almost laughed. Was confronting Morgan the Tomato really my entrance into the 'real world'? I may feel like I wasn't liked, not blatantly by Tiffany or certainly not by Morgan, but did that mean people were really pushing me around?

All I could say was, "Okay. Thank you."

I really didn't want to be a pushover. I am still not interested in conforming to the complacent culture of the preschool. No, I am certainly not a conformist! Any sixteen-year-old without social media or a crutch of a boyfriend is definitely not average. Sure, my friends in Missouri may have all of that, but was I about to cloud my mind with other peoples' lives by scrolling on social media when my own life was barely held together?

I had to be present. I had no choice but to devote all my mental energy to holding this family together. I wasn't going to rely on any artificial escape. I was fulfilled by no other thing than my personal time with God praying and journaling, and thankfully, those things will always be consistent and reliable.

Korie was right. I was separate from the 'real world.' I didn't know why I was so strict about my lifestyle. People often ask for my defense against why I do not listen to certain songs. Sometimes I just didn't feel it in my spirit that it was right. I didn't know why I was so strict with my entertainment other than it's how I had always lived. My views weren't even derived from strict rules, I sometimes walked away from family movies as the only one convicted by certain things.

Why was I the only one in my family who got up early and ran on hills?

I thought about how sick and tired I was of surviving in life and not thriving. I was supposed to out of the season of sacrifice. I was supposed to be blessed after moving to Oklahoma and following God's will for my life. Did it all really boil down to hopping around like a frog at a preschool? They say there's a grand scheme that someday we'll be able to see, someday we'll say, "Ah, that's how it all works out." But what if that wasn't true for me?

Playing 'Mom' every day, at home and work, seemed to last longer and longer. Was it not strange that my siblings, Angel and Jordan, called me Mom occasionally? My friends from private school were cheerleading at football games. But choices brought consequences. I was learning that first-hand. I chose to stay at home. I chose to accept a part-time job. I was sacrificing now for blessing later. Except I didn't know what *later* meant.

Work went well. I stayed in Savanna the whole time, and Korie seemed protective of keeping me on the playground with the kids, even when my boss came out and asked if I wanted to be moved back to Ocean with Helen and Jenny. Of course I didn't, but I did not have to respond, because Korie was kind enough to explain how well I entertained the two-year-olds.

Birthday parties were now a daily occurrence. While some children were too bashful to join in, many new faces scrambled into the playhouse today, including Coulter.

Toward the end of our time outside, I was wet with play, having hopped around like a frog for the majority of the hour. "C'mon everyone! It's someone's birthday today!"

Faces were red, and several children's eyes glittered with tears from sudden gusts of Oklahoma wind. A birthday was just the thing we needed. "Whose birthday is it?"

All faces looked around. Some even pointed to the last person we celebrated. My heart wanted to burst. What a joy it was to teach them a new game!

"It's Coulter's birthday!"

Coulter was shocked and a bit scared by this attention, but when his peers stopped clapping, his little face relaxed. After singing *Happy Birthday*, I cupped my hands around the imaginary cake and he blew out the candles, after Liz and Ollie showed him how to do it.

It was remarkable how the children's minds could envision the cake and candles. They knew to clap once every candle had been blown. Sometimes I liked to play with them: "Layton, you missed a candle. Blow this one out." Sometimes I let them open imaginary presents where they decided what they were. What flavor was the cake? Did they want ice cream, too?

Imagination at its youngest. I am so glad I said yes to the challenge, and continue saying yes, even on hot days. Life is opening up in a dozen different ways as I learn something new every Oklahoma afternoon. How much my life has changed because of this blue-collar job!

CHAPTER 4
THE CONSEQUENCE OF IDEAS

Don't be an error.
—*Unnamed classmate*

Studying Philosophy appears to be an adventure in the dark. I am only slightly thrilled because I may find something rare and obscure and be mentally transported outside of rental house life. Philosophy is a core subject for all 11th grade students in the homeschool co-op of which I am currently enrolled, which includes the study of secular and religious philosophers, of genius minds and ancient fathers from who knows when and who even cares.

Philosophy is also one of the credit classes I am taking virtually at Southeastern University. According to my college syllabus, my assignments will semi-overlap with my regular junior year papers, which is wonderful, except this means I will have to actually care about getting good grades. I have many philosophies about life, and I wonder if they're going to be resolved this year, but it's rather unlikely. What my new professor does assure me and my invisible classmates online is that our study of philosophy will stimulate the love of logic and reasoning and I will develop an appetite for it. This is possible but also unlikely. I don't have any sort of urge to debate—not yet anyway. Why I traded homecoming games for the solitary study of dead people, I'll tell you when I find out.

The dig began today. I, Candice, strode into my first in-person day of school wearing a diamond necklace and white lace camisole pressed under my shirt, really excited, because hey, this could be my graduating class! This may be my new group of friends! I was ready to actually try to, I don't know, be academic. Not because I liked school, but because I was already in a *make war* kind of season and the aggression level was high. I was used to running uphill in wind. I could handle a new school for the second time this year. I was also excited to make new friends. Something was bound to impress them.

Wait until they hear I went to private school, I thought with a little snicker, flinging open doors with my shoulders back like the cheerleaders taught me, briskly and with great importance, head high so my hair wisped like a pompom. My new school building is right beside Oklahoma University's football stadium, so I feel very preppy. I did a little 'tut' at the sight of a student without a backpack but a rolling cart spilling over with Milton's poetry. *Nerd.*

The doors were tall and narrow, most swinging without handles, and the off-white walls were made of giant cinder blocks. I caught the breeze from the door to a bathroom, which I observed seemed like a rather small cell with no windows or even a big enough mirror to check your shirt. Definitely no room to invite friends to join you during an escape from class.

Carissa immediately flashed in my mind—her little cheerleader's face, the first locked in my mind on the day I toured private school—my key to observing how popular girls should act, which affected everything from my mid-morning snack to the length of my nails. I studied my own sparkly ones; the nails I begged Mom to let me get done for this momentous first day where I would meet my new circle of friends. Carissa would be proud.

Bunch of geeks. I huffed my way up more stairs, my backpack stuffed with intimidating Shakespeare. Girls were looking at me like I was a spineless princess. It couldn't be helped.

What also couldn't be helped was the state of underwhelming shock I fell into upon emerging on level three of the building. I had been transported back in time. Students, most younger than me, were hurrying in and out of classrooms with strong, sweatered arms cherishing authors like Mays and Borton, Rhodes and Liebert. Here was a little cave of geniuses with their own language and ideals of not only popularity, but presentation, which sounds absolutely shocking coming from private school. But I can only assume there are still customs of this sheltered world because of the creasing reality that I haven't really acknowledged in Oklahoma: *I was one of them.*

It was all so infuriatingly familiar. Here they were, brisking down hallways with their homely desk partners and homemade lunches tucked in crocheted crossbodies. Here I was looking like I thought I was special. The irony was I was raised in a very classical program which taught Henle and Lutz and Kern. I knew these textbooks. What's worse, I could quote them.

Why was I acting superior? Had private school really made me feel so 'above' my fellow homeschoolers?

A girl with wide-rimmed glasses studied me with what I caught as a slight sigh of pity, like I had no depth or brains. It was suddenly clear I was the worst of both odds. There was no sense in committing identity suicide in such an intellectually honest environment. I was terribly stuck up. I was also beyond marginalization.

God, I give up all facades. I prayed, breathing in my new academic home, upstairs and down a dark, blue carpeted hallway, walking in my classroom and smiling at no one in particular. Hopes rose and fell as each student entered, either quirkily well-established or complacently beyond repair.

This all leads to right now, where I hopefully clutch my invisible spade and expect to find gold or something else tantalizing, like a new beautiful best friend or a tall, athletic boyfriend …

"Welcome to your junior year, also known as Challenge III in this curriculum." The teacher leans over with thick, black-hair in gray-streaked curls, simultaneously swinging a stack of books to the floor, throwing a bag of markers on the table, and popping a rolling cart against the wall. "Where did summer go." She mutters.

Her level of enthusiasm is matched by every set of inattentive eyes but mine, scanning the room and realizing not only there is a complete absence of natural light, but this is a literal boardroom. Our table is rectangular with rounded edges, a raised center with built-in power outlets, and executive-looking swivel chairs of luxurious black leather. I sink into one on the right side of the classroom and, to my surprise, a little hint of aggression kicks in.

I decide, *I am going to own this chair for the rest of the year.*

It's a sad day when the location of your chair becomes the highlight of your school year, but I find a strange sort of solace in it. Some parts of me, out of survival, are falling into passivity, while aggression spikes at the oddest times. It could be a hormonal imbalance. But at least action is moving back into thought. Before this year, I wasn't always so passive, so chilled into letting life hit me without retaliation. But at private school, I was scared to breathe. Running was my channel of aggression. All else in life, left to fate.

A bearded man slumps into the classroom. "Junior year sucks." Surely he wasn't sixteen.

A small, scholarly boy pushes the swivel chair beside him with his foot. "Here man, by me."

As more students trickle in, the sea divides evenly with boys on the left and girls on the right. A white board extends in an L shape around the center and right wall behind me. I speak a few words of social obligation to the girls to my right and left, and then wave to the boys across the room, because hey, you've got to keep your options open.

Eh, never mind. There is absolutely no chance I would date anyone here. I gather the feeling is mutual: everyone is staring at me like I am a misplaced 40-year-old who thinks she is to be prom queen. This is so disappointing. Imagine being labeled a social outcast for trying too hard.

I look left to right and wonder if I'm in the wrong place. Maybe this was the class for people who didn't care about being excited on your first day of school? But alas, the teacher is writing 'Challenge III' on the board, the name of the junior year program, and I can't help but stare at the theme of the year written below it in black ink:

CHOICES BRING CONSEQUENCES

What kind of choices would I be offered? What sort of consequences would occur? Do we ever really consider the word *consequences* to be positive?

Well, here is my consequence of friends after opting out of cheerleader functions:

Boy #1 is asleep.
Boy #2 is a literal nerd.
Boy #3 is the teacher's son.
Boy #4 lied to the teacher but seems nice.
Girl #5 has oily hair (she may have never been told).
Girl #6 is stuck up (her problem).
Girl #7 is an artistic genius (intimidating).
Girl #8 is argumentative (dangerous).

In all fairness they probably see me as overly dressed and prideful. I have a good reason to believe there is more to these students than first impressions, and I dare not judge—not after being the new kid at private school, or the new teacher at work. Still, a little balloon deflates in me when I realize that none of these teenagers will probably want to be friends with me, this tan will soon completely fade anyway, and I will probably begin to slouch in my seat. I may even wear pajama pants like the boy across this boardroom table. I feel like I should be in a suit with a briefcase of notes spread before me, like a real executive—ha! This may be as close as I get.

"I'm Mrs. Loose." The teacher states without smiling. While the building is cool, it is also stuffy with the remains of summer, and I am thankful she flicks on a fan in the classroom. Mrs. Loose seems stable and authoritative, calm and self-depreciating. I already like her, but I don't know if the feeling is mutual. "Get out your math books." She instructs.

And the year of consequences begins.

I don't want to become one of those people who call books room décor. Yesterday they stained all the wood in our new house and finished painting my bookshelves, but I don't know what I am going to put in them. Abstractly—and this is a very out-there thing for me to say—I want it to be a room of books never written, a background of stars in space, a realm of light and color and music and imagination. Kind of like a playroom for teenagers.

So weird, Candice. Maybe that's why you don't have friends.

I went for a run yesterday not because I had to or even felt sluggish but because it has become instinctive. It's like animal survival, like a lone deer that wanders around looking for its herd—running and hoping someone finds you or hoping no one's chasing you. Really, the only three challenges I am hounded by are college classes, work, and this metallic taste in my mouth from flossing too hard, which reminds me I have chemistry homework due.

I believe I may enjoy poetry and philosophy, but there is no hope for liking math and chemistry. All those *numbers*. I have never really liked school before, but I have recently prayed for God to make hard things easy. Particularly that I wouldn't fail my college classes.

Mrs. Loose stopped by the rental house and loaned me two books for poetry. Mom was behind ordering my textbooks, so I was the only junior without *The Roar on the Other Side* on the first day of school. It makes sense why I had flicked out a composition notebook and drew sketches of my new room. I have so many ideas: a secret bookshelf, a sliding pole escape into the garage, perhaps even a tunnel from the wall to the attic on the other side of the stairs. But then Mrs. Loose asked me about iambic pentameters, and I confessed.

"You can't take poetry without these books this semester, and you don't want to get behind," she warned today.

I was deeply ashamed. She had a right to consider me an avoider of work, and it wasn't far from true; this ruined my plan to be exempt from the first poetry assignment.

"You are so kind," I said to Mrs. Loose on our steep driveway. On the inside I was thinking, *Ha! 'Get behind.' I've always been a 'behind' sort of girl. Behind in comprehending math, behind in seeing a need for reading and writing poetry. I still don't see a need.*

"Take good care of them. My son never creases his copies." Mrs. Loose said.

I squinted back, thinking quietly, *a creased book represented a loved treasure. A creased book means it had been digested by a serious reader. I don't own many creased books, apart from maybe a Melody Carlson novel. Yes, she could expect this back in perfect condition.*

"Thanks!" I told Mrs. Loose, and we hugged. She said she lives close and offered to help if I needed anything. I told her thanks and that I would, but the thing I needed most was the roar on the other side of this rental house to stop. She laughed.

Mrs. Loose' minivan left. I walked barefoot up the steep driveway. *Should I run today?* I eyed the street. *No, someone has to cook dinner.*

My book based on my essay *Obedience, Sacrifice, and Blessings* is official. I started writing it in the most professional way possible, or at least in a way that *sounds* official, by outlining it. I have no idea what I am doing! Finding the time to write is excruciating. You should see the garage right now! Not like the clutter has anything to do with my procrastination to write my book, I really don't know how it's affected, but somehow it seems when the new house will be ready, and everything is situationally in logical order, I will have some sort of magical passion to actually *write*. My rental house routine has funneled into a sort of high-intensity morning-focused situation:

- 5:30 a.m. Bird-chirping alarm; swing out of bed without hesitation. Devotions.
- 6 a.m. Breakfast; make kids lunches for school; clean house.
- 7 a.m. Drive with Mom to the gym, workout and shower.
- 9 a.m. Reading and online college forums.
- 10 a.m. All execution required for school (essays, speeches, projects).
- 1 p.m. Lunch/study while I eat, clean the kitchen.
- 1:30 p.m. Get dressed and walk to the school for work.

- 2 p.m. Work in Savanna (or Ocean or Tropics).
- 6 p.m. Make dinner for family (and if time, practice my cello, Quincy).
- 9 p.m. Read Psalms and go to sleep as fast as I can!

It is often interrupted, but at least I have attempted order.

Writing the book comes super early or distastefully late, and I have to just go with it and do it even when it is inconvenient. Sometimes I wake up as early as 4:30 a.m. to allow time to pray and journal before the house stirs. I've claimed a little place for this in the pantry, which doesn't have a lock, but it is, straightforwardly, the only place I can go without interruption. Otherwise, it is in Big Roy the Suburban.

I am also almost finished reading through *The Message* version of the Bible. It is written in a sort of narrative form, which I like. I'm a little tired, but my spirit has never been better. God's obviously preparing me for something, and I am eager to walk in His will.

Learning the true cost of leadership—whether leading a class of two-year-olds or leading myself—is eye-opening. Sometimes I pause, step back, and study the faces of curious children behind me at work, watching my every move. My inner self begs me to skip an impromptu story time with Angel and Jordan, so I can write a college essay, or clean the house, or scrounge for dinner food. But I don't always listen to my inner self, and it pays off. I value staying close to my siblings.

I still believe I will pass on any sort of celebration for my seventeenth birthday. This year is the sad reality all my Missouri friends being tied up in work, school, and adultish lives. Most are older than me. I'm not a ten-year-old throwing an *American Girl* sleepover party. I want to be respectful of my friends' time so we can keep our relationships healthy. It is always difficult to discern how much to write friends, if at all. I did write one of my childhood friends recently of some inner revelations, as she has had a similarly difficult year:

> Moving to Oklahoma was an opportunity for me to pray about what friendships God desired for me to cultivate and which to let fade away. I want you to know that I value your friendship, and I hope we will always stay close. You have an anointing

over your life as a leader. I admire your faith and sensitivity towards God and how you run from evil. I've learned so much from you. Thank you for being a godly example to me and many other girls. I have been praying for you a lot this year as the enemy tries to pull you down. In track terms, "Keep running." Don't lose sight of who God's called you to be just because you've lost sight of God. Your daily work can be an important fulfillment, even if the outcome is completely out of your hands (Eccl. 9:10) (1 Thess. 5). Know when to leave and when to say 'no' because at the end of the day, is it worth your soul?

It surprises me how letter writing seems to reveal parts of me, and certainly explains things in me, that may otherwise never be written. I almost seem to be talking to myself.

We learned last week that half of my in-person co-op classes are student-led. I volunteered for our philosophy strand this week, not because I know what I am doing, but mostly out of fear of being called out when I didn't want to. Unwilling to be led by a leash, I highlighted pages in my philosophy book and handwrote notes to be prepared. Who knows how this is going to go!

Humor seems to be the only safe entrance.

After asking the class, "Who is Socrates's worst student?" I answer my own joke that it's *Mediocrities,* and someone comments my meme passed around is spicy. Now I feel the need to defend the meme to Mrs. Loose, yet saying, "It was just a joke!" just makes me feel more and more dumb, like a yellow lump of Play-Doh stuck on this table I've been staring at for the last four hours. Is philosophy a joke?

The clock ticks loud and I can almost feel Plato the philosopher laughing at me from somewhere in space. This is going to be the longest hour of nothingness.

"So, as you all may recall we are entering the second chapter, which discusses how Plato was a realist and an idealist …"

I wince. *I don't even care about what I am saying. Why would they?*

"You can be an idealist about some things and realistic about other things." A girl dismisses. "Like how Plato saw mistakes but saw the potential of the world."

Whatever. I invisibly roll my eyes. Then a deeper side thought hits me, important, but not profound. It's something I've never thought to say aloud. "As we are in philosophy, I think it is worth considering what we even define as good, conceptually or otherwise. Like how everyone knows there is such a thing as good and evil, but they may not necessarily see their actions as inadvertently right and wrong. Consider heroes and villains. No one's like, 'there's no such thing.'"

It seems so undebatable, but by the stares of students across from me, I wonder otherwise. My chair spins. "Really, it all goes back to the spiritual world." I think of the art of story. "If anyone ever was like 'there is no right and wrong,' I'd trace it back to that. When was there ever an absence of ally and enemy?"

"But do what we consider 'good' or 'evil' change based on what society values?" Mrs. Loose challenges. "Is good entirely objective?"

The philosophical wheels are turning in my head because I've just remembered something I read, which is absolutely insane. I rarely recall something I read. Ha! I rarely read at all!

"I think he was right on customs and ethics specifying different rights and wrongs. But I don't think it means good actually changes," I process aloud. "I think people just embrace evil. People say that's what they believe and that's what's right for them and therefore declare it justified. It goes back to whether perception equals reality. Just because they say it is right, it doesn't make it good, or true, for that matter."

The nerdy boy is staring dead into me, like he's somehow found a screw loose and wants to pull it. "But no one has the authority to define truth because all perceptions are tainted. Objective truth is the most disappointing deception of humanity."

Before I can open my mouth at such a statement, the argumentative boy grips the handles of his executive chair and speaks. "Except that it isn't."

The nerd's face reddens. "That is absurd. How do you classify truth if everyone believes in a different truth?"

"Even if everyone is in opposition to it, there still remains an ultimate truth."

"Well, who gets to decide that?" The nerd exclaims.

"Candice is leading this discussion today." Mrs. Loose interjects.

"Yes ... er ... back to our notes." I cough. There are too many strings to pull, and I feel like I'm falling into a black hole of voicelessness. "Recollection, also known as the Theory of Reminiscence, is another topic discussed in this chapter ..."

I am struck by my own intellectual slight and dishonesty. *Am I afraid of being a philosophical failure, unable to answer in sophisticated terms?*

Astonishingly, the next question I have written down defies every non-confrontational bone in my body: "Plato was a student of Socrates, who believed knowledge comes through reason and not experience. But is this really an either/or? Does experience truly equal perception which equals reality?" I feel a little flame inside, like I'm suddenly on the verge of punching someone ... but my hand isn't strong enough.

"It's like a deception." A girl speaks up.

"I mean, does reason equal knowledge? Is reality truly objective?" I direct.

"Do explain," Mrs. Loose raises her eyebrows, redoing her thick bun of curls.

"Well, do you have to experience a car wreck to know it is bad?" A boy who hasn't spoken yet proposes. "There are some things you just need to miss out on!"

"Perception doesn't always have to come through experience." I clarify, passion dwindling when I feel a real pang of hunger accompanied with the realization that I forgot to turn in an online forum response associated my Southeastern University college class work. *Bummer.*

"Where do we even get our ability to perceive?" A girl asks.

"It isn't mere physics." The nerd corrects. "It's neurological digestion."

"That reminds me of what Plato said," I sit upright and flip through my notes. "Something about appetite being the desire for physical things …"

"What are we told to do with those fleshly things?" Mrs. Loose asks.

"Put away with it." I answer. Mentally I think of Romans 8:6 but keep quiet.

"Like the idea that there is no objective truth." The argumentative boy spits back.

"So grass isn't really green?" A boy jokes back. "My whole life's a lie."

My eyes close. All I see are splattered little yellow dots as we continue intellectual paintball. I am baffled, infuriated, and invigorated. Hunger and all other troubles seem to vanish as I realize the famishment of my soul. How do you answer everything at once, how do I know how to answer anything at all?

"Anyone have any burning questions you need Candice to touch on before we dismiss?" Mrs. Loose' eyes glimmer with mild amusement, albeit impatience at our own naivety. Everything's been in and out, up and down, side to side. I haven't even heard each comment, let alone answered every question.

The argumentative boy points to the nerd boy in utter horror: "He —he just said justice is nothing but the advantage of another!"

"He's right." A girl agrees. "Justice is a concept for the weak-minded person who lacks the will to discern himself. That's what we are learning, isn't it?"

"It all goes back to moral relativity …" I trail off.

"Is there such a thing, Mrs. Loose?" The nerdy boy demands desperately.

Mrs. Loose laughs. "Let's discuss morals and ethics next week. But rest assured there is such a thing ultimate justice. We have an imperfect view of justice, but all of you will have moments where God reveals something to you, moments of spiritual revelation. Those are like memorial stones. You *will* wrestle many questions. But you can always come back to the pillar of the ultimate justice of God. Once you've wrestled something down, you can let the sand fall where it may. Reconcile now the fact that there will be things you may never understand, but that doesn't mean there aren't ultimatums."

The nerd's eyes are going wild. "So you're a believer in ultimate truth!"

"I am a believer in God." Mrs. Loose' voice is firm.

A small girl coils lethargically in her chair. "Mrs. Loose, is philosophy dead?"

"Philosophy is thinking. When-people-stop-thinking-philosophy-is-dead." The nerd interrupts hastily, repulsed by her question into a slur of words.

"Yeah. We're just a bunch of people sitting in a classroom thinking, so I don't think philosophy is dead." The argumentative boy agrees.

"There are a lot of people that just don't think. Are they dead?" The girl mutters.

Mrs. Loose breathes deep. "Many people are contemplating, 'What is life?' They don't figure it out for themselves. They wait for the obvious answer and when it doesn't come they don't think there is an answer. Many people think, *Oh, it's all been done, it's all been thought, I'll just live my life*. As if society will tell you the right answer for everything. A lot of people just want the answer right away, and if they don't get the answer right away, then the think, *There is no answer, and it's just alright.* I want you all to sit on this during the week and come back with your reflections."

We dismissed from the heated boardroom, entangled in wild thoughts.

Music and nightlife filled the streets of Naperville, Illinois. It is in the 40s, really feeling like fall. I am with my dad on one of his speaking trips. There is a downtown riverwalk that's currently flooded here, but floods don't scare me because we grew up in a town that was often flooded. The trees are edging bright yellow and kids are exploring downtown on their own in huddles and the shop owners seemed to know them by name. I like journaling places and cultures like this.

Yesterday we visited to a famous grilled cheese place called Everdeen's before eating cupcakes at a fancy bakery that had swings as seats hanging from the ceiling. I got a pumpkin cream cheese cupcake and Dad got a crème brulé one.

Today we ate Giordano's Pizza downtown before walking back to our Indigo hotel where I took a three-hour nap. We then went to a smoothie joint and jogged to Barnes & Noble where I now find myself touching each book's spine, irritated.

Traditionally, books scream one thing to me: boring.

But there are so many concepts and ideas in here, and I am starting to think, if there is ultimate truth, that automatically classified a multitude of works as false.

But we don't think they are, do we? Books are just entertainment, aren't they? It doesn't matter whether the ethics align with ours because, ultimately, it could be a work of fantasy where murder is the highest glory.

And why should we care if we read a book that does not align with what we believe? Isn't all entertainment mere personal pleasure?

Why is it then that some of these books bother me?

Why do some seem to be haunted with a sort of amused wrongness about them, as if the author knew they were going against truth and rejoiced in it? Beyond bloodstained horror covers, beyond the attraction of mystery and action, why did it somehow seem some books were deeply wrong?

It appears this feeling is far beyond my background of reading exposure. I am not a student of theology like Kelly Grace, but I am aware of a certain spiritual presence behind certain books. Genre is irrelevant.

Why does this hit me so different today? That's the thing about philosophy. Once you open the door, it never closes. Alone in this massive bookstore, reasoning overtakes me, and I almost start to cry, thinking about if lies were without consequence, if life were without objective truth or good and evil, nothing we ever did would matter. But it all does, and that bothers me. If the root of all morals is exclusively objective and found in God alone, and if God was sovereign and would eventually bring absolute justice to earth, then there was such thing as spiritual death. The question of entertainment's involvement in our spirituality seems worth exploring. People are walking, like magnets, to light or darkness. And I, having just begun to sort deeply into this, am about to turn the handle to knowing more of both worlds.

CHAPTER 5
EXPLICITLY CHILDHOOD

*O, what men dare do! what men may do!
what men daily do, not knowing what they do!*
—*Much Ado About Nothing (IV.I.19–21)*

"Protagoras believed objective truth is neither possible nor desirable." I open today's philosophy discussion. "But is an absence of complete objectivity really undesirable, and does this lack of desire perhaps force us to deem it unachievable?"

The door to our boardroom-classroom opens, and a teacher slides in like a lizard. His hair, like his skin, is slick and white, but not from age. Rather than eyebrows, he just has indentions carved in the top of his forehead. I smile at his appearance and my automatic prejudice, for I realize I judge too quickly. I am friends with everyone in my previously deemed ill-tempered class of juniors. Mr. Drake, I know ambiguously, is a highly respected board member, also highly involved in the day-to-day classroom learning of the school.

Today, he finds us interesting.

"Mr. Drake, please, take my seat." Mrs. Loose quickly rises.

Mr. Drake dismisses it with a wave, leaning his lanky frame against the wall. "Continue." He motions to me.

I stammer. "The … definition of the Socratic Method is to discern truth through provocative questions. Again, we're back to the concept of truth. When we do the Socratic Dialogues in Socratic Circles, we are given a chance to hear a range of opinions that may redefine our perspectives." I ramble. "It's a positive approach to differing opinions."

Mr. Drake raises a finger. "Ah, excuse me Miss— ..."

"Candice."

"Your last name?"

"Gibbons." I choke down an inappropriately timed laugh. It happens when I feel uncomfortable, which explains inappropriately timed funeral giggles. Justifies? Hardly.

"Ah, yes, Miss Gibbons, you mention going back to the concept of truth ..." Mr. Drake laughs, and I catch a hint of an unclear accent in his voice. "What is truth? Hmm? Anyone care to elaborate?" He scans the room of lowered heads. "This is a dialogue, is it not?"

"Well, um, I personally love our Socratic Dialogues." A girl chimes in, avoiding his main proposition. "I love it when we talk about truth and discern it with questions." She blushes at the sound of the *T*-word, probably having meant to avoid at all costs. "Sometimes it gets heated." The girl snickers nervously, her voice sounding like squeaky pipe drains. "There are times when somebody can say something that is totally wrong and we'll tell them in a polite way, like, 'Yeah, sure, but no.' And there are people that will just totally shut you down, and that makes you want to turn around and be like, 'Oh, and I still argue about it.' But with these dialogues, you have to convince them that they're wrong before you actually tell them that you're wrong."

Mr. Drake's eyes widen.

My eyes widen, too. *Poor girl is digging herself in a sandpit ...*

"At least, you have to listen to what they have to say." She explains hastily. "Once you do that, they're actually interested in this. And so if you listen to someone, they'll listen to what you have to say. Which is really what that's about."

"If you're telling someone they are wrong, then there is objective truth." The argumentative boy speaks up, perhaps for the benefit of the opposing nerd to my left. "That's like saying 'All statements are false.' If that's true, then you contradict your own statement."

The girl shrugs. "But even then, one person's objective truth may be classified as subjective in the first place. So we're back to there not being any sort of objective truth at all."

I look at Mrs. Loose tentatively, "I guess that depends if you think God is objective, or not good." I avoid Mr. Drake's wide, eyebrow-less stare. "The idea of a God who is not good seems to slash the utter concept of an ultimate God in the first place, given our basic understanding is, in essence, a God of perfection and love." The conversation is not taking the lane of debating the goodness in God, but of objective truth. Still, I can't help but sense Mr. Drake is more aggravated in the former per his coughing red face.

"It's necessary to say," Mrs. Loose offers slowly, "if you really aren't a believer in objective truth, then there goes Christianity, so make sure you wrestle with that a little bit."

"Quite right, Mrs. Loose. But I gather these students aren't interested in religion." Mr. Drake slices with his tongue.

I stare back blankly. What is this surprising feeling—a little hint of aggression? Not of proving thoughts wrong, but of testifying experience.

"I'm with Candice." The argumentative boy speaks up, and I somehow feel it is wrong to keep referring to him as that, given he's defending my own position. "It says in our textbook how moral rules, or ethics, if you will, merely express customs or conventions, which are never really right or wrong. Ultimately Christians' concept of right and wrong come from God, so if you don't believe in God then these are just guidelines. Let's get that straight. The argument isn't really 'Are ethics objective?' but whether the ultimate reality of God is objective. If one has this base of authority, ethics are objective—*secundum litteram legis*, if I am using that right." He adds in a whisper to Mrs. Loose. "Comparatively, law itself is confusing without a lawgiver—*obiter dicta*." He stops and appears to be repeating the words in his head. "Am I making sense?"

"Yeah, well, I don't know Latin," a girl speaks up, "but I agree that even for certain individuals who are not affiliated with a religion, there are laws that govern, like, their state or country, not just maybe social customs, but, like, I don't know, everyone can agree on them. And those would be subjective because they are derived from man and not some divine source."

I acknowledge, "It would be essentially impossible to derive right or wrong if you didn't believe in God. It goes back to Dostoyevsky's proposition how if God does not exist, all things are permissible. My conclusion is that Protagoras' assumption that morals and ethics are really just social customs is taking it too far."

"Ah, but Protagoras himself said knowledge begins and ends with man," Mr. Drake interjects. "How do we know the Bible or other religious texts are, as they say, *divinely inspired?*"

I think, crossing my arms. Mrs. Loose has a flow chart of thoughts on the wall-wrapping board that makes my head hurt. It's all a bunch of circles to me, an endless roundabout as meaningless as ethics without a purpose. *I am still wondering why philosophy matters apart from free headaches and enemies. If we were to understand every aspect of God and His ways, we would be His equal. Reasoning, like the ocean, has its limits. Deep down it is impossible to entirely deny there is a God, no matter how much one conspires.*

I want to say my thoughts aloud right now, but Mr. Drake is raising his invisible eyebrows and muttering something about childhoods, and I can't help but picture some unfortunate circumstance in which he lost his eyebrows, perhaps in third grade during a fight over existentialism.

But oh no—he's saying something against my childhood.

To this I feel my own hand clenching the side of my leather chair. *What is this inner enthusiasm?*

"I personally loathe the man who believes in God and had a rosy childhood." Mr. Drake mutters. "There will always be deceit and dishonesty in their work."

"Mr. Drake, these are *juniors.*" Mrs. Loose hastens to whisper.

"I forget." He raises his hands and relaxes with a laugh, then eyes me with peculiar interest. "Miss Gibbons, forgive me again if I impose, but will you tell me in honesty, that you had a particularly good childhood? And does this not support your belief in a good God?"

I stare at him speechless, hoping for a window of air or a gasp or a faint, anything to cut the knife of the spotlight. I am thinking, *All our childhoods seep into our beliefs, good or otherwise.* But I'm not sure how to say this yet, or even how deeply to wrestle how this is true, and so I reach far back into the caverns of my blue-collar job for some bit of a scientific response: "I do think part of our conscience is formed through parental upbringing. Age zero to five is when the brain learns the most. That is when parents are telling you what is right or wrong. However I do not believe that one's conscience is solely derived from environmental circumstances."

"Do explain."

"The age gap of zero and five is so influential that some describe it as being brainwashed." I continue hesitantly, formulating. "It's not exactly your own opinion, but it can be eventually. None of us are free from feeling what our parents imposed. It will always affect what we consider right or wrong. But it seems deeper than that, doesn't it?" I turn to Mrs. Loose, who smiles, and I can't tell if it's out of praise or pity. Either way, I'm left hanging by myself. "It seems there is unmistakable evidence to support that man was given some sort of pang of conscience, regardless how that ends up being affected by culture."

"Present it." Mr. Drake says.

But rather untimely of me, he demands this as I mutter, "Maybe it is too deep ..." And I can't help feeling very small and dumb.

You could have refuted. Inner Candice defies. But I am not used to thinking this deeply, not this deeply so quickly, and instead of ending philosophy like a smart Englishman with a pipe, I flee the classroom like a squiggly worm being chased by a lizard. Intellectual dishonesty, appeal to ignorance, or emotional escapism? Perhaps.

I had a journalism teacher who told me to treat my brain like a hard drive. I'd like to say I try, but at this stage, I am beyond finding a manual. The problem isn't that I am an overworked hard drive, but perhaps I was not meant to be a hard drive in the first place. The more I listen, the more incapable I feel of retaining information, possibly from a history of poor academic achievements, or perhaps just because of this full year. Ultimately, the real issues are that I don't have friends, and I can't sleep because of these roaring philosophies in my head that are incapable of being drowned out by Kelly's sound machine.

When I explained this to my parents, they laughed, and before I could call a friend to vent, I found myself back in my blue-collar shirt, sitting in an early childhood education lecture, feeling like a hot air balloon about to pop from an exasperated amount of statistics.

Why am I working at a preschool and singing with toddlers on a playground? Why am I taking a philosophy college class and enduring intellectual ridicule? Why am I still waiting on some supernaturally derived blessing after nine months of restarting my life?

The lecturer asks the room, "How many of us would say we have a fixed mindset about ourselves and something?"

I already feel ashamed.

"Many of us might say, 'I'm not a good artist,' or 'I'm not a good singer,' 'I'm not really good at math, I'm not really good at science.' You've trapped yourself by stating that it's unchangeable, right?" She goes on to say how Harvard released a study where a group of toddlers were followed, and their teachers had to worry about their language and what they were saying and how they were responding to children in the classroom, and when those children went to kindergarten, those children did not give up as quick as their counterparts.

"They persisted because of the verbal positivity and intentionality from the teachers." The lecturer's face beams, like she is one of those teachers. "We're seeing it across the United States where children are not persisting. They are so used to moving. Things are moving quickly for them, life is moving quickly for them, but we can get them to understand that they can focus and do hard things just by intentional wording and encouragement."

All this helium is promising to burst my own misconceptions—if not my entire brain by the end of this year—by first attacking any deep note in my voice in philosophy tomorrow. I think I am losing my voice. Was it from today's round of *Happy Birthdays*, or perhaps the cooler weather hoarsening my voice on early morning runs?

Is it already time for philosophy class again tomorrow?

Is anything about my sixteen-year-old life turning normal?

Why can't I stop asking such troubling questions?

Oh, this year of consequences!

"Statistically, *statistically*, you don't come to your own opinions until age 10." The class nerd follows up on my reference to brain development. "Personally, the idea that everyone is born with a conscience seems like nonsense. If you were put around absolutely no influence, chances are you would create your own moral code. Consider how the consequence for telling the truth means you end up in jail. Survival instincts would kick in. If we do not steal because of the consequence of it, we would be doing it for government alone, which is rooted in egoism."

My comrade, formerly known as the argumentative boy, presses, "It seems unfair to deem something as wrong based on what kind of consequence occurs."

Another girl speaks up, "Well, I've been watching this series, and they're in New York City where social norms are different. For the people on the show, stealing was rewarded. Does that mean 'good' and 'evil' are interchangeable?"

A knock interrupts the exchange.

"*Excusez-moi*," Mr. Drake enters with a bitten apple. "I couldn't help but peep into the most troubling junior class of the year. This really is gold for me, if you all will permit me to polish—all in great fun! Where are we, hmm? Objective truth?"

"Welcome, Mr. Drake. We are on good and evil." Mrs. Loose rolls her eyes. "Continue." She motions to us.

Mrs. Loose is becoming more favorable to me, more stable and assuring, even despite my unstable math grades. I think she caught a glimpse of my mother and thought, *Wow, poor girl.*

"I think you need to clarify justice," a girl says. "I think justice is what you deserve."

My comrade shakes his head. "But keep in mind justice is not man-enforced."

I suddenly think of Job 8:3 and how God cannot twist justice.

A boy endowed in history speaks. "I think justice is a relative term.

Technically, there's no such thing as perfect justice in this world. Law is nothing more than a reflection of the ruling class in vested interests. Ideally we want to see the law as a way to make all people equal."

"You also have to keep in mind what philosophers were pre-Christ." My comrade proposes. "Their only view of God and justice would be Old Testament Jewish law. Still, ultimate justice is the very essence of God's character. Christ was the fulfillment, not any sort of negation."

Psalm 97 is in my head. I can't believe I am recalling passages of scripture! That's unusual of my brain to reference during conversations. It shows how what you study is retained, even if you don't think you remember it. And it may not even be what you classify as 'study,' but whatever your eyes see in repetition. *Maybe I really am turning into a walking archive!*

All the same, I don't want to sound like a textbook. "Justice would not be true justice if there weren't an ultimate basis for truth. When we stand before God, it's not going to be like you *kind of* have justice, as if God plays favorites. Without the basis of God, we have this imperfect view of what justice is. Therefore it has to be trod upon carefully." *Like eggshells.* I think, partly out of hunger, partly out of sudden recollection of the human brain.

Fascinated by the medical world, I watched tumor removal surgeries as a child. I recall one doctor not being able to remove an egg-like tumor in one piece; it had to be picked apart in tiny pieces, else the operation would fail. Somehow the boiled egg surgical picture mirrors philosophy. Rubbery and bland, and … perhaps … deadly?

"The unexamined life is not worth living." A student blubbers in his hands. "There's just no point in all of this if there's no judgement, no grand crescendo."

"Unless you're here for the game," the nerd smirks.

"You've lost me." A girl slumps down.

"Nay, good fellows!" Mr. Drake crunches down on his apple and I feel another pang of hunger. "Let's chat on paganism, shall we?" He says with a slurpy mouth.

"Oh, shoot. We're so over time." Mrs. Loose glances at the clock behind him, "Thank you, Mr. Drake." The room murmurs in relief.

"Hey, class, make sure you have your assignments done in spite of these rabbit trails. Tending to be a college class in here."

"I'd like to think they're beneficial," Mr. Drake winks, and right as I go to exit, his little pointer finger wiggles for me to come hither.

Great.

I take as long as I can to stuff *The Roar on the Other Side* and other beasts into my backpack, trying not to bite my lip and taste blood.

"What are you going to study in college?" Mr. Drake asks, rather nicely to my surprise.

I can't help but laugh, not only at his friendliness, but at the thought of me going to any sort of university. "I may study writing. Maybe film. I've always had an interest in that." I try to sound convinced and excited (totally not) but again to my surprise, it is Mr. Drake who turns an excited shade of tomato.

"I've got a screenplay idea just itching to hit the theatres," he shakes his accusatory finger now like a ravenous scientist, eyes darting from spiderwebbed corners, real and unseen. "I taught psychology, you see," he adds, perhaps to fill in fragmented thoughts on my face. "I'm rather an eccentric guy. Must be in part from my bohemian father. Anyway, while my old girl was studying fashion in Paris, I tinkered with producing a *Cinéma-Vérité* screenplay. We moved to the city after living in *Hautes-Pyrénées,*" he waves absently. "Quite a place for the mind to unravel other worlds ..." he snaps twice, "fiction or otherwise."

"Ah," I nod, like yeah, everyone knows where *that* is.

"I am quite amused by such—how shall I say it—*innocence* in your class's philosophy discussion. Yours in particular, so cloaked in morality. I hope you don't mind." He winks again.

"Of course," I readjust the weight of my books, trying to think of something French-sounding to say other than *bon appetite*. I start to open my mouth to say this because he seems like a sort of character partial to comedy, but it happens right as I notice a piece of apple nudged between his crooked teeth, and all I can picture is Emile from *Ratatouille*. I withhold.

"Carpe diem, young writer!" He pats me and leaves. "Thought is action! Action is history!"

Sure, I think, descending down the staircase in my private school

HOCO sweatshirt with a bit chewed out of the cuff from my dear C.S. Lewis, that faithful rat of a dog. *We could say I have a belief that I am not academically smart, which is true when we consider my comprehension of chemistry and mathematics. But I don't think just by telling myself I am smart I can become smart. That's like thinking I am an Olympic runner and expecting to make it to the United States Olympic Trials. Just because you think it,* cogito ergo sum, *it does not mean it is true. Surely perception does not equal reality, in this light.*

Regardless, I can't deny the association between thought and action, nor the fact that I am turning into (dare I say it) a mental nerd.

"What on earth are you *doing?*" Mom catches me at the kitchen table in surgical gloves, bent over a glass container with a boiled egg.

"Shh … I'm in the middle of surgery." I whisper.

"Candice, you are hilarious. But this … this is strange. You're what?" She laughs.

"Tumor removal." I employ a pair of tweezers. "It's life or death."

"Probably a coping mechanism." Kelly walks by with a thick book.

"Clearly …"

Mom shakes her head and leaves.

"It's … action … to … my … thoughts …" I murmur to no one.

"I was once a minister for the Church of England," Mr. Drake confided to me before class to my utter shock. "You may find it odd that a man of such open thinking would be enslaved to a book of rules by a tangle of contradicting fathers." He licked one of his fingers as a comb. "But I am half-English, half-Irish, and that is just the sort of thing people do. Religion, *objectively*," he leaned in, "is a hierarchy of self-pretentious …" I tried to unhear his language, picking up with his hand-gestured statement: " … and I resent anyone who refuses to listen to the logic against it."

"I see," I had said rather flatly, although I hope not too flat. You can't be too careful with a half-English ex-minister, bohemian psychiatrist, especially one who's on the school board.

I carried in a tray of white chocolate blueberry scones to today's philosophy class, partly to win the favor of Mrs. Loose in an effort to smooth the grading of a particularly lousy chemistry lab with my name on it, and partly because while everyone's mouths were full, perhaps our discussion would rabbit trail less, and we could get on to reciting our Shakespeare lines before I forgot them. We all should be very proud of Candice, staying up late to memorize the wedding scene of Hero and Claudio in *Much Ado About Nothing*, even when sleep called.

Just a few minutes ago, I was daydreaming about the relationship not of Hero and Claudio but between my good friends thought and action after the boiled egg operation. It was silly, I know, and something I may never do again, but it helped my brain process the intangible weight of thoughts that had burdened me, pieces that needed to be picked apart. Perhaps out of fatigue or nerves, I thought of something random and felt the need to say it in class. I was already talking about something but couldn't really hear myself, so I hesitated, arms rolled up in my HOCO sweatshirt, waves of hair on my face, and voiced: " ... what if ... thinking is an action?"

It hit me more profound than it was, but the class roared with "Ah's!" It was an unforgettable triumph of Play-Doh-morphing thoughts. Just when you thought you saw definable shapes, there it was smushed and pounded again.

I liked pounding thought. Even after you've rolled a ball and perfectly rounded it, someone's fist pounds it into a plump. At least it was morphable.

Yet that was also the worst part.

The thing that scares me about the power of the human brain's philosophical dough is how it can directly inflict disdain for God.

"Come, Candice, be brief ..." they tell me now, and I find myself feeling deathly faint as Hero herself.

Still, I play the part to perfection. It was a romantic scene of passion. I almost forgot entirely of self-preservation as I fell to the floor in the heap and applause rose.

"Ah, romance satisfies all." A girl says.

"Does it though?"

"It is the Great Longing, and the Great Attraction."

"But surely it points to the Great Beauty? It itself cannot be the ultimatum, for it is fleeting and restless."

Not time for that yet, I think. *This is my time to learn.*

I wish I could explain how religion is man-made, a twisted version of God's incomprehensible love that recklessly bleeds outside the lines of justice, and yet fully encompasses it, due to the ultimate victory of light. But thinking this deeply, and even more complicated, putting it to words, is too hard to define.

Of course, Lord, You have revealed Yourself to me. I do not doubt You exist because I know You and have tasted Your love. Your existence is not containable in human vocabulary.

Online in my three college credit classes at Southeastern University, discussion is quieter but just as evident. Indirectly, heat surfaces, one click after another. Someone posts; you think, you respond. But my in-person classes are in real time. I also do not work a slow-reaction job: I hear children, I respond, they react. There is no time to think deeply, but to move quickly to the point of perspiration, and as swiftly as Korie's khaki knees I shift thoughts in my in-person philosophy class. Of course this is good training for me, though I don't exactly know why. Why am I learning to think about philosophical matters, to even care about debating? Like Mr. Drake in the back of this classroom, in the back of my mind sits Mom in a dark corner.

Oh God, also please help Mom. She is hurting so bad this year.

I got a 'bad' grade on one of my (personal opinion) best English papers. 97.4. My virtual professor said I had too many quotes and needed to paraphrase more. I got my hopes up when Mrs. Loose complimented it, she had even recommended entering it in a contest. I guess writing is a bit subjective. When I say I am not naturally inclined to good grades, I must explain my reasoning lest I appear intellectually dishonest. To provide an overall average of Candice's academic scores (pretty consistent—except for math) throughout my whole life, see these stats:

- Elementary: Bs, 80s-90s in English/History, Bs, 80s-90s in Math/Science
- Junior High: Bs, 90s in English/History, Ds, 50s-80s in Math/Science
- High School: As, 90s in English/History, D-, 30s-50s in Math/Science
- SEU English Average = 100%
- SEU Philosophy Average = 99%
- SEU History Average = 98%
- Math Average: 75% (before redo's)
- Chemistry Average: 30% (and decreasing)

Looking at D's and F's on my current report card, the future is not looking bright.

Would I like to go to college? I mean, yes! Football games and friends sound highly appealing, considering I lost all of that in high school.

Will I get into college? Not at this rate. Earning college credits in high school may be as close as I get. I don't think I could even do community college, if they required certain gen-ed scores. *Haha.*

Free writing: Mom has been yelling at us saying things I've never heard her say. Out of nowhere, explodes. She's mentioned leaving us, going off to do something crazy. She nearly kicked Bria out of the house. I try to manage the family, cook and care for the kids, clean house, etc. But that's not it. I can't give Mom what she wants, and I am freaking out. Charlie the dog has been sulking around the house like a Benedick. I really don't like Shakespeare's Benedick. He is too opinionated. Hero seems nice, and she does not often speak out of turn. Claudio should have investigated her background before assuming things. That reminds me how sometimes I assume things that aren't accurate and I need to step back and look at the big picture. I need to learn to listen with the right perspective. My reasoning is, although perception does not always equal reality, perspective directly affects action. It is imperative to have the right perspective. Whether I am lending an ear to a negative coworker rehash her unfair life or trying to understand where in the world my mother is coming from, I discipline myself to maintain an open mind. There is no greater opportunity to practice understanding people than with Mom himself.

"I just wish seven people didn't act like I was the crazy one for taking some time to sort through my emotions. I just need to heal." Her words replay in my mind.

Internal conflict, like a hidden disability, can sometimes be worse since people don't directly see it. Suppose teenagers misunderstand how hard a move can be for the parents, strangling out pre-existing tensions within the relationships. Everything had flipped upside down for her, as it had in a small way for me. Except Mom is still hanging upside down.

Freedom of thought brings choices.

Choices, like actions, bring consequences.

The consequences of my ideas now will shape who I become.

Oh God, may I make the right choices!

Reluctant to go to work today, I gave God my evening and stepped in with a good attitude. An opportunity to show if I really walked by faith arrived immediately: I was put with the task of training a new girl. And the Lord helped me!

Yesterday it was my first day seeing Morgan the Tomato for a while. She said, "Candice!" loudly, excited to see me. Dad reminded me my work is so much more than a paycheck. Yes it's about the children, but also about the adults. What were their childhoods like?

My favorite verse right now is on an index card from one of my old track coaches:

But they who wait for the Lord shall renew their strength; they shall mount up wings like eagles; they shall run and not be weary; they shall walk and not be faint.[1]

I feel like that verse relates especially to me because I have POTS, a blood pressure disorder that makes me severely lightheaded at random times, and it also reminds me I am more than a conqueror in Christ, and my day-to-day strength comes from time with my Lord.

What a great pleasure it is to live beyond little things that used to bother me! I'm grateful cleaning dishes no longer frighten me, a new school isn't intimidating, and attacks on my mind aren't undefeatable, thanks to prayer. *Thank you God, for growing my capacity.*

"Compliance is not self-regulation, and this sometimes gets confusing." This week's early childhood lecturer explains. "If I tell a child to go put up their jacket, they go put up the jacket and follow my directions. But we want to get children to a point where they innately know the right thing to do."

She looked at me right when I yawned, and unfortunately, I look eighteen and qualified for late night lectures rather than a sixteen-year-old running an eight-person household. This may be a form of self-preservation, or like a layer of ice guarding the heart, a sign I really am going insane, but I am beyond feeling any need to prove myself—to her or my coworkers or really anyone else anymore.

"I took an old oatmeal can and covered it with construction paper. I then took pipe cleaners and tissue paper and made each one for children and we put a picture of each child in the middle. When I caught them doing something that was helpful, following directions or helping another child out, I would say, 'Go get a sticky flower and put it in the pot!' A lot of us have reward systems in our classrooms like that. The one thing to remember is when you take it out, you've just taken away that effect. You're not teaching them to innately do the right thing. Where does self-regulation begin?" She prompts, and our table discussion begins.

Sitting up, I realize I do have something to contribute.

"For me, personal regulation begins with an early morning run. Sometimes I have the thought that I am going to be disciplined that day, but it stays a thought. However if I connect it to action with a run, I am training my brain to do something hard even when it doesn't want to. Running then prepares me to tackle mental challenges later in the day."

"What a great thought, Candice," Gina, one of the older teachers compliments. "Can you elaborate more on the science behind this connection?"

"I am no scientist," I laugh, "But I have seen direct results that ideas often become consequences. A lot of times people assume they don't have ideals, but they do."

"Well, I'm not a scientist," Morgan suddenly interrupts. "But apparently information about us is stored in dark matter until the end of the world, so some physicists think."

Now the table has shifted into two conversations, one about the mysteries of the cosmos, the other on what brand of running shoes I wear. I am more interested in the space conversation, but Morgan's broad shoulder has turned away from me. I am clearly alienated.

"Do you run by yourself?" someone asks me, "on hills?"

"Yeah, I find hills and wind strengthen me. The rainier the better!"

"What time of day do you like running?"

"As early as possible. 5 a.m. or 6 a.m."

"What do you listen to?" a younger teacher asks.

"Oh, all kinds of things …"

"Can you share your playlist with me?"

I could, I think, *but that's pretty personal.*

Why does this scream philosophical warnings to me something isn't right? I obviously feel the need to hide what I put in my ears, words that, whether I admit it or not, have indoctrinated the way I think—therefore my actions have been affected.

"Sure," I finally say, thinking, *after I delete some things.*

"Great—if I could have everyone's attention," the lecturer's voice picks up. "I hope you all concluded that for infants and toddlers, it begins with co-regulation, and we just continue to build on it. We want to be mindful of 'How are we building them a secure environment?' Structure the environment. The neurons for attachments are connecting right now. The brain architect of this is happening at such a young age that our impact affects attachments for the rest of their lives."

Who knew early childhood development was so foundational. I ponder, writing a few notes on a legal pad I brought to look smart. *Might as well play the part, even if I don't plan to become a scholar.*

Something that does interest me is what the lecturer says next, strangely more acute than anything else I have heard in this fluorescent classroom turned lecture hall.

"Think about lighting in the classroom, too. Lighting, sound, color, temperature, and even smell. Think about the *five senses*."

Now here was a cosmic star, an unborn sense of light on which I could dwell deeper.

CHAPTER 6
THE MAKING OF CANDICEYLAND

Lose no time of what may be,
but boldly grasp what is real.
—Dietrich Bonhoeffer

Midnight-sky and rain: the perfect day to turn seventeen. I enjoy my traditional early morning birthday run to clapping thunder and rap, damp under the darkness of a windbreaker, the secret dawn of a solid age. *This Is a Move*, among some rather aggressive songs, beat into a new pair of headphones. I laugh aloud. *This is a move to my favorite age and a new house.*

Mentally, seven is purple, and paired with a blue number one, it seems like such a royal age of becoming. Seventeen reminds me of a brown-haired missionary named Rachel who had the sensitivity to find little Candice introverting in a corner at a conference. Rachel shared about her adventures in Africa, challenging my nine-year-old self to think beyond sensory overload.

Seventeen also marked the last year of life for Rachel Joy Scott, killed for her faith and who left the world her journals. Since I was fourteen and first watched her story cinematically, I have kept four daily journals. This began nearly one year before the big move to Oklahoma.

I know seventeen is going to be clear and focused and documented.

Kelly just gifted me my fifth day-to-day journal for my birthday, reading LOVE NEVER FAILS in dark colors, which is perfect because I have long assumed in my seventeenth year I would instantly mature, darken my hair correctly, and fall in love.

You may expect me to say none of this is happening, but I met a new hairstylist who gave me lowlights yesterday, I have already conquered a hard run in the rain, and the greatest thought-turned-action has arrived: our new house is complete!

Even if romance isn't evident, *philia* love is certainly precursing things. Mother gifted me a trip to the *Chateau on the Lake* in Branson, Missouri, with my best friend, Adalie, and our sisters, Elianna and Kelly Grace. It was the first instance I found myself alone at a hotel with three friends, surrounded by refreshing springs of water in the lobby white noising a dinner of porkchops and chicken breasts and a cheese platter. Afterward, we talked of dating expectations in the hot tub before licking ice cream while wrapped in hotel towels in the chateau's parlor, and sunset pictures led to stories, giggles, and opening presents in our hotel room.

Early the next morning, Adalie and I drank coffee on the deck of the hotel and watched the fog rest over the lake before shopping downtown, where I spontaneously bought a blue formal dress (it looked very seventeen). Yet my favorite gift of all is neither dress nor journal, but Adalie's birthday letter:

> As I grow older the more particular I become about my friends. I love that even though every year you become more beautiful, wiser, grown up, creative, *Candiceish*—for there is only one word to describe you and everyone who truly knows you knows this is right—you are still the same girl, same values, same beliefs, only stronger and drawing closer to God. Every year is a step further toward God, a step saying to the world I choose God. Stay strong and true to what you believe. Be content with what you are given because anything extra will be blessings. I can't wait for next year! And this year! I'm glad to have a friend like you in the dark dangerous world!

I want to write more letters. Mother gave me a set of stationary at my birthday breakfast. Letter writing can seem tedious and overlooked, but all it takes is to receive one good letter from someone to realize the power of the written word. Written words of affirmation speak of the deepest love anyone could ever give me aside from physical touch. I am so thankful for Adalie, though this may be the last time we see each other for a year. I miss doing life with friends.

My mother's parents, Annie and Papa, surprised me with a beautiful ombre blue beta fish. I named it Chesapeake, Chessie for short, after a series we watched together last fall. Now a fish holds the essence of caramel cappuccinos and head massages at their house—a fish that, after its little time swimming in circles in my new room, will go down to its watery grave.

For everything has a season …

I don't think I will buy a large bed for my new room like my sisters are doing. Now does not seem the time for that. I plan to stay in my white daybed with its squeaky mattress that launches me out at dawn to the sound of birds.

I need to jump from just thinking about all I want to do in my room to acting on it. I want to turn my room into a place people could visit and feel something like the Christmas spirit.

How will all of this be done? How will I put light and sound and texture all in this room?

I am too excited to analyze, too adrenalized to overthink.

No more talking about it. No more dreaming and thinking and wishing and hoping. Time has run out, and it is the best birthday present ever.

We're moving to our new house!

What better way to start off seventeen than stepping foot in your new, navy bedroom to stick glow-in-the-dark stars on the ceiling. *Thank you, Lord, for this long-anticipated feeling of going home.* I pray while driving up the hill to our new cottage, smiling at its loyal shade of blue.

I wish I had friends to help me decorate, to hang pictures and play music and eat the first bowl of popcorn on the daybed. But just because this monumental day isn't shared with a friend, it doesn't mean it's not a blessing. And I have this truly unconventional eight-person family, who really deserve an entire series dedicated to their personalities.

"It feels like fall!" I run through the house.

Autumn Leaves is playing on a little speaker as men in moving trucks beep up the driveway, carefully rolling out Mother's grand piano. Lining the front lawn is another moving truck, waiting for a chance to unload the eight mattresses, golden-leaf mirror, and dark wood television hutch to their proper places; whilst ahead of that, Big Roy the Suburban is parked appropriately out of the way. Closet boxes have accumulated in the black-and-white kitchen, shoe boxes in the open brown-wood coat room, and piles of trash bags stuffed with plush toys have landed in a laundry room with two shiny stainless-steel machines. *That is certainly a change.* I think with little nostalgia, recalled our eggplant-colored tiles and 20-year-old washing machine back in Missouri. Nothing nostalgic about half-dry clothes.

Yes, the English cottage is abuzz, and I can't wait to visit all the new rooms, but one in particular has me gliding down the slick tiles and up sixteen stairs to an attic, teetering as if tiered on a ship. The gray hexagonal ceiling and slanted blue wall is prime for dreams and ideas, whistling "Come up here!" through the wind of a happy, howling window. The little room still smells of navy paint and sawdust, and I savor the rich feeling that this is all mine to behold, to create. Just weeks ago, I came in and wrote scriptures and quotes on the wall frames, praying over its structure, like, "A simple life prepares us to take the unexpected adventures ahead," and, "We will all die, but the way we live determines the life we live tomorrow."

"Are you Candice?" A designer named Brooke with a pen in her messy bun smiles broadly as I enter the room. "Cool paint you have in here! I have several fabric options here for window curtains."

Curtains! It is all I ever wanted, ever since I saw Mary Poppins peek through the lace to talk to the birds from Jane and Michael's nursery window. Core childhood.

"Also, your mom mentioned you wanted some kind of window seat cushion," she slides her hand on the cream bench under the window. "Take a look in this print book. I think you'll find several patterns appealing."

"Oh yes, thank you," I say stately, flipping through the booklet.

Patterns! This wasn't just another decision. I have waited for a window seat since I watched Stephen James pray out the window in the 1998 children's movie *Prayer Bear*. This is literally a lifelong fascination. (Who knew films affected so many of my ideals?) The real joy will be tonight, after everything was more or less settled in, sitting on the window seat, staring up at the real stars, then staring back at my own. A dream realized. Finally—thought turned action!

"Were you thinking a ripple fold, or perhaps a tailored pleat?" Brooke works on happily as I move Chessie's fishbowl to an empty bookshelf.

Pretending to know what any of these are, I put the book aside and scrutinize the large cream windows that overlook the east wing of the cottage, a perfect waving view from Dad's office windows, even though they're on the opposite end of the second floor, split up a separate set of six stairs. "Yes, that sounds lovely. Or whatever you think." I smile graciously.

If only I owned a pair of plaid pajamas ... I really could be Stephen James.

"Your mom mentioned you like blue, so I gathered a few fabrics you can touch here."

What textures did I like? Oh, Candice, don't overthink it ...

"It all depends on what you're envisioning." Brooke licks her thumb and flips through the ring of texture squares. "A nice cotton or chenille is practical and cozy, while a leather or polyester adds a level of modernity and sophistication to your room. This isn't an office, so I don't recommend those, especially if you plan to sit here to read."

Haha! She thinks I like to read! I smile and nod, like yes, of course I read. She probably does not guess this fresh-faced high schooler plans to become an author in this very room. Better yet, an author who doesn't like books. "What about the fabric patterns?" I direct.

"Well!" Brooke lights up passionately. "The choices really aren't endless, given you have your preferred texture."

"I do like chenille," I rub my fingers down the tiny rows, "however, I am also particular about the pattern being just right for this space. What do you think?"

"It really depends on what you like. There's houndstooth and harlequin and tattersall and tartan, madras and gingerbread, argyle and glen check …"

"What about … er … polka dots?" I point to a velvety-woven square that already has them in blue and white, simple and predictable, very early 2000s. And I can pronounce it.

"Ah, yes. Very cute. I like it." She notes the number of the pattern on her legal pad.

"And as for the curtains …" I peruse through a list of names. "Let's go polka dots too."

"Polka on polka? Done."

"Wait, are you sure that isn't too much … polka? I hesitate.

"No!" She laughs. "There is *never* a wrong time for a polka dot, Marc Jacobs tells us. I do recommend a distinction in the size of the polka dot, which I have ideas on how to do … thinking sheer …"

Sure, but Marc Jacobs isn't the one who has to stare at all these polka dots. I think as two men come up with boards of plywood. What if it starts looking like white freckles after a while? Bouncing atoms? Bouncing *thoughts,* even!

Chill, Candice.

The designer opens her mouth upon seeing my deepened brow. "The consistency of the polka dot can be surprisingly cleaner than if you were to do two different patterns."

Interesting, and I guess logical. I nod now without a crease in my forehead, save the line from raised eyebrows, giving her a courteous *'ah,'* for the ostensible genius I obviously lack.

"Excuse me, ma'am," some workers ascend to us. "Just fixing up the bookshelf room."

"Ah, the *secret room*," I whispered aloud.

"What are you going to put in there?" The designer peeks, flicking out a tape measurer.

"Storage, I guess." I say vaguely.

No sense in telling the world. I discern, eyeing her carefully. She probably means no harm, but designers tend to be on the craftier side. Chemistry class had given me all sorts of ideas for utilizing this tiny space I can't stand straight in—I figured it means more for the world's good that Candice carefully designs her writing home during class than memorize the periodic tables, given all the books I planned to give the world. The first idea I have for this attic space isn't necessarily even a place to write, but walls to pattern with 4x4 squares of scenes from not necessarily *favorite* films, but inspirational ones. I have already started printing pictures.

"*You* certainly have an eye for design," Brooke tells me before shaking my hand and moving down and up the hill of stairs to the west wing of the house and into Kelly's room, where I hear the same delightful curtains presentation begin and Kelly's signature hesitancy as she murmurs: 'Hmm, now may I see that again?'

The only thing bigger in joy than that secret space is a place I know I will spend more time, if not every day, growing in—the garage space where my future car will go is going to become a new workout room. I begged and begged for a mirror and really did not know for sure if it would make it in there, but one day after returning from school when we came to check on the house progress, there it was waiting on me. On that day I clapped my hands so they echoed like the taps of metal shoes and exclaimed, "Just think of all the things we're going to do in here!"

"It's literally a dance studio! I'm adding a ballet bar." Allison said.

"Mom's punching bag could go in here, too." Bria added, for Mom had recently begun to take Mixed Martial Arts, a shock and surprise to all of us. Everyone needs an outlet.

What a space! No more planks on carpet in the bedroom. No longer breath sucked in, held underwater, waiting on a change to spread out and really fly. If spaces really defined who you were, one step in each of our bedrooms proved the five girls were their entirely own people. Every room provided a space for personalities to be distinct: Candice's stage; Kelly's sanctuary; Bria's ice palace; Allison's pink drink; Angel's … well, it's a mystery at this point.

I visit each of these rooms before returning to the east tower, the side of the staircase that holds my little attic room and shower that you have to lean your head inside lest you hit the ceiling. The bathroom is pastel blue, with glass lights on either side of a modest-sized oval mirror elevated above a silver sink head. One rectangular wall vent releases a distinct chill and little howl. The knobs, like all my jewelry, are silver. It's a formidable space for a single girl.

"All done here." The secret room workers move out of my room just as more footsteps arrive, carrying my chipped cream dresser and daybed. I am glad we got to move in our stuff today, even if workers are still shoring up details.

"Hello, thank you. This wall." I motion to the space carefully measured out weeks before.

It's amazing to see dreams become visible. The loose plan formed in chemistry class was to use the center wall that faces you upon entering for a wall-mounted mirror, something no one else decided to do. It could have fit my desk, or I could have hung my cello, Quincy, but it just didn't seem right. "Are you sure you don't want it in your closet? You have room for it. Or you could even mount it on the back of your bathroom door." Mom had advised me. But I wanted it front and center. Priorities must be visible.

A little Irish tune is now playing in my mind, a reel with a high BPM that makes me stand on my tip toes and wish I could go dance in the garage at this moment, but a man is asking me whether I planned on using the outlet on the blue wall before a mover covered it with the bed. Here is where I realize this space cannot be completely ideal; if I am to have a wall solely devoted to the mirror, other furnishings will have to be given away. There are only three walls that can technically be used: the mirror wall, which may have room for a portrait or clock, the music wall, where I planned to eventually mount Quincy the cello, and the desk wall, high enough to hang a white board above it.

"So *you*, Candice." Kelly walks in to survey the progress. "This is such an exciting day! What are those drawers for?" She points under the window seat.

"Toys and archives, of course."

"What do you mean 'toys'?"

"You've got to have somewhere to put your Play-Doh set!" I laugh seriously.

It was apparently caused by an underdeveloped nervous system stifled somewhere in the womb that I was an uncoordinated and overly sensuous kid, scared of everything from ballet tights to seatbelts. This makes sense when you see me rub the edge of a cardigan between my fingers or run with a twist in my legs. Occupational therapy (OT) and physical therapy (PT) as a grade schooler was fun only because Mom took me to get an orange sherbet shake at Braum's Ice Cream between appointments. It was the rhythm of this routine, OT being first, that involved laying on your stomach playing *Perfection* (the memory game) to riding on your less dominant foot on a scooter around hospital atriums. I was okay not joining the soccer team. My therapist doctor wouldn't allow *that*. I only wanted to because the cleats looked cool, anyway, so when Mom found out she bought me a pair of Velcroed look-a-likes at Payless Shoes. I played with the straps and pressed the base of the rip until tiny red dots appeared on my fingers. Satisfied.

Today at work during an early childhood development lecture, I find myself wondering how perhaps these experiences may serve to be more than just a memory of the past, but something to still play with between fingers.

"Using a rhyming or chanting style often captures children's attention and helps them learn about speech, patterns, and rhythm. That rhythm and speech pattern, well, that's the beginning of biological awareness. Do you have the tools to incorporate the physical touch component?"

Glad I have polka dots chanting in my room now. Hehe. I can almost see the polka dots marching with little knives. It reminds me of my childhood fear of lima beans marching off my plate to eat me ... I shiver.

"Face-to-face play and gentle touch are important ways to build a secure relationship with a baby. You should be asking yourself, *Do I have a squeeze vault? Do I have sensory stations? Do I have colored paper that relaxes the amygdala?"*

What a great idea! I nod to the lecturer.

Whatever a squeeze vault is, I certainly need one. I could make my secret room a sort of vault—a vault of ideas that squeeze themselves out in such a space dedicated to the work of geniuses. I am not sure what to call my overall room yet. All I can think about are Savanna and Tropics and Ocean right down the hall in this school, the texture books I played with after school, the body sock I rolled around in during occupational therapy, the bubble motion tumblers and kinetic sand and surgical brushes that littered my bedroom as a child. Thankfully, messes were something Mom tolerated, from doll clothes stuffed under the bed to stethoscopes in the closet. I plan to bring a sense of order to my new room, and a great deal of imagination.

"People thought the brain must be complete because the weight of a baby's brain maximizes to that of an adult's between the ages of three and five, but of course that is a total lie. At this stage, we are in the heart of neurons connecting. We play a big part of not only what's going to happen but what is happening right now. And I'm not talking content, I'm talking about personal emotional stories for the rest of their lives."

These lectures are continuously eye-opening. Here I am, thinking early childcare was where people worked if they didn't know what they wanted to do with their lives (i.e. me), but clearly it is bigger than that. This role I play as Officiator of the Happy Birthdays on the playground may very well cement into the minds of toddlers like Jaxon and Layton. My love for children, and really, my heart to nurture as a doctor and mother, suddenly evokes more meaning than the monotonous tasks of marching with toddlers.

There was surely worth to my work hours, to my voice, to my actions.

What do I do with these raw senses? They're like beautiful wounds that have remained untouched, scars of DNA never fully processed. It is wise to never classify an injury as good or bad, just as you would never call a sickness 'ugly' though its effects can be thought of as that, but you see it as merely something calling for attention. In the real medical world, you see it objectively, not emotionally. But since my memories are intangible, I feel more at liberty to connect emotion with them. I call them wounds because they seem to need treatment. All these memories and miracles and magic and mystery in the last seventeen years, all of it buried under moving boxes and fitting in at private school. It seems there is a deeper layer of knowing the past, perhaps connected to a deeper layer of genius (or eccentricity, as some may see it) which I have not yet uncovered due to an invulnerability—not ready to fully admit who I am or where I came from.

But this isn't good for a memoirist. To be a good writer you must be honest with yourself. I am not fully ready for this, but at least I recognize it at this stage of life.

Studying early childhood development and creating this new room is pulling wires that have carried ten years of dust in my brain for the past seven years. I am not ready to go back to age ten, but it was my favorite year, and I hope to do so someday. I may need friends again to pull it out of me.

"Don't forget, in that very first year of life, 702,000 neurons per second are connecting in the brain. Language is developing. Learning and content is developing. Resiliency is beginning to connect. And if we don't use it, we lose it."

Like Latin, I mourn. I used to be able to translate paragraphs of first-century Roman texts. Now all I can remember is *sunt corpora in flūmine*. It's fine; someday I will be in a dire situation when an eager Gaul will ask me, "What is that?" And I will respond that there are indeed bodies floating in the river. I suppose I should be grateful that my massive digestion of philosophy these days seems to hold more meaning than translating a dead language. I really should hold onto my memories though, before I lose them as Bing-Bong did in Disney's *Inside Out*.

"Give them the words that they need." The lecturer's past words replay.

Strange how everything seems connected to childhood ... and writing my first book.

"Any thoughts on dating?" Mother asks me as we stand on the driveway unpacking boxes in her new garage. What an unexpected question. Not that every seventeen-year-old girl isn't already thinking about it, but it's such an alarming thing to ask me in public when I have a negative answer. Are the neighbors listening? Am I being videoed? I really can't be too careful.

The sun is hidden beneath cotton clouds and the air is just silent, which I like. No wind or squinting. Like the sun, I am guarded.

"I will someday," I reflect. "Given I find someone worthy of dating."

"Well, don't be too particular," she warns. "Little Candice is like that."

Sure, I thought, spinning the wheel of my bike. *Except you only get one chance, right? Unless you're Elisabeth Elliot, I suppose. But it's not like you can plan to have three husbands.*

" … you don't want to be waiting around for some perfect person. And then you get to your forties to realize you were waiting for a fairytale." Mom continues.

Fair. I make an inner note to warn myself of the danger of a façade. The lie that everything would be better because of a new room—or, more pointedly, a new relationship. Still, everything is just perfect the way it is. I don't need a boyfriend; I have a space to call my own now, and I'm going to be awfully busy writing my book based on moving to Oklahoma.

Shadows move across the cement. I sense a breeze of peace but also of fear. I feel a gaping hole, but not one that is about to be filled. Not yet. "He might not even be here."

"What do you mean?" Mom asks.

"I don't know." I shrug. "Suppose he is right down the street. But sometimes I wonder if he's even in Oklahoma at all … he just feels so far away."

I have never admitted it aloud. It's honestly discouraging thinking he is somewhere very far away and I won't meet him soon. But, in all seventeen's disappointment, I genuinely feel it.

"Why do you hope he's far away?"

"I don't *hope* he is. I just *feel* like he is. There's a difference."

"But there are so many good boys at your school and church!"

"Mom, I don't think he is my age, or in any way already connected to me."

Such a weird thing to think—let alone say. Too late to take it back.

"Candice! You have no idea!" She laughs. "You just wait how God is going to surprise you. I vowed to never marry a man named Scott, and look at me now! He could live super close to us. He could be someone you've known your whole life. You just never know."

"Of course I don't know." I add my hands under her lifted box. "For all I know, God is just keeping him generic and far away in my mind because it isn't time yet. Perhaps it is just because he is not in my current circles that I feel so isolated from him." I reflect on this for a moment, then this strange image of a globe—as clear as beach glass—pools in my mind, somewhere in the righthand corner of the real sky above an empty lot across the street from us. "Yet sometimes I wonder if he is somewhere else in the world."

"Who knows, Canzie." Mom eyes me warily. "He might be here, and you're just not awake to him yet. I just don't want you to be weird around boys I introduce you to."

"Of course not, Mom."

"Well, you are weird sometimes! You've got to be friendly, even if you don't like them."

"Sure." I smile. But at this shadowed hour, love feels a contented million miles away.

On a crisp morning in this brand-new, quiet room, I tell God, *Nothing has changed with me. I give You my whole life.* I say this to clear any gray area of being attacked by the feeling that I have everything and don't need

God. No, nothing could ever fill His place. Not this room, not my book, and certainly not a friend or boyfriend (I still have neither).

"Christ is enough." I say aloud and fling my feet over the side of the bed. The smell of homemade pancakes and bacon gradually fills the room and voices from the echoey kitchen float up the stairs. Before anything is officially nailed or hung in this Candicey-land, full of potential for ideas and execution, I need to go on a run.

Candiceyland.

It sounds timeless and iridescent, like a sharp crystal with sun sparkling on it, a spoon clinking on glass and settling in a warm hand—perfect for winter-blue dreams.

Candiceyland it is.

Carved with steep hills and stone bridges, our neighborhood is like a medieval desert of citadels and cottages. Red clay oozes from the cracked yellow road connecting cul-de-sacs, so the neighborhood has the lighting of constant summer even though it is fall and chilly.

Legend has it a rattlesnake den is in alarming proximity, in addition to the common problem of indoor scorpion infestation. One of the first things I realize while running is not how scary that is, but how scary these empty lots are to my right and left. Plots that scream construction is coming. My dad might think of this as progressive, and he may even admit that this will bring out the snakes and we should be careful, but my thoughts are elsewhere. Construction means early morning noise and people watching my painful route of death. It's so embarrassing being such a crooked runner. I can't even keep my hips moving straight forward. I'm like a dancing puppet, gasping while climbing a mountain (not an elevation of twelve feet).

Good grief, I need to get my first book out there, I think while loping up the hill. Moving feels like so long ago, and no one has even read about it.

Isn't it exposing to publish your journals? I ask myself. *But what were the journals for in the first place? Just to vent, or to actually help someone else?* I recognize.

It's funny how paralyzing new things are.

Running away from writing.

Writing, and even procrastinating running at times.

Yet even if I am lying to myself by saying "writer" when I have less than a hundred book words, calling myself a runner when I haven't even done a 5k, surely taking neurological steps in these directions is progressive.

Even if my name isn't Rachel, I still feel like I'm becoming what she inspired in me. I am ready to step into that leader role I assumed came upon her with this beautiful number 17.

A part of me feels like I shoved away very honorable parts of childhood incorrectly. So much life happened before I moved, still unrecorded. Before I trusted. Before I sacrificed. It's all packed away—not in a forever kind of way, but like I am supposed to do something with it. My childhood feels like it isn't meant to stay in a box; it's supposed to be reopened and examined. That's strange to think about for me, an unknown seventeen-year-old, so anxious to grow up and be like the Rachels I admired. Like when we moved, I said goodbye to Missouri, but saying goodbye did not burn the memories. What am I supposed to do with them? Who knew I would be here to start my most anticipated year alone and friendless? I don't even have a car! At least I am out of yellow sixteen. Never liked the number. I do like the thought of writing in this year. Seventeen sounds very author-ish. Let's see if it actually is.

Everything sits in silence except for the clicking of the clock in Candiceyland. I find it soothing in a fearful sort of way. It reminds me time is running out. I am constantly aware of the fact my actions equal consequences. As the weather stiffens my bones and the days fall short, I feel my body slowing down. It's customary now that it is December I feel this way. Last March's drive to survive private school is history, and so is any sort of competitive summer spirit or September determination like I had in the rental house. Yet this the most crucial time of the semester. I have finals this week in both my Southeastern University classes and Challenge III homeschool co-op classes! I found out at school yesterday that for the Lincoln-Douglas (LD) debates, a strand in the Challenge III curriculum, I am going against a girl who's known to be an extraordinarily competitive debater—and I have never done LD once! I am slightly competitive, but I don't care for conflict, unlike her. Everyone's been telling me scary stuff about her. My advantage? I am pretty organized and thorough in my research. That's about it.

Another project that looms over my head is my philosophy class speech. I am supposed to do it on my 'big ideal,' my most passionate cause, but I don't think I have one. Apart from the new significance of early childhood and the making of Candiceyland, I am not sure what I really care about, except … thinking about philosophy now, there is something that still hurts my heart.

"Do that," Mrs. Loose suggested when I mentioned it.

The problem isn't my own reluctance to defend something so ultimate, but something so sensitive. It is people like Mr. Drake the atheist and skeptical classmates who make my spirit deeply troubled. I do not want to be the cause for their resentment towards God. But I realize I am thinking of it all the wrong way.

Truth did not need defending.

God Himself would remain God whether I represented Him well or not. Of course, I can't imagine suggesting He was anything less than good and perfect to my class, but I also don't see myself being ready to answer every question.

"Having a relationship with God is so personal," I explained to Mrs. Loose. "How could I ever describe it to others?" Although it was a relationship not built on bullet points, I have to present it as such.

"You already do by the way you live," she acknowledged. "This speech is meant to be an overview of what you've learned this semester in terms of our discussions, not a defense for your salvation. I think you are more than capable to lay out the facts."

Real writing begins now. I'm in the secret room, not entirely perfected, but *here*.

As a writer you have to get over imperfections quickly. You don't just wake up and have a perfect secret writing room hidden behind a bookshelf. If you have the structure at all, you're stuck with a toxic-smelling attic space, perceptively hot in summer and deathly cold in winter. It's endearing when you picture yourself wrapped in a shawl like Jo March in *Little Women* clicking away by candlelight. Except I am not allowed to have candles up here, and the sound of outside construction is noising the space that is supposed to only circulate Michele McLaughlin's *The Descent*.

Writing is less endearing when still in workout clothes from a mediocre run. I didn't feel like changing into anything else, but now I feel rather dirty and can't shower because there are issues with our new water well. The water is turning orange. Add in oily hair.

Don't think about how you feel.

It's time to start writing. No matter what it is or how it gets done or when it gets done, it's all about adjusting to this new stage as a real writer. God has a plan for my words, even if my mind feels like a blank piece of tissue paper that belongs somewhere in someone else's basket of genius. Rather than basking in imaginative ideas, I feel like clamming up and spending all my time reading other peoples' work, especially as it is winter now. Katherine Woodfine's *Sinclair's Mysteries* are calling me, along with a cup of peppermint tea. But I have no right to become a consumer. *No, writers write,* I tell myself.

The secret room is still in progress, but I have hung a strand of Christmas lights in the L-shaped space so it wraps a candle-like glow around the cloud-ceiling cocoon. My dear friends of stuffed bears and porcelain dolls sit on the puffy side of the wall with foam stuck over the edge. I am part-marshmallow, part-hidden war survivor … with my stuffed animals.

God, why have you chosen for my life to be without friends? It would be so much more fun to share this space with someone who is actually alive (no offense to you, Cornbread the bear). To have them help me hang pictures and letters on the walls. To watch movies and read books and talk about boys …

It is what it is. If God is preparing me for something big, chances are He will take me through a season of solitude, like what I am experiencing right now. It is obvious that I am not ready for a relationship because God has not brought one, so why would I talk about it and stir up feelings prematurely? Yes, I am glad I am not talking about boys. I need to learn that I can't lean upon anyone but God for my confidence so I can gain the strength to stand alone even when no one else stands with me. I need to learn to trust Him more, then have the faith that He will help me step out in faith even when I don't feel brave. I suppose all brave women are scared at times. As long as I still rise to the occasion, I am a brave woman.

All in all, I cannot stay the way I am and go with God.

PART TWO
ACTA NON VERBA
(DEEDS, NOT WORDS)

*It is with composers as with all of us:
what we believe affects our total lives.*
—*Beethoven*

CHAPTER 7
JO WRITES

11TH GRADE WINTER, EDMOND, OKLAHOMA

*I write not for the sake of glory ... the sake of fame ...
the sake of success. But for the sake of my soul.*
—*Rachel Joy Scott*

Public speaking terrifies me. As in, paralyzes. Suffocates. Turns me into a lightheaded, nauseated, trembling mute person. Too bad the end-of-year philosophy assignment is a speech. As in, too bad for the people watching.

It's Friday, December 6. The last in-person philosophy class of Challenge III for the year. Candice Gibbons is on deck to offer an eleventh-grade stance on morality, basically a defense of ultimate truth and good and evil against ancient philosophers' conclusions. No big deal.

"Ensure you are recording," I whisper to Mom, not because I want to see myself stutter for five minutes, but because my online philosophy professor at Southeastern University demands footage to pass their class, too, as this assignment overlaps with their curriculum.

"You've got this!" Mom whispers back. She gives me the hug I've wanted for a long time and even kisses my forehead. But it hits me wrong in this moment.

"I am so proud of you. Little Canzie is graduating with an A in her first college class. *Little Canzie!* Tee-hee!"

"Not yet, Mom." I pull back in a wave of nerves.

The lecture, formally titled *Morality: The Nature of God* (I thought throwing a colon into the title sounded very academic) is not a clean punch. To my seventeen-year-old brain, it hits me that I am basically signing up to defend *the earth is round*. Super controversial and, then again, maybe not. The whole earth debate is much more laughable; this is serious—not just because it has the letter *m* in it evoking feelings of royal business, but because it is spiritually intertwined.

One eleventh grader in a windowless classroom isn't going to make an explosion in modern philosophical thought. This speech does not solve all the questions we had debated or strived to fully refute (how could one?). But having this foundation of morality, it is deep in me like tight abs—hidden and stabilizing when life is uneven. It didn't matter what anyone thought or said. I cared about it so deeply it made me cry sometimes. That's why I can't just embarrass myself here and let it all out emotionally.

Persuasion requires composure and logic. This matters like the accuracy of a tossed lifebuoy. The fact that thought affected action which affected where someone spent eternity was the highest crisis at hand.

And here I am, holding a little green index card scribbled with points from a lengthy, meticulously worded paper that I could not fully take with me to this corner of the classroom, about to walk up and defend objective truth to a room of people who may or may not receive it.

Oh Lord, nothing I say is good enough. Nothing I have written is evidence enough to convince people of the validity and certainty of Your love and justice, that there is a way to live that keeps them from both earthly and eternal destruction. Please go with me.

"You're up." Mrs. Loose points, and to the applause of the last presenter, I walk to the front of the boardroom failing to breathe.

Mr. Drake slips into the back.

I try not to look at him nor the phone positioned to video me. With each step, heart-pounding lightheadedness gives me blurred vision. As all sets of eyes meet my own watery blue ones, I realize I can't just start and dissipate the awkwardness of silence because the timer is not set. Mrs. Loose whispers something to my mom that has me trying to read lips.

This is so awkward.

"Alrighty, let's get this set up." Mrs. Loose adjusts the portable red timer situated on the boardroom table. "Er ... hold on a minute."

I lean into my left hip, retreating to a habitual stance of insecurity, though it feels like security to me. I slip the edge of my black-and-white-striped cardigan between my fingers, wondering if I should crack a joke, run through a song in my head, or rewrite my entire exordium. In regular overthinker fashion, all three run through my head like three streams feeding into one another, colors yellow, pink, and blue.

Stop staring at me, nerd. I'll never date you.

Why is that girl looking me up and down? Is my shirt tucked in right?

Lock in, Candice. Morality. Morality.

"Alrighty." Mrs. Loose says. The bold five-minute countdown snarls back at me, eager to run excruciatingly slow, I am sure.

Oh God, help.

Suddenly, He does.

Like the sound of a favorite person's text notification, I recall a scripture verse memorized in seventh grade. It really hits right now—and it's not even for me to feel less insecure.

> *For since the creation of the world God's invisible qualities—his eternal power and divine nature—have been clearly seen, being understood from what has been made, so that people are without excuse.*[1]

The thought struck again: truth did not need defending.

God certainly did not need me to say anything in order to speak to someone. He did not need me at all. But He chose me. Broken, ill-placed, and certainly not in my element. But obedient. And trusting.

That was enough to slip a smile into my first words.

Breaking it down with a lyrical reference opener in a calm, clear voice, it begins and flows with clear enunciation, a precision far beyond what my own trembling nature could allow. Despite not having access to the full paper of notes I so practiced, I am able to recall specific points and deliver them calmly, without exaggeration.

> ... Protagoras stated, "Objective truth is neither possible nor desirable." Future philosopher Soren Kierkegaard agreed with his own words, "Truth is subjectivity." ... While this may be convenient with preferences when arguing chocolate is superior to vanilla ... if there were no objective truths in our world, everything we sense and perceive is, in fact, deceitful.
>
> ... Aristotle perceived there to be "a demand for justice, a demand for black and white answers and math, science, and even more law." He recognized it to be orchestrated by a supernatural being with ties to humanity.
>
> ... Thomas Aquinas protected Aristotle, proving virtues need a moral basis. Aquinas believed all virtues, charity, love, and faith, the like, are rooted in God because they are the nature of God.
>
> C.S. Lewis addressed an idea he called the Law of Human Nature in his book, *Mere Christianity*. He writes, "The Law of Human Nature, or of right and wrong, must be something above and beyond the actual facts of human behavior. In this case, besides actual facts, you have something else, a real law which we did not invent and which we know we ought to obey."
>
> ... Russian novelist Dostoevsky gives us the thought that if God does not exist, all things really are permissible. If there is no God to face on Judgment Day, no authority to reckon with at the end of times, and no powerful governance enact when choosing right and wrong, don't color in the lines for man's sake.
>
> ... Because we are created in the image of God and the nature of morals is rooted in God, then we must make moral choices. ... history tells evidence of destruction when man bases his decisions on his perception of reality. The root of truth is exclusively objective and the demand for ultimate truth and justice is found in God and God alone.[2]

With a firm "thank you," I smile and excuse myself, blurring past Mom's thumbs up and Mrs. Loose's smiling face. The longer I can stand outside the classroom and watch the slow bar upload on the video of my presentation to my online portal the better. I don't dare to watch it before clicking 'submit' and sliding into the bathroom to check my falling bun of curls. It certainly gave off a sense of height. Now it's fallen; like everything else, deflating from sucked-in adrenaline that got me to this place. Dizziness is replaced with exhausted relief. I did it.

The bathroom door creaks open.

"You did it!" Mom says with another hug. "Did you watch the video yet? Did it upload okay? I've got to run and need my phone, baby."

"Yes," I say. It comes out in a relieved sob.

Mr. Drake is standing in the hall when we emerge. He studies me intently before saying, "This was, perhaps, one of the most complete set of responses to this blue book exam. Exemplary rhetoric. I trust you gained more tools in your pursuit of knowledge, wisdom, and … er … truth. I was thoroughly compelled by your presence in our classroom this semester to do an in-depth study on such topics as morality."

Rather, I think sheepishly.

"An indefatigable struggle." Mr. Drake huffs long. "Someday …" he eyes me mournfully, like he can't decide whether to tell me some grave news.

I know what he's trying to say. I don't accept it.

"You'll stay on with philosophy, I hope?"

Wheels turn. I feel my face lighten.

"Forever, I'm afraid."

I almost forget to thank God for helping me when I return to Candiceyland, now festooned with a little blue Christmas tree reflecting off iridescent-blue tinsel draped over the newly hung polka-dotted curtains above the polka-dotted window seat. The air is staticky and cold but has that fresh house whiff of newness, and everything has once-in-a-lifetime afforded innocence.

No one had ever showered in the pebble-floored space with the slanted ceiling and high glass door before me. Mine were the first hands to hang blue coat hangers in the warm space of closet. When it was time to be quiet and write, I could simply shut the door, and all fell silent. Beyond my little pun-of-the-day calendar and white board with a list of black to-dos was the essence that my bookshelves were inspired by the two sides of the brain: the left side neatly rowed with an ode to classicalism, thanks to my recent philosophical exposure; the right side, creative, with artifacts like an antique pirate ship inspired by the movie *Tintin*. Quincy the cello is reclined in the corner, his scroll head nodding to a row of southern magazines in dedication to my grandmother, Gigi, working on me becoming an appreciator of such things as homemaking and hospitality; above that are my two favorite fiction series' by American YA author Melody Carlson and UK children's author Katherine Woodfine, the two women who are working on me becoming a reader. All these things say that I am becoming someone quite 'learned' but my favorite thing on the shelf is the PARADISE FALLS jar full of money. The iconic movie element symbolizes a tangible possibility that somehow, someway, something may happen and I have to be ready for it. Once that jar and my alive little fish, Chessie, found their corners, I was settled into a hot air balloon, ready to take off.

My books, on the other hand, aren't totally transportational. They may just sit there with their bright spines forever. But they do look very nice, and that's what matters. It's one thing to own books; it's another to do something with them. Naturally, I go for the appearance. And preparing for an unwritten adventure.

Ignorant, I'm sure.

Distanced by the bench of thought where I sit to write deep at night while gazing out the window just like Stephen James, are the righthand shelves full of journals, notebooks, binders, and photo albums. Ideas. Projects. Creations.

Right now, the Lord is speaking to me, very softly, that I need to study. Go into the woods. Do deep work alone.

Sure. I see it happening later in my secret room when snow is on the ground …

But you're out of school now, I counter. *Now is the time.*

Suddenly, a frozenness in the room slides its hands around me. A frozenness not of thought, but of body. A stillness turning me to stone. Dry, meaningless wind. A kind I sense I am choosing.

What am I missing?

Oh. Adequate praise!

It is in this moment I start a practice. I drop to my knees at the window seat.

Thank You, God. You completely helped me today! I am so sorry I forget that I could not have done what I did in my own strength. You didn't take away the fear; You taught me I can be strong even when I feel insecure. Thank You! I give You this book I am trying to write. It is meaningless without You in it! I really have no idea what I am doing. God, You know I don't even read my favorite authors often. I don't like to read! Please give me a love for learning. I know I don't study well. I don't like to study, but You can help me. I will try to pray to You more consistently now that I have this window seat. I'm sorry I did not pray consistently before. I know I shouldn't rely on outward circumstances to dictate my happiness. Please help me be more versatile. And let this bench be my reminder to come to You in prayer about things. Thank You again!

With a weight-relieving sigh, lights spring on in my head. Permission to write.

Outer Oklahoma Christmases aren't the snowy kind tucked in rosemary and thymes, but the dry, western plains of orange spice and mulled wine, wild with a wind and ice so dangerous in the gingerbread grids of four way stops. Sliced into five main roads, you can cut left or right to hit the next main street, with various coffeehouses available to the many students in the multi-university region. With an emphasis on the arts, as well as professional sports, the power of Oklahoma City's diversity and progressiveness is new and empowering, showing me a new and broader scope of the world than my hometown, Ozark, and yet it is still a midwestern centralization point for farmers, fishermen, and ranchers. Cattle, horse, and chicken farms commonly line everything from backroads to highways, not to mention an unusual amount (in my opinion) of cemeteries. 'Cowboys and Indians' and the ghosts in these stories are the folklore told around riskily high bonfires, either handmade from piles of burning sticks in a homesteader's yard or an in-ground firepit in a multi-million-dollar neighborhood.

Another such element that highlights much of the culture of Oklahoma City and its suburb of Edmond are strings of lights on trees in gas station parking lots. Electric blue and Christmas red and sour green. Modernity and community spirit at their finest. Even the radio tunes are different here: instead of one version of a holiday classic, I hear a completely unknown one, and rather than driving through Ozark, Missouri's Finley River Park's Christmas lights, we drive around Nichols Hills in Oklahoma City, marveling at four-story homes with entire light show displays synchronized with music. I can't return to Missouri to participate with friends in our annual gingerbread house making contest, but I can make new traditions with my family, like picking out a Christmas tree from Sorghum Mill Tree Farm, or ice skating at Mitch Park. This side of Oklahoma I am seeing is certainly a step or two ahead of the Missouri I left. The sentimental side of me can't decide if she likes this, though I've learned at least one important thing this year: Wherever God has you is where He has you.

Of course, if your heart isn't right with God, chances are the misplaced feelings you have are signs that you need to get in the center of God's will. That is the safest place you can be. For me, it means working at the preschool, being homeschooled, and writing my book.

Socially exciting? Not exactly. But fulfilling? Completely.

Sickness is inevitable when you play with viral toddlers on a playground for a living, but that is where God has me right now, and I have embraced it. I am fevered and all the things, missing a drive-around night with the family, but I am content. I've been off and on sick ever since I started working there, but I don't want to fill my journal with useless cries about headaches and sore throats when that is where I am supposed to be.

You need to be careful as a writer. Just because you seal a moment in a journal, it does not mean it is private, or somehow forgotten, that you can release it forever; rather it is the opposite.

Still, I don't feel well, and no amount of editing, reading, or writing can satisfy or distract me from my headache. I have no Christmas list, and it isn't an option to eat Christmas food or listen to Christmas music. I just don't want to! But I have a soft hum of some of the deepest worship, a large container of water, my Bible, and journal spread out.

This is the first holiday season I am not in Missouri. Every song reminds me of some smell, some person, even the place I listened to it. In the end, it's about the people, the memories—a feeling richly sewn into my childhood. I am thankful we will return to Riverview Ranch where Annie and Papa and Poppy and Gigi live for a family Christmas dinner. I refuse to let Christmas be a remorseful season of past nostalgia. It is too significant! You can't have an Easter without a Christmas. This gets my writer wheels turning, and I step into the secret room and put pen to line.

Finishing the task, my eyelids slide low, rolling me in a horse-drawn carriage into dreamland, and I crawl out of the secret room to Candiceyland turned dark, minus the glowing stars above me. The year of change, about to close.

CHAPTER 8
REBEL INTRO

Where does self-regulation begin?
—Early childhood lecturer

The new year begins promptly for me at 4:30am. Casual in a sweatshirt and braid, I turn to Proverbs, intent on digesting a few words of wisdom before spinach frittatas and writing about the year of sacrifice, currently titled *A Time to Trust*. On my way there, pages flip to 1 Corinthians, where I spot a familiar but not always practiced verse:

I discipline my body like an athlete, training it to do what it should.[1]

Rats! Convicted already!

It is easier to read something about wisdom or virtues, to silently put them into practice, than to do something physical, like running. But I know I need to put action to my thoughts, action to the scriptures I read. I've run enough laps to know I will be stronger mentally if I am stronger physically. What in life isn't connected?

Fine, fine.

I journal this before putting on my tennis shoes.

I decide to call 2020 the Year of Health.

Our garage: dark, drafty, dead. The cold room of fluorescent lights and fumes is a blank galaxy of mirror and white. At first I think, *This is so gross, doing pushups beside the trash cans in the garage!* But it is the energy of the scorpion-infested space that marks me to push myself through the inconvenient. *Make war … don't settle … push yourself …* I breathe, feeling absolutely no aggression whatsoever.

But energy must be created. And this is where I decide that I like the absence of warm lighting and a space heater. There is something serene in the uncomfortable.

This is the kind of rebel I need to be—not a black-haired artificial one, but the rebel that decides to take on a new form of living in order to become what they neither see nor see coming easily.

I mark my progress in a notebook gridded for math homework. Can't look at any English lines, those composition spirals open for dreams in words; got to think like a grid, like Oklahoma.

~~10×3 pushups~~
~~10×3 sit-ups~~
~~15×10×3 squats~~
~~8×2 1-legged bar squats~~
~~1-mile speed run~~ in preparation to run long distance (my dream).

I am going to track my schedule of waking up consistently by at least 5:30 a.m. for an hour or longer workout before school. Noticing changes in my health, my attitude, my resilience and aggression. Things just seem easier. Still, internal dialogue hits just about every day I hit the light switch in the garage.

Candice the Writer: *Why, pray, do you attempt such inconveniences?*
Candice the Runner: *Because you can't not do this. Just because your*

feet hurt, or you're lightheaded, or you're tired or sick from work, or too busy to want to go on a run before it gets dark, you can't give in to excuses. Candice doesn't do that.

Candice the Writer: *Why out here? Can't one do light yoga in Candiceyland?*

Candice the Runner: *Because you can't play it safe. Not all work is done in the secret room, but the secret garage. You can't just be a writer who sips tea and thinks.*

Candice the Writer: *Fine, fine.*

In the garage again doing that hidden work. Rebels rebel against the norm.

It's February now. The norm for Candice is to procrastinate—to conjure a census of ease and certainty with the least amount of effort required. But if I am leading my personal life like this, I don't stand a chance at outward opposition.

You can't *not* do this.

Even if I feel like a random writer, it must become part of the routine of who I am, even if I hate every part of it. Even on the days when all I want to do is curl up and write and read and think lovely thoughts, I need to put on my boring workout clothes and go to the boring garage to do an isolated workout that hurts which nobody cares about but me. Even when I feel swollen and tired or sick from working at the preschool and fed up with doing anything physical, I must lock in mentally and shut myself in the garage.

This is a consequence I want in my life. It is the *choice* to do it that is the hard part.

Seeing progress, one rep at a time.

Lifting heavier.

Planking longer.

Face purple.

Vision blurred.

Becoming an athlete, even if I don't feel qualified or 'there' yet. Because I have to start before I become.

You can't wait to *be* in that place before you *walk* to that place.

Candice is an athlete.

Candice is an athlete.

Candice feels lightheaded.

Made it through another Valentine's Day without a date or friends. I always thought I would start dating at seventeen. It just felt so perfect! But until God makes it absolutely clear it is time to open myself to love, I must guard my heart and stay focused on all that's before me. I convinced Mom to let me join an independent track team to keep me accountable in both my workouts and my mental health. I know that the physical and spiritual are connected, and I feel best when I am active and healthy. Recognizing that actions lead to consequences, I can keep my heart guarded by focusing on pushing myself on the track. This will allow me less struggle and distraction before it is my time to love. I can't expect myself to stay guarded if I am choosing to listen to love songs and dream about romance; I have to be proactive in my mental purity. (Again, being rebellious here, because culture isn't exactly screaming at girls to be pure in their minds.)

I am so excited to run with a team again! I want to beat my 400-meter sprint time, and I think I can. I really like my coaches—tall, 50-something former multi-athlete Coach Barnett, and four-time Olympic trial qualifier Coach Robnett. They're tough and level-headed and listen seriously to my health conditions. But best of all, they push me.

The only strange thing is, being on the track this season gives me a startling new kind of fear, because I have a new kind of pain. It is still fun competing against other runners, but the results are freaking me out. I had to sit out from the final exercise because my right foot oddly hurt. I don't want to risk an injury this early in the season. It is probably just me getting back into a rhythm.

Tonight we eat Italian chicken, rice, and green beans at the family dinner table (a new round one with a particularly Lazy Susan that gets stuck halfway) talking about all the exciting things that seem to be just around the corner.

This fall I am a senior. Next August is my last time competing at the fine arts competition I do every summer. We will plan a road trip as usual, perhaps go to Florida again, or maybe the mountains, like I have always dreamed.

"I'd like to request a Missouri writing retreat this summer to finish *A Time to Trust*," I tell the family.

I obviously want to stretch myself by doing things like writing *A Time to Trust* and following God's will for my life, which is what I am doing, because I do feel a peace that has not come from any outward circumstance. It is still sad being attached to friends and a school you want to graduate with only to be ripped away and shipped to Oklahoma. Even though it was difficult to find a place at private school first, at least there were hundreds of people to choose from! I nearly cried yesterday in that tiny boardroom classroom asked embarrassing math questions, the narrowing eyes of Mr. Drake and snarky remarks from fellow debaters. It's not a big deal. I just need to learn how to process these random atmospheres that I am sure will mean something later on.

God, thank You for track. Even if I don't have friends yet and it hurts my feet, I really enjoy pushing myself physically so I can be strong mentally. Thank You for wiring me that way. All I want is Your will to be done in my life, whether it's at a nice school or the same damp classroom. Please give me patience to receive all the blessings You promised me if I moved to Oklahoma.

I can't run track.

Two months of pushing through an irregular amount of foot pain led me to x-rays with a new foot doctor who has the voice and smile of Dr. Dorian, the psychiatrist in the movie *Charlotte's Web*. He's great; the diagnosis is terrible. I could have promised you the screws in my right foot were loose when I walked into the office. I despise that kind of discernment. It felt like an attitude, immature negativity, a cloud of dread I created over my head.

But I was right.

"It appears as if one of the screws is pointing down and pushing further and further when you run," Dr. Dorian said sympathetically as he reviewed the x-ray.

So there you have it: I am getting the screws taken out in mere weeks. A surprise surgery has replaced my calendar of track meets and 400-meter sprints. I've already covered it in prayer. I am at peace knowing God has everything under control. But I am still crushed and trying to work through my emotions. Forget this year's records.

I angrily sweep the toddlers' bathroom at work. Not just angry about losing my ability to run during what I thought was going to be my 'Year of Health,' where I could make new friends and become an athlete again, but the fact that my other dream has felt like a sick nightmare.

Am I really ready to write a book? I realize anxiously. *Aren't I still learning trust with this unexpected surgery? But I can't not write! Words seem to drip from my brain at every second—words that come from my fingers but didn't come from me.* Thinking about this makes my already pounding headache feel as if the back of my skull is now dripping with blood. I wipe my neck to confirm it's just a feeling.

"Candice, you're needed in Tropics." Morgan yells through the hall, sounding ticked off.

I can't stand this job. I cough. *I'm getting paid minimum wage to be sick all the time.*

What else can I do? Writing itself is a pain right now, I can't write! Every time I walk into Candiceyland and see the bookshelf door that leads into the secret room that's supposed to be so magical and enchanting I feel guilty because I feel sick. I feel sick of procrastinating writing and sick of feeling sick for procrastinating writing. It feels very hypocritical to be writing to other girls about trusting in God when things don't make sense and here I am questioning where I am placed at the very job God provided.

I storm into the Tropics classroom turning into a mean Tomato, just like Morgan.

This is literally the worst. I cough again, this time getting a napkin and seeing blood.

"Can you lead story time today? I heard the children love you." A substitute teacher asks.

Find someone else, I think wrongly, but outwardly pulling it together by redoing my side braid that has marked this junior year. I smile loud enough that the children hear my raspy breath that sounds like little toddlers Layton and Elizabeth, who both have colds. What isn't there to love about lonely winters and rain? In my mind reading Longfellow …

The day is cold, and dark, and dreary
It rains, and the wind is never weary;
The vine still clings to the mouldering wall,
But at every gust the dead leaves fall,
And the day is dark and dreary.

My life is cold, and dark, and dreary;
It rains, and the wind is never weary;
My thoughts still cling to the mouldering Past,
But the hopes of youth fall thick in the blast,
And the days are dark and dreary.

Be still, sad heart! and cease repining;
Behind the clouds is the sun still shining;
Thy fate is the common fate of all,
Into each life some rain must fall,
Some days must be dark and dreary.[2]

I journal on my window seat to the piano song *Lavender Hills*, thinking of all the good amidst all the bad, like something that happened at work towards the end of the seemingly endless day.

A mom stared at me through the glass window for an awkward amount of time. At first I was flustered. Who was she? Why was she watching me so closely?

Come to find out, she is the mother of the new little strawberry blond girl named Hayden, who was terribly scared of everyone but found my khaki knee at story time safe. By the time her mother came to pick her up, she was jumping around with all the other kids. "Thank you," the mother said when she picked up Hayden, who waved shyly at me. It was a strange encounter in which I felt too dazed to process, but looking back, it meant something to her.

Ah, I see how You work through my weakness. I tell God, looking at the stars He hung. *I see how You can still grow me without track, perhaps even more so through a surgery. I connect my physical brokenness with a mental surrender. I'll do my best to let go of ideals and let You take it from here—my job, my purpose, even my health. It's all Yours, anyway. May I be a rebel to everything easy, familiar, or comfortable, no matter the cost.*

CHAPTER 9
LOCKDOWN

11TH GRADE SPRING, EDMOND, OKLAHOMA

This paralysis is my greatest mercy.
—Joni Eareckson Tada

Crazy to think mere weeks ago I was running on a track, and here I am now, plugged into an intravenous apparatus about to be slit open. Thanking God for a surgeon who got me in so soon, even if it cut into track. *So* ready to get this over with and run again.

"Surgeries suck, don't they," my nurse says rhetorically, dabbing blood on my arm. I am lightheaded, and unashamedly cried a little at the needle, but I am beyond caring.

Friendless.
Anonymous.
Unpublished.
Zero degree.
Zero makeup.
What do I have to lose? Two screws in my right foot, that's what.

"Oh, girl, that's tough," the nurse says when I tell her I was going to run track.

"God has a plan." I shrug. "I trust Him."

She ignores the God statement. "So you're a runner?"

"Oh, not really. I just like it."

"Well, runnin' is lot of pressure on your feet."

"Here's another irony," I say, a bit loopy. "I like surgeries."

The nurse laughs at my slurred voice, thinking I am out of it, but I repeat to her that I really do enjoy hospitals.

Better not say anything else, I think, praying words of surrender as I am wheeled into the operating room, a deep weight lift of letting go …

…

It is at the exact moment I am "letting go" that a crisis beyond the walls of the operating room prompts Natalie Evans, Edmond's City Clerk, to issue a Declaration of Emergency:

> NOW THEREFORE, it is hereby declared that a State of Emergency now exists throughout the City of Edmond, Oklahoma; and … IT IS FURTHER DELCARED AND ORDERED that all previously approved special event permits … are hereby revoked.
>
> This DECLARATION shall continue in effect until such time it is terminated or amended by issuance of a subsequent declaration. Approved this 18th day of March 2020.[1]

Basically, the world shut down.

All I could do was laugh when Mom told me in the car, my right foot dangerously propped on the dashboard, rain and clouds hovering above. It certainly felt as if my world had closed, but in a cozy, good way. If Panera still served chicken noodle, I'd be in good hands. I looked forward to sleeping a lot, being excused from homework and that snotty-nosed Savanna where I worked, and doing the dishes, my first-born duty in the winter months.

It was so beyond my young brain the intensity of uncertainty and suffering that lay ahead for the world—a kind that would mark history books for my children.

The city was on lockdown, and I was paralyzed in bed.

In my little seventeen-year-old world upstairs draped in Christmas lights, I enjoyed feeling tucked away with coloring pages, some fantasy books, and staring at my cello on the wall—until the unexpected hit me post-surgery, and I could not scream. I experienced sleep paralysis repeatedly. It felt like some being was going to kill me every time I took a nap.

"It felt like I was falling into an endless abyss," I finally explain to Mom.

"You ought to try and pray or journal." Mom tells me.

Anyone who's experienced sleep paralysis and its effects knows how scary it is. You can't control your movements or speech, and many people feel a presence of darkness. I am thankful I have the power of God, who rules over all demonic strongholds.

I read the Book of Daniel. He was a man to whom God gave the ability to interpret dreams. I'm too tired to think deeply about things, but too desperate not to read something to give light to this eerie room where monsters seemed to have entered. I spot something right away.

"Don't be afraid," he said, "for you are very precious to God. Peace! Be encouraged! Be strong!"[2]

Outside, streets are bare, signs are apocalyptic, stores out of food. I don't usually get bored or lonely up here in Candiceyland by myself, but it has felt rather heavy in my room, so I have determined to worship out loud. There is something freeing about singing, clapping, even shouting at times. It gives off a tangible feeling of victory.

Missouri friends have been texting me a lot, texting about stress and anxiety and parents losing jobs and their graduations postponed, and I am stuck in bed with my own sleep paralysis nightmares, helpless and unhelpful. The Lord must want me to be close to Him in a new way. Still, I am so scared to close my eyes. Sleep itself is a paralytic nightmare.

Surgeries themselves are untangling, humbling me to dependance and vulnerability. *But once I recover, I'll be stronger*, I remind myself, thanking God that the pain is completely bearable compared to past pains.

When you have to shower on one foot, swashing around with a trash bag on your cast, when you have to push and scoot up and down sixteen stairs, ask for help with everything, you just feel like one giant dumbbell: awkward, big, and loud.

I wish to twist my ankle, but I can't. Yet though everything may feel like it's unraveling (everything but this foot, which I wish *would* unravel itself out of this cast), God is my hope and strength. His goodness is not defined by my circumstances.

I can't believe how fast things happened to test my trust in Him this year. With all my heart I can confirm that God alone is my ever-present help. Not even my own bed can save me. When I was scared in the hospital of the IV (I tried not to let on), Jesus was there with me. I felt peace in the room. And even though this worldwide lockdown has everyone quarantined and scared, even though my senior year and basically my whole future is up in the air, God is good. Thank goodness I wasn't getting too excited about college! I am so relieved to have the screws out of my right foot! I hope this means I can run soon without pain.

The world is falling apart, journal. And what does God do? He confines me to bed with a broken foot and tells me I must write a book. I laugh and close my spiral-bound journal.

This is seventeen. This is my junior year. "This is all part of the story," I yawn. *Surely.*

CHAPTER 10
AN ENGLISH SUMMER

11th grade summer, Ozark, Missouri

*You don't change the world simply by looking at it,
you change it through the way you choose to live in it.*
—Amelia Wren, The Aeronauts (2019)

June is like a melting star-lit sky reflected on lake water, spent entirely outdoors amongst the lemon-lime colored fields of haybales. I stand by the therapy of running on eighty acres of farmland with dogs as the best way to unwind, whether after a lockdown and surgery, or simply while living the stifling life of a writer in front of a computer screen.

After I requested a Missouri summer with both sets of grandparents, I quit my job, packed my overalls, and now my head sticks out the window on the four-and-a-half hour drive from Oklahoma to Missouri, where my mother graciously drives. I watch a hot air balloon rise and float away from the eastern sea of green lining the familiar Highway 65, like me, lifting off for adventure.

Things really haven't changed. I undo my hair and let it fly.

I don't know why I am so apprehensive about driving. It's like every time I am on the road I think I am going to crash. I wish people would stop asking me about driving. It makes me feel behind. Honestly, transportation is not on my mind. I wish I lived somewhere where I did not have to drive. I am lost in jumbled papers of confusion in desperate need of an editor. I thought it would be assertive of me to say I needed a writing retreat in Missouri since I am learning how to write a book completely on my own. I am also learning the art of teaching myself to do hard workouts without track motivation and a foot recovering from surgery. I plan to run at the farm when it isn't so hot.

Missouri feels timeless: shoeless river dancers are splashing in the banks of the Finley River; farmers are on tractors doing what they do. I see Missourians on walks and bikes, even an Amish family in a buggy on their way to collect an electric weed eater. Missouri is like that: tipping between the points of modernity and tradition. As go the summer vibes, I've got my rope bracelets stacked, smiling out the window at the iron gates to yell, "Farm!" as we enter Riverview Ranch, breathing in the sweet blue asphalt of having *arrived*.

The air is thick and maddening, like that humid rust of an old garage or unventilated basement, but it is also endearing. It was in these garden-ripe months I used to pick raspberries and blueberries and little cherry tomatoes. Some of the boot-trekked trails have overgrown since my days running in the woods with a shark tooth necklace around my neck.

But rather than the expiring feeling I felt upon leaving home in Ozark, Missouri, this feels all new. We've visited Missouri many times prior to moving, but this trip feels unusually different, like there is something waiting on me here to find out or explore. Maybe it's my book.

The blueberry bushes are dried up, but Poppy's garden is popping with heaping large watermelons, and plain squash I don't typically like. The big playground's zipline is rocking in the wind, and I am tempted to climb up the ladder and lay high in the tree branches. It was deeper in these woods where we stuffed Ritz crackers in our pockets; it was on my grandfather's land where my cousins and I raced breathless with wind tears down our cheeks with the dogs, like my favorite, Hailey the golden retriever, rest her soul. There are parts of this land I have never explored, like inside that red shed to the right of the farmhouse. I found a birdhouse once in the field beside it, and Poppy said I could keep it. I have a feeling I'll find a lot of treasures here this month. It is rather a long time …

"Oh, darlin'! You made it home!"

"I made it home!" I repeat back. I am barefoot when I get out of the car and meet Gigi, who is in a long turquoise linen dress, stooped over pink hydrangea bushes.

Inside the cool-drifting farmhouse, an Irish reel plays in my head and my duffel bag tosses on a sofa. Gigi washes her hands in warm, slow-MO water, the soft kind that smells sweet. I hold on to the edge of the counter and stand on my toes. Feeling 'old self.'

"We're thinking about cooking the squash and zucchini tonight," she says. The sink has a window looking out on the outdoor kitchen plotted with flowerpots. "I've got some work to do on the porch this afternoon, so make yourself at home. Oh, *do* sleep downstairs this time."

"Really!" I try to twirl on my foot but it sticks to a kitchen floor brick, so I skip down the hall to one of the guest bedrooms with heirloom furniture.

At the door I stop. The carpet is like a freshly iced cake: absolutely flawless with vacuum lines. It is the nicest of the guest rooms, the *sparest of spare*, the only private suite on the front of the house.

"This can be *your* room now." Gigi says with her signature emphasis behind me.

"It's beautiful." I sigh. "Too beautiful, actually." My view is of the front lawn and two trees, a plot of garden, and the narrow, far-stretching driveway leading to the silver barn.

"The drawers are empty except for some blouses you may enjoy. And there *are* dresses in the closet you can try on as well. You're *welcome* to come outside with me. But I *know* you have writing to do."

"Thanks," I answer Gigi who is fluffing the pillows on the very high bed. It reminds me of a Princess and the Pea mattress. "I'd really like to write this whole trip, but I haven't been inspired yet. Not about *moving*, goodness." I shudder, already adding southern drawl with my own wild-eye reaction. "Missouri has my breath at the moment."

"You haven't even seen the half of it!" Gigi tilts the stem of a hydrangea on the nightstand. "Come find me once you settle." She leaves with a kiss.

This is definitely a different half to Missouri, almost like the half-and-half Gigi drinks with coffee, Italian Sweet Cream, in its a purple container with a gold lid. Such a creamy visual of how royal and exotic I feel in this room. What kind of lessons would I learn this summer on the farm? I mean, what would I really be learning, no longer a ten-year-old running in the woods, no longer a private-schooled socialite with aims to please certain friends and get into college?

I move into the sunset lines on the new carpet, doubly cushioned after the result of post-construction flooding. Gigi insisted on a double padding under the carpet in replacement of the hickory-colored wood flooring in this room for important guests. And here I am, a sweaty junior in shorts and a t-shirt, standing in the sparest of spare rooms without so much as appreciation for the freshly cut hydrangea drinking from a crystal vase next to my princess bed.

As a child, visiting the farm meant I would be sleeping in what is called the Girls' Room, a blush-wall bedchamber upstairs through a glass door with no handle. Those were the Nancy Drew mystery book days when I read by pink lamplight and nestled under Egyptian linens that smelled like cherry blossoms. I wore a Duke or Spartans t-shirt from an athletic uncle or cousin, and I slid on a cloth headband to airdry my hair while I played outside. I got deeply tan and speckled with fiery mosquito bites, ate blueberry muffins and drank orange juice, and took showers every night to get the dirt off my burned feet from walking on the pebbly driveway.

At the farm, you didn't care about late nights or too much sugar because you were at the farm and that's just how you lived. You begged to stay, begged to leave when you were homesick, and dreamed about it when you weren't there. It was magical.

I feel like I have checked in to the wrong hotel room. This room is too big and grand for me. Really, everything is already grand at the farm; from the two grandfather clocks in the entrance hall and foyer to the ashy hearth room fireplace that wails of Christmas fires past, down to the littlest details of style in each of the six bedrooms on four levels of cream walls and unusually tall doors. All the rooms are dark and echoey with cast iron handles, the blinds dusted by our Amish friends who visit to help in the garden or inside the house in the summertime. As a young girl who loved to watch these bonneted women, I was living simply in my little overalls, sleeping in the Girls' Room's cozy familiar quarters. That is really the only 'safe' room I know here. Above the bed there was a picture of a woman in a white dress standing in a field with her hands on hips, explained to us girls, of womanhood's tenacity. We girls knew it would become us someday, a day we would dress like a woman and help Gigi and the aunts in the kitchen rather than playing with the boys and dogs outside, but it was an *eventually* sort of beckoning to become, like it may never happen, or was only for certain girls in the family, like Kelly Grace.

Now, however, I am forced into a hands-on-hips position, a real woman in a real bedchamber. Did Gigi now consider me ready for sophistication—at seventeen?

Kelly Grace practically grew up under Gigi's wing, baking pound-cakes and wearing a pink floral apron. Sometimes I helped them, but only if we were playing a game. Kelly and I used to stuff costume dresses in our backpacks and put them on in the girls' room before tying on what we thought were such old-time aprons, and while the Amish matriarchs stood shelling peas in the outdoor kitchen, we scrubbed the glazed bricks in the kitchen floor to classical music, pretending to be girls from the 1900s. It was such fun, but all pretend.

Lord, I'll grow up if You want me to, but You'll have to help me! I run outside to zipline.

My southern accent has come back with a huge, sweaty hug after only being here a day. Poppy's garden is confirmed to be ripe for the picking, and so I stuff round cherry tomatoes in the pockets of my grown-up overalls before climbing up my old tree fort. It's the childhood place of my elementary summers, laying at the top of the tower, the trees dotting speckles of light on my face. After this, I plan to run back to the house and learn what I can for how Gigi has made this place what it is, for it is surely not by accident. My goodness! She has taught me the importance of perfectly folded towels, of having seasoned, homemade lentils ready in the fridge (along with dumplings, cinnamon rolls, soups, and pies), of recording peoples' shows in advance and serving drinks according to the visitor's tastes, of ironing sheets and putting scent sachets in closets and drawers, or of arranging fine antiques on shelves … good grief, this one has been hard to grasp because I grew up with the opposite mindset of thinking I am in no need of unnecessary décor. Out here in the branches, now that's something I understand as being necessary.

But what should I teach myself? I can mature.

Surely I can merge the two mindsets. There is so much to note about Gigi's style: the painted family portraits hanging in gold frames, the pantry bookshelf designed to hold the dozens of cookbooks in Gigi's supply, not including the family southern recipes stuffed in notecard boxes for things like stuffed eggs, Mississippi butter beans, sweet spinach or cheese toast or the famous Amish sandwich (*love* these), or strawberry salad or cranberry salad or real sweet tea that brews all day. I have already developed the habit of magazine collecting as Gigi does, piling them on tables, centerpieces, in sitting rooms, on nightstands and what not. I love her sitting room—seeing her in her China blue-and-white cotton nightgown with a blueberry waffle in hand next to a tall, green mug of Italian Sweet Cream coffee, reclining on her mint green sofa overlooking a wall-sized window of mountain hills and farmland and garden. Beside her would be a nightstand atop with home décor magazines and a designer something—be it as simple as her glasses case or as elegant as her diamond earrings or Chanel perfume.

Luxury was not in what you had, but how you lived, as Gigi taught me, in reflection of her mother. My great-grandmother, Mimi, was a respected real-estate woman who would invest in top-of-the-line skin care products which resulted in the smoothest, most vibrant, youngest-looking skin in the world. She served ambrosia on crystal plates, entertaining both businessmen and neighbors in her Mississippi home and garden.

At this point in time, I *cannot* relate to ever wanting to spend a penny on such a thing as makeup, but perhaps someday I will see the value in things like crystal dishes and all that stuff, like Kelly Grace does, so classy and beautiful as she is.

"Gigi?" I enter the house like a boy, stomping and dust visibly on my arms.

I am about to ask if she has any cherry popsicles from my childhood, but I am struck still noting the open glass cabinets displaying all kinds of dish patterns that are strictly to 'see and not touch' beside a wall of family portraits, painted and pristine.

"Gigi, how and why did you collect all of these things?"

"Oh honey," she walks in slow, glasses on her forehead of thick blond bangs. "That's just how it *is* in southern families. Some of these things are handed down from your Mimi, others given as gifts, and of course, your Poppy goes to different auctions."

We walk into the ashy hearth to watch something she recorded for me. "Why, see that lamp in the corner? That was *quite* the discovery, and such a purchase!" She remembers.

It just looks like any other lamp to me, but I still give an impressed *"ah,"* and settle on the couch with a light, sage-colored blanket all the same. I snagged a bowl of green grapes while she was talking, which is about to hit the spot on this hot day that I've been running around like a kid again. I've even balanced it over a napkin of crackers and cheese. Yum.

"Oh, did I leave that there?" She says kindly, her eyes on the blanket. "I'm sorry."

"Oh, it's fine! It's just like a blanket." I ruffle the blanket, warily setting my bowl on the table beside the expensive lamp of which I now know its history. "Super comfy." I crunch a mouthful of crackers and cheese. Cracker crumbs rain on my lap.

"Well, now, thank you darlin'. You *know* what's mine is yours. I just would be careful eating on that cloud linen blanket. You may care for one of these other ones until you shower." She hands me a blue and pink plush blanket with the Walmart tag still attached.

Offended? Nope! How would I have known not to eat on such a blanket, one that is ... er ... conditioned to absorbency, cut from natural fibers and all that? I read the in-seam tag rather ashamed. Still, I am a little too stubborn to admit I didn't know plush from linen and simply remove the precious fabric from my sweaty legs and pop off the tag of the Walmart blanket. "Thanks!" Is all she hears between the two grapes in my mouth.

An American Aristocrat's Guide to Great Estates

The show Gigi recorded is one I have never seen nor ever cared to see. The first episode is of a place called Inverary Castle, toured by Julie Montagu, Viscountess Hinchingbrooke. Never heard of her, nor the castle in wherever-it-is Scotland. But the accents are cool.

"Isn't that wild!" Gigi says during the intro. "She was an American who married into British aristocracy, and now she is a Viscountess!"

"That is wild." I say, sipping an Olipop. Gigi knows it's my favorite soda.

"Would you ever want to travel, *Re Re*?"

Aw, I haven't heard my name in a long time.

Candice Marie Gibbons: the 'rie' in my middle name is often what I am called at the farm, or by my dad. "MARIE-RIE!" He'd yell, chasing me as a kid. I'd laugh and scream. Gigi writes it like *Re Re*.

But nah, I'm not into travel. Not after a worldwide lockdown.

"What *is* cool," I offer, "is how spectacular the castle is. There is clearly an attention to detail in every room." I am thinking of my own little space, Candiceyland, and my future home. "I think it would be grand to run an estate someday. I do have a good model." I wink at Gigi.

Estate or not, *Re Re* is committing to learn more about this lifestyle of elegance.

Ryan and Hannah, my tall, athletic cousins a couple years younger, come over tonight for dinner at the farm. Ryan goes fishing at Finley River just down the hill on Riverview Ranch with Weston, one of my other favorite cousins. Hannah and I decide to watch a dance show with Brooklyn, Weston's fun younger sister. We start to make fun of the dancers and pretend to host our own show in the hearth room, relishing late night immaturity.

"What are y'all laughing about in there?" Gigi yells from the kitchen.

"Candice is going wild!" Brooklyn yells back, laughing hysterically.

"She's teaching us how to Irish dance, Gigi." Hannah says evenly in her usual way.

"Oh *my*," I hear Gigi say above my horrendous, stomping leaps. "Candice, you better watch that foot!"

"Gigi! It's the climax! Come watch!" I say as the sound of the song *Heartland* crescendos, the clacking of precision building in sound and speed on the television.

"Don't you have writing to do?" Gigi says, and of course I do, but I'm doing what I was made to do before I even started writing—dance!

I don't know when it hit—perhaps when I was in the upstairs workout room earlier listening to soundtracks from movies that have this sound of the sea, of sailing to faraway places where lilts lift voices and walks turn to skips. I distinctly recall looking out the window from the second floor to the orange pebbles on the road while lifting weights, thinking, *Where will I be this time next year?* It was a gesture distilled in time, a feeling that I would someday look back on this time at the farm before adventures came. But none of that is more relevant than this tucked away feeling I have here to relax, settle in, write that dreaded book.

I am told I have Scottish blood; but without an accent, I don't feel qualified to call myself anything but plain American, born in Missouri, stuck in Oklahoma, frozen in a country still half under lockdown. I may never leave the country. I'll definitely not be going to college. Might as well call it quits to studying anything. I mean, if we are restricted from trips to the grocery store, I might as well get rooted here and enjoy Poppy's garden on my own two feet (thank God the cast is gone).

Hannah, Brooklyn, and I end the night in hysterical tears, feasting on Gigi's homemade poundcake topped with fresh berries and cream, and I laughed my way to the princess-high mattress, both feet throbbing, thinking about Inverary Castle and waterfalls and dance.

Lord, how much I have to learn about Your world!

As endearing as it is, the farm proved to be distracting with its Amish friends and cousins in and out. I pack my bag and switch locations to focus on writing my book and swing on the back of my grandmother Annie's porch, serene with birds and flowers and fluffy pillows. Annie has a canopy over an outdoor bed for the naturalist to be in heaven. I feel more like a wilderness lover turned imposter writer.

"How is *A Time to Trust* coming along?" Annie brings out a hot slice of Neighbor's Mill's bronzed honey wheat goodness, a local treasure and filling piece of home.

"Terrible," I bite into the bread and laugh. "But this bread is amazing."

"Why don't we go cruisin' to get your mind off it?"

"Deal!" I slam the lid to my computer and hurry through the house that smells that faint scent of caramel cappuccino—just like the weekends I used to spend at their house before we moved. Annie's house has rows of bookshelves and so many boxes of photographs that I could dance with joy. I am starting to realize I like things like that—archives, I guess? It's sounds so ancient and confusing. Now, I don't know what I would *do* with all those papers and things just yet, but it feels worth my time to explore. But first things first: a writer must cruise.

Annie is a deeper form of mother to me. Blond like Mom, she even smells like her, so I never feel homesick staying at her house with Papa. Perhaps Mom and Annie use the same hairspray or perfume, but there is something so intimate about being with her, like I was always made to be with her, like she knows me inside and out, like she wiped my very first tear.

Down Highway 65, Annie surprises me by letting go of the wheel.

"Your turn to drive!"

"But—but—I'm not ready to drive!"

"Girl," she drags out in her Alabama accent, "You gotta learn somehow!"

I manage to talk her into pulling over and nervously clam behind the wheel.

"You're telling me writing a book is easier than driving for you?"

"At the moment," I sigh, shifting gears to drive. "Both seem impossible."

I write best at Annie's house, specifically on her porch, gaining thousands of book words in mere weeks. At nighttime, Annie, Papa, and I watch historical dramas. One night she shows me a movie about two aeronauts with British accents. I study it with an endearment to the soundtrack and characters, their tenacious search for knowledge. Does film attract you to certain things, or does film merely affirm what you have always been attracted to forever?

'Southern-wild' sounds like crickets, grasshoppers, bumbles and birds, all incessant, but volume fluctuating come evening. It feels like 112 degrees and the Missouri humidity has my hair in frizzy, dainty ringlets, but even with a full writer's brain I still make time to see my friend, Adalie, before I return to Oklahoma. In fact, I *need* to see her.

There is no other Adalie in the world. I love her bootcut jeans, clipped up caramel curls, and striking smile. How fast she talks, so logical and deliberate, her thoughts surprising. I love how we often disagree; her candid nature, her honest feedback, and loyalty to engage in my hearts' problems and respond in an unapologetic way.

"Coffee?" She texts.

"YES!" I respond, minutes later, hopping in her truck.

"How is it really in Oklahoma?" She asks after we talk of her college plans changing due to the worldwide lockdown.

"Lonely and busy." I say, and we both laugh at the common theme.

"Did you make any friends at track?"

"Kind of. I mean, I like the coaches."

"Well, that's better than nothing."

"Yeah, except I left them to have foot surgery."

"Oh yeah," she reached a hand up to me. "I'm so sorry."

"It is what it is. At least it's not both feet."

"Oh, my. Eighth grade. I remember those days." She rolls her eyes in her Adalie way. "You had to craw all over Meghan's basement at the Gingerbread House Party in knee-high casts to film a movie. I don't know how you did it."

"Well, we won the film competition. And I won the Gingerbread House contest."

"That was the shocking part. You filmed your movie from a ground-level angle. The other team had much better cinematography."

"I'd give anything to go back to those days …" I dream back to campouts at her house, staying up until 4 a.m. not merely talking about boys, but praying, crying, laughing.

"Don't say that." Adalie corrects. "You are centered right where God wants you."

It is good to hear her firm voice.

Before I leave, Adalie's beautiful mother says hello. I can't help but note that her house has several things of design nature that catch my eye as being similar to what I saw in the estate show with Gigi. I am learning about how these things don't just happen.

"Your house is so … beautiful." I say awkwardly. 'Beautiful' can be overused, but it is hard for me to think on the spot, so I walk around and take it all in …

Her element of style is what I would call calm and detailed, hot or cold, whichever the most fitting for that room, candles on random trays and tables around the house; fresh veggies and flowers on the counter, windows open, nature greetings all around; really, it's an appreciation for atmosphere, a slower pace in life: eating slow, cooking rich, savoring coffees and teas on a foggy screen porch, allowing delicate, purposeful noise and music only, no running, shouting, or damaging property. There are kittens roaming, hot bread and pies in rotation, and something Italian simmering on the stove celebrating their family heritage. It is a lifestyle of cleanliness and health, hospitality and charm, and European influence: Italian cookbooks stacked on a cabinet, a plant and candle on the high counter, fresh dates and savory fruits by the latte machine, a fountain in the living room, a second parlor of different color scheme in the kitchen for unexpected visitors, old books with great meaning, and another lit candle resting 'just because' on an old chest in the walkway. There is a soft, thick towel and smooth marble bathroom counter (non-sticky) in the bathroom with lit cabinets, large doorway plants, a French café table outside the front door, and Persian rugs beneath every furnished room.

Lord, teach me to appreciate this slow beauty so foreign.

Returning to Oklahoma, wheels that have never turned before are moving around in my brain, the kind that crank up a song when started. It sounds a lot like *At Wit's End* by Hans Zimmer. The wheels have a force about them that gained traction from Missouri but is not bound by it. It is like they are being moved by an Immovable Source— like God is igniting this churning of thoughts, ideas, and actions into a big consequential burst of enthusiasm to … go to the library. It is like being embodied in Kelly Grace. I feel this urge to stare at words and drink them like broth. Not just my own book words, but other peoples' masterpieces. Ones I understand and even ones I don't know *how* to understand. It's like inserting a new SD card in your brain.

All at once, I am excited for school, and not just what my first day outfit is going to be. Transitioning homeschool co-ops to a new location in Edmond, Oklahoma, a suburb of Oklahoma City, I am neither daunted nor dreading it like my junior year in the rental house. I am excited to school myself at home—even after the pandemic spring of doing this exact thing. I am excited for the final tests, final speeches, and final first day experience. Missouri refreshed me.

Even after meeting my new class (which was again a little sigh of disappointment as I realized no one ever would be the Bricks, my original high school friend group), I wasn't fazed. Junior year was a letdown. Now, it's like I am beyond even thinking about having friendships. This could be a sign some sort of wall has built up, something I need to process and deal with, but I'm okay to let it ruminate. The main thing is I am excited to actually *learn*—and we're not even taking philosophy. Restless, as if I am on the verge of *something*. Expectant, but increasingly withdrawn from activity.

Who is this Candice, energized to be what she had always despised?

CHAPTER 11
IT'S JUST ENTERTAINMENT!

12TH GRADE FALL, EDMOND, OKLAHOMA

… never use relevance as an excuse to compromise.
—*Heath Adamson*

Here I am, about to die on the first day of my senior year. What a way to go, crashing on this hill with my sister in a thunderstorm as a new driver in my newly earned Jeep, all because I forgot to find the windshield wipers. Thank goodness I don't have college plans.

"Drive straight!" Kelly screams.

"I can't tell if I am!" I scream back above the torrent of Oklahoma City thunder.

Getting drenched on picture day as a sophomore at private school should have taught me not to place my hope in my appearance—my own knowledge and judgement, especially. I should have known good jeans don't guarantee a good senior year.

By God's grace, I find the windshield wipers eventually, and it stops raining by the time Kelly and I open the glass doors to the wide staircase leading to our new academic home. The chairs are stiff, and the air is cold, making me wrestle the senior confidence I held at 6 a.m. in the mirror when I slipped on my blue shirt and chose straight hair to accentuate my new highlights. As much as I care, I don't.

Why?

It is the strangest thing. The stage every American girl waits for has arrived for me. I am finally a senior: jangling my keychain and allowed to skip the last class, about to soar through the year without caring about anything, minus one last ACT test.

Senior perks aren't why I am hyped. The desire to learn is giving me an unusual adrenaline much associated with the thrill (and fear) of running far. It is all neurologically connected I am sure, but what really makes this new season so anxiously dependent on the joy of books?

Returning to Oklahoma after a summer in Missouri amid Irish-English influences, I am inclined to narrow my thoughts down a tunnel I was afraid to walk during my junior year. A tunnel beyond just the desire to study philosophy—an already loved subject—but of science, of cultures, of histories that aren't my own. Is this my love of cause-and-effect rubbing off a bit too far, my intent to see the connection between ideas and consequences going zealously extreme? Would this school year perhaps make me, a non-reader, hard-to-comprehend-anything overthinker more endeared to the books in Candiceyland I have stared at all these years without daring to understand them? Is this a prayer answered beyond the depth I even prayed it would be given to me?

Doing this for someone other than myself is absurd. Mrs. Loose's wise head of curls isn't even shaking at me to stop drawing room blueprints. Mr. Drake isn't even at this school! No one around me is pressuring me to go to college, to be smart or impress teachers or relatives. Most colleges are still hesitant to reopen. No one knows where the world is headed in the next year.

But here I am, jigging in nerdiness. Alone.

Why not?

For a rule-following overthinker, nearly crashing from lack of driving knowledge could sink me into despair all day, but I am beyond feeling sorry for myself. A sharp wavelength of knowledge vibrates in front of me as I make my way through the classroom, pulling me towards the unknown. Books on my back include Lewis' *The Abolition of Man*, Hesiod's *Theogony* and *Works of Days*, Homer's *The Odyssey*, Boorstin's *The Discoverers*, and Homer's gemstone, *Illiad*. We are also studying poetry dating as far back as the sixth century.

And Old Testament history, I remember, choosing a seat on the right side of the classroom. Thank goodness I remembered to pack my small Bible, the copy I fearfully clutched back in private school. A requirement for the New Testament class back in 10th grade, it never seemed as 'real' to me as the highlighted study Bible flipped open nearly every morning and night. To think it held the same words was a bit hard to grasp. I am still working on not letting appearances affect my affection.

Now, in an entirely new school, I will open that small book again, this time to the Old Testament.

Time transportation, as an older version of Candice.

What a failure, I think as the teacher murmured something about us analyzing the Psalms. *Here I am, living in personal relationship with Jesus, and I hadn't even read all of God's Word.* The realization hits me and is especially alarming right now, as my teacher, Mrs. Burk, a glamorous Italian mother of eight, asks us what we hope to gain out of the year.

"Everything," I breathe at my turn.

Past Candice would have turned right and left, reading faces to see if that answer made sense, if that helped her socially, but it's just so fluid in me like a gentle stream of water, I don't even care when a girl laughs next to me. In fact, I barely see faces at all.

Is it chronic loneliness that has me in this dimension of only numbers and words?

Some girls answer with the senior perks: sweatshirts, yearbook quotes, prom. I was right there with them. All I mostly cared about was my hair, my nails—everything that was expected in private school, in the relatively affluent Edmond culture. To a degree I still care. But materialism doesn't overwhelm my thoughts like it did in the past.

When Mrs. Burk probes us for depth and articulation in our

responses, a few students moan about college applications and the excitement with belonging to a university for the social side of it, while others say they are taking a gap year for travel. I search faces for anyone who looks excited like me to be here—genuinely excited to learn not just for an ACT score, but for the sheer joy of growing in wisdom and knowledge, but no one seems to be with me at this point, not for school, at least. Whether I will be included in any sort of friend circle, I was here because, like every other new place I have walked in before, God has sent me here to ultimately learn more about Him. The learning part, both spiritually and academically (although I realize my academics are spiritual) is becoming more and more open and appealing. Finally.

"Candice, what has you so obviously excited about learning?" Mrs. Burk's bracelets rattle as she asks me, her onyx curls swaying like mass church bells. Absolutely capstone.

"My whole life I have avoided books. But this August feels different."

I visualize a moment in Candiceyland that just happened yesterday: curtains drawn, my chandelier light illuminating my new books in polka-dot shadows.

"When I held Virgil's *Aeneid*, I actually felt like, wow, there were subjects I didn't have to just say, 'Oh, I'll never be able to understand that.' But I could actually open my mind to learn it. I guess I am ready to embrace knowledge, not just in literature and history, but in science and language. I want to learn to think more critically, read more broadly, present better cases. Prepare for the future, I guess …" I explain.

Whatever the future is for America, I inwardly roll my eyes.

"Well, you won't be disappointed." Mrs. Burk says. "Challenge IV is all about leadership. Understanding the requirements for leadership is essential to you thriving as part of this personally rigorous class. As such is the case, I am not your teacher, I am only a resource." She points at each of us individually with tipped red nails, "Every strand of this curriculum is student-led. Every hour, one of you will be leading. Because that's what it's all about: *intellectus consequentia definit ducibus.*" She spins out of her chair and writes on the board the statement that will mark my final year of high school education.

I hold my breath.

UNDERSTANDING CONSEQUENCES DEFINES LEADERSHIP

Consequences no longer scare me, and leadership seems already in the trajectory of my days. Being alone, as author Elisabeth Elliot tells me, is a requirement for such a future role of influence, and I am definitely enrolled in the 'Be Lonely' course.

Still, I can never be too sure a year with the word *consequences* still largely intertwined that it won't beckon surprising choices in unforeseeable bends. Bends that might bend my character, sharpen me as iron, purify me as gold, but could literally cut me to extreme discomfort.

This could mean more than stiff chairs but a pop in my back to literally deny or accept things which, like academia, I had formerly rejected as "not something I did."

This, like being a good student, is something I will put on myself as a leader of my own thoughts. No one is responsible for my actions but myself.

Oh great. God is giving me two little somethings to chew on during our first strand of school, which is, to my surprise, coloring time.

First of all, I want to read the entire Bible. I want to *actually learn* everything He tells me to do. It's about time I took the studious part of my faith seriously.

"I want us to start every day using our hands to color as I read poetry." Mrs. Burk says.

I can appreciate anyone who gives dignity to childhood practices.

"Think about your creative influences during the school year." Mrs. Burk adds. "Everything you do this year outside of studying will directly affect your studying."

That's interesting. I color fast.

There is something else that God is saying ... something that, as she reads the poetry, makes me wince.

I have been excusing a little green centipede-ish word with a lower-case *e* when I am alone and often trying to have fun: entertainment. This is something I curate myself, and it is not all good. It is cute and nice; always there for me, just a tap away. It gives me a high when I run. It makes me feel like I could do and be all that the hard-core lyrics boast. It leaves me feeling like I was a beast myself (in the most attractive, girl-power sense). It also gives me a high when I drive with the sunroof down and feel flirtatious. It gives me permission to look a certain way that results in clear approval from people my age. The little word also helps me in dressing up on a formal night downtown; in going to sleep when I was anxious or had insomnia. I am not clueless; it holds more power over me than silence. The scariest part is, I am uncomfortable without it.

Career-wise, entertainment is the world I sincerely feel I am about to step into. Surely exposure to more entertainment means more knowledge, more respect, more creative genius to overcome technical problems on the stage and screen, two things I have distantly admired. Sure, the correlation between entertainment and spirituality is confronting, but I hardly have the time to consider whether the music that motivates me to roll out of bed aligns with my spirituality. Even if there is science to prove entertainment was morally connected, research seems irrelevant, even messy. I will color and think about this later.

An unknown text pops up on my phone from someone named Stacy. It is business-concise and cordial, inviting me to intern at the office of the church I attend. She says she is the executive assistant to the senior pastor, and that she has heard I am a writer and would like to meet "whenever it is convenient." I open the message then close it without responding, only because I don't know what to say, and who needs to answer a random person on time?

"It is kind of her to reach out," I admit to my parents when they ask why I haven't responded, "But I have a full schedule. I already volunteer at church on Sundays."

"You ought to respond right away, Canzie," Mom says. "It's good manners to do that."

Yeah, to people you are loyal to, I think, reluctantly pulling out my phone.

I am an actual nerd these days, wearing turtlenecks and drinking tea. I definitely won't be making friends in Oklahoma anytime soon. Still, it has been a splendid few days of fall in Oklahoma, which doesn't even celebrate the best of fall like my hometown of Ozark. Hot cinnamon apples. Homemade pumpkin bread in the oven. Braids toppled upon my head. Dresses of sleeves. Cool wind. Dark sky. Whistling chimney. Maple trees inching towards gusting yellow. Fall will forever hold birthday memories, lighting candles, and hanging banners …

Not this fall. This is a surprising time of loneliness in my life, a cost of discipleship, a call to sacrifice. But is it really sacrifice when you're giving up *good* for *best?* I have a strong sense this has something to do with school. Maybe since God has turned my attention to that, the spirit of stress has been overwhelming me.

I am so nervous to do an internship in—get this—an executive office. I don't know who Stacy is other than a recognizably tall, northern assistant with sharp instincts and a stellar reputation.

"Stacy gets things done," people say.

Meanwhile I spend time procrastinating, counting glow-in-the-dark stars on the ceiling.

I am learning so many things about God's character that I've always heard about but never personally grasped. I am a senior and turning 18, and I know I am supposed to be excited for all that comes with adulthood, but it all seems too hyped, like unnecessary celebration.

I am learning to be content while friendless in Oklahoma. I must remember this is only a season, and soon I will be in a different world, longingly looking back on my treasured life as a seventeen-year-old. Right now, I can wake up early and eat a hot breakfast, pray and write.

I run freely, drive in my Jeep (named Jerry, for the affectionate old man that he is), twirl my keychain, and even have a little parking spot at school. I have so many books I can't fit them all in my bookshelves! Imagine that—Candice reads!

I have a nagging feeling that I must deepen my trust in God—fast. Something is coming. It just feels like I am supposed to prepare my heart or something. I have such strong convictions against certain music and such fervency in my overall lifestyle to live pure. I have not fully given all my entertainment to God, but most of it is God-honoring I think, and I haven't really been too bothered by where I am at with everything. And yet I have struggled with sleep paralysis and very scary dreams, which have made me realize my helplessness and drawn me closer to God. What fun is it to have an immoral spirit knowing it displeases God?

I miss my dark hair. My blond highlights from August which I originally liked now look so opposite of Candice. Oh well, I should learn to stop getting my hair adjusted anyway. At least it's not black. I need to grow it out, take care of it. I feel more firm that I am not going to college. I just want to write books and travel. I want to be wide open to whatever is coming.

That reminds me, I think while I take Charlie on a walk in the hilled neighborhood. *I need to look at all my playlists and make sure nothing is terribly wrong on there.*

It's something I've thought about since that first day of school, something that low-key scares me. Not that anything is terrible on there, but what if there is something in my songs that wormed its way in there as I to prepare to drive down I-35's interstate with confidence? What if it isn't blatantly evil, but more harmfully toxic to who I am trying to become?

It's hard to be relatable to the girls at school. I'm trying to find Jesus' balance. He was so in tune with people; I feel like an untuned cello that's been in an attic for a hundred years. But I cannot go back to the girl I was who only cared about the material world. I have come too far to become spiritually desensitized. Girls are feeding themselves on the world and left hungry and broke. Entertainment without discretion seems to be at the forefront of everything.

No progress on finding a book publisher.
No letters from old friends.
No new or promising friends.
No book in my hands.
No boyfriend (or anyone I even like).
No clarity on college next year.
No energy to wake up early tomorrow.

But I worked hard today and honored God. Between those things I know everything will eventually fall into place. It is hitting me that I will have to work really, really hard to see my dreams come true. I just hope my entertainment choices aren't stopping me from God's best.

"Could that actually be a thing?" Adrianna asks me during lunch. She is a fellow senior nerd with an easy smile, wide brown eyes, and a mutt named Butterscotch. She reads fantasy.

"I mean, why wouldn't it?" I crunch into an apple. "What we read affects who we are."

"I've just never connected the two." She takes a long sip of her beet-red smoothie. "I mean, I guess the dragons in the book I'm reading make their way into my dream. But I can't really say music impacts me. And if it does, that seems to be for the good. I tend to do calculus a little faster. I really don't listen to anything other than Vivaldi."

"Yeah, I don't really either," I say without thinking.

You totally do. I convict myself.

Adrianna pauses thoughtfully. "Violins aren't a bad thing, are they?"

I see I have a fellow overanalyzer.

"Nah, I don't ever think certain instruments themselves are bad, it's just what we do with them. Kind of like how thoughts can be good or bad. But it doesn't mean we should not think."

Calculating this, Adrianna turns a queer shade of green. "I once read that what you think becomes who you are. Well," she leans in, "My sister thinks a lot about velociraptors …"

I laugh. "You've got to keep it all very logical when you think about it. Otherwise we get wrapped up in too many particulars. Yet sometimes it's not all cut and dry."

"What do you mean?"

"I haven't researched it enough to know. But my guess is it's less about 'this artist is bad' and more about how you see yourself being positively or negatively affected after consuming it."

She nods understandingly.

It still amuses me to think I would research anything. I continue, "I am thinking about doing my senior thesis on entertainment and the brain. I have always liked watching brain surgeries, and entertainment is kind of my future as an author."

"Don't you want to be an English teacher, or a professor?" Adrianna asks.

"Oh, no! I just think there is an importance to our entertainment. We often excuse it because it is related to pleasure, but that can sometimes be the fall."

I can't help but think of today's reading in Book XVI of the *Iliad*:

But the mounting cries of war could not escape old Nestor,
pausing over his wine. He turned to Asclepius' son
with an urgent, winged word:
"Think, noble Machaon, what shall we do now?
The cries are fiercer-fighters beside the ships!
You sit here, keep drinking the shining wine now,
till well-kempt Hecamede draws you a warm bath,
steaming hot, and washes away that clotted blood.
But I am off to a lookout point to learn the truth." —Homer's Iliad

"Are you sure you're not an academic student?" Adrianna says when I reference it.

I wince.

Yesterday, Stacy officially asked me in person if I would be interested in interning in the executive office. This sounds amazing except for the four things listed below:

1. I am already busy with school and writing my book.
2. I am not a technical writer and know nothing about copywriting and the like.
3. Working in a cubicle is definitely not appealing (or cool for someone my age).
4. This won't help me make friends because everyone there is literally forty.

Closed-minded? Maybe, but I've got too much Greek mythology waiting on me to think deeper about not turning down this out-of-nowhere opportunity. Plus, Chapter 6 is waiting on me to write in *A Time to Trust*.

The days are getting dark. Sunlight disappearing, sunset rays out the window. It is currently 5 a.m. and nearly time to drive myself school. I am tired from writing, but I must splash water on my eyes. Must turn off Writer Candice and become extroverted. It's funny; everyone in class thinks I'm a people-person only because I try really hard to be kind to everyone, despite the inner nerd that is taking over. Now eighteen, I am excited because I have control of my mind, thanks to Christ. I can take cold showers, wake up early, stand while I study, actually write a book, drive places (I finally learned how to navigate the dashboard properly), jump rope (it took me all summer), and love family members. Next up are learning how to file taxes and vote. Oh, and figuring out if I am going to do an internship I feel entirely unqualified to do. Not looking forward to becoming a grown woman in that sense, but I am the happiest I have ever been because I live entirely for God.

What a way to start adulthood! All my priorities are straight.

Wait. Except for my entertainment ...

"The senior thesis is the capstone of your year, and, emphatically, thirty percent of your grade. That being said, you will need to start your research now. This will be a substantial project and perhaps the largest paper you will ever write, apart from those of you bound to doctorates." Mrs. Burk eyes Adrianna and me. We now sit together. "Anyways, here is your flashcard. Write what you are most passionate about right now. Write what you think the world needs to hear."

God, are You really wanting me to do this? I am scared of what I am going to find out!

God seems to let me know that it's scarier not to know.

Clearly I am crazy, lost in my own controversial musings, teetering on the edge of modern insanity. Students come up to me all the time asking about how I am choosing to research entertainment for my senior year thesis. Some people assume I am out to get them, as if I desire to monitor their entertainment like a sort of, I don't know, moral authority. Intimidated, perhaps, that some scientific evidence out there supports that brain cells exploded every time they listen to E-marked songs. Of course, I just laugh. This is as much an attack on me as it is my classmates.

There are some who are directly opposed from the beginning. They don't need to hear from Harvard or national medical associations; they certainly do not need a random senior judging their playlists. Still, there are others who, like me—although we are scared of the truth—

have to know: is entertainment intertwined with moral decision making? If so, the consequences are eternal.

In some respects, this is far more serious than philosophical debates on morality. That is nearly impossible to wholly articulate because what could not be expressed in words was the unfortunate reality that people would not choose to believe in God. As morality crumbles without the base of this absolute truth, it would be a useless argument that would be 'lost' in the wide majority. That did not mean the case was wrong or invalid, but it certainly proved limitations. That is why the entertainment dilemma seems more on the front end of things in need of urgent research. It has affected all of us and will continue affecting us until someone says something. Teenagers, both those who accepted God and those who had not, are openly asking questions about their entertainment, like whether it improved their sleep or affected their view of relationships. My job isn't to hate on certain artists but to simply prove the connection between the brain and entertainment. The rest would be irrefutably conclusive for those who reached their view of thought and action and the issue of morality—and ultimately, if they dare to think deeply about it, it will affect their perspective of God.

No one (including myself) wanted to really think about how this thesis could change everything. But the ice had been cracked as I turned in my thesis topic, and I held the axe.

I have officially accepted the internship with Stacy in the executive office.

Books. Words. Numbers. Calls. Texts. Stoplights. Four-way stops. Gas. Car wash. Smoothies. Radio. Budgeting. Dark mornings. Cold classrooms. Winter static.

This is my senior year.

Today is the day all students stand before the senior class and pitch their thesis ideas. Nerves set in that I am about to defend one of the most controversial hot topics in my world. But so does the flame that strengthens I really am onto something, cued from controversial opinions.

"So what you're saying is that I am affected by the songs I listen to?" one of the natural public-speaker-girls throws out from her chair. "Well, I think that's already been proven."

"She has a point," Adrianna acknowledges, "but I think what you need to consider is that it doesn't just affect your personality but your spirituality. Isn't that it, Candice?"

"Yes," I turn to Mrs. Burk. "The idea is more than just that entertainment affects you neurologically, but spiritually. If the physical and spiritual are indeed intertwined, this is more serious than we realize."

"But Candice," Will, whom I have come to appreciate in respectful disagreement to just about everything, interjects as I move away from my presentation space up front, "you have to realize this is going to offend people. It's too gray of an area. You can't just say it and walk away. Are you ready to be polarizing?"

"But that's just it, isn't it?" My thoughts suddenly connect. "Not that I have to define and determine everyone's entertainment standards, but merely that I have to prove that it is connected to the moral side of the brain. People are then left draw their own conclusions."

Students are starting to shift uncomfortably. If I had a chair, I would be too. Instead I am in front of this classroom, having forgotten to eat breakfast (extremely rare, but isn't everything these days?), ready to give it up and defend the polar bears or something else less-sensitive in this thesis, like that girl over there curled up with a blanket.

"So what is it you are really after?" Mrs. Burk asks, and I see my time is almost up.

All of a sudden, a flame seems to melt any icy feelings of inferiority, turning me from feeling incapable of defending anything to being built to defend this very subject since childhood.

"This is everything to me. This affects me as much as anyone. If entertainment really does affect a person's moral judgement and I am going to write books, they could directly affect someone's stance on

God, which ultimately defines their eternity. Everything's on the line here."

"Good luck to you," a girl researching the effects of vaccinations offers.

Neurological research behind sound and image became personally affective. I had the effects of electronic light and sound in my head, but now it prompted daily changes. Suddenly it wasn't just a playlist, but a flaming sword that kept swinging at me like one of those toxic meltdown inflatables. It meant that there were things in the lyrics, in the spirit behind the artist, that would either draw me closer or away from God.

Why would we want to filter our entertainment? Couldn't we let it slide as one of the minor pieces of our faith? Didn't God understand that music was a gateway to stress relief, an outlet for vocal expression, a platform for the creative process?

I was suddenly reminded of when I was fifteen and wondered why we would move to a new state to follow God. I wrote it in the manuscript of *A Time to Trust* about how I didn't see the need to have more of God. Why did we need to move to get more 'Christian'? My mom reminded me that it wasn't because of that at all. If you really loved someone, I mean really wanted to please them, would you hold back anything that wasn't 'cool' in their eyes? Especially something that was, in a way, disgusting to them?

If I really want to honor God with my life, I need to see what entertainment truly glorified Him. I couldn't decide this based on whether or not I liked the sound of the song. It would have to come through prayer and a strong wrestle within.

And yet there was another icy layer. Once one decided that their entertainment played a part in their moral judgement, there had to be a reconciliation with their choices. It would forever affect the songs they choose, the premieres they endorse, and could even play a part in the friends they choose. Knowing this, I had to completely take an inventory of my own influences.

First, it started with my own sheer quantity of music digested. It usually began as early as my morning run and ended with an evening strength session or cinematic bike ride. But sometime this came even *before* reading God's Word. Even if it was worship, it was still *noise*. The act of silence itself was missing from my life. It had to be won back.

I began to research the history and beliefs of the artists I supported. Perhaps I did not have to agree with every lifestyle decision they made, but it was worth considering what influenced their lyrics. It was a tightrope I had to walk and keep from turning into an extremist.

Did the artists not matter as much on instrumental albums? Or was it merely that the lyrics themselves added a whole new layer to the filtration of the song? Songs had *become* me. Lyrics during certain seasons of life had marked my thought process, and this would continue to define me. Surely in adulthood I wouldn't live off music like bread (it seems only a teenage thing), but it still mattered I figured this out. Whether or not anyone cared to change their own lifestyle, I had told God He could have all of me. Just because He was now shining light on a formerly irrelevant area for me to bring before Him, it did not mean it was, in some way, something that I could dismiss as not from Him. It didn't make sense that darkness would want to shine light on my entertainment, other than the temptation to fall into overanalyzing rigidity. I would have to watch myself on this.

Remarkably, conversations around this topic involving other peoples' decisions were all around me. People were throwing authors' names at me, testing me with album cover illustrations, daring me to watch certain things and deem whether there was a limit to the number of profane words, if in some way that meant the movie was good or bad. Of course, I tried to reiterate it wasn't as much about the specifics for me to decide (although that would inevitably confront one who saw the connection) but to simply prove to them that it mattered.

A girl once said to me, "So, I just started watching this new Netflix series and I really like it. It's not that there is anything really bad in it, I just feel weird after watching it. For one thing, I start to notice myself thinking like the main character. It's like their voice gets stuck in my head. I never really thought about it until after your presentation."

Nothing could be more relatable! Here we were filling ourselves with perspectives that may or may not benefit us. It wasn't about the positivity per say, nor even the relatability—surely there was health in hearing alternative perspectives—but what if it really was about the consumer quantity, or the way we thought about a certain thing, perhaps some things affected some more than others? I thought of Paul:

> *Be careful, however, that the exercise of your rights does not become a stumbling block to the weak. For if someone with a weak conscience sees you, with all your knowledge, eating in an idol's temple, won't that person be emboldened to eat what is sacrificed to idols? So this weak brother or sister, for whom Christ died, is destroyed by your knowledge. When you sin against them in this way and wound their weak conscience, you sin against Christ. Therefore, if what I eat causes my brother or sister to fall into sin, I will never eat meat again, so that I will not cause them to fall.[1]*

In this situation, the entertainment dilemma would have to be more than a thought. I decided to pray and fast to prepare myself, because I know the physical and spiritual are connected. If I was going to come to the conclusion that entertainment affected the depth of one's spirituality, I would have to wrestle it alone, and ultimately, publicly defend it.

It is here: Senior Thesis Day.

"18-year-old Devin Moore sat in the police station waiting on suspension for stealing a car, when he impulsively grabbed an officer's 40-caliber Glock automatic pistol, and, with great precision, killed three police officers, all with shots in the head. Then he stole a squad car and attempted to get away. What made him do it? Experts were convinced that Moore had only implemented what he rehearsed for hours upon end playing *Grand Theft Auto*. Is it possible for entertainment such as that video game to lead to such tragic consequences? Maybe Devin's own words would influence your thinking. After being found guilty of murder, he was quoted as saying, 'Life is a video game. Everyone's got to die at some point.' My name is Candice Gibbons, and today I will be defending the thesis titled 'On the Basis of Entertainment.'"

As confident as I looked in black heels and a suit, inside I wanted to cry.

The searing pain of two-sizes-too-small heels was worth the intimidating walk up to the stage but not worth it for the next hour of defense now that I am standing here. This is the moment I had prayed about, the time when I shared my wrestle with entertainment.

Moments earlier, I sat outside the room with Adrianna, still and cold.

"I don't think I can do this."

"You've already done the work," Adrianna encouraged. "It's just time to talk about it."

"*Or* get eaten by three hungry lions prepared to counter every proof." Will retorted.

I laugh disarmingly in my sportscoat and white, flowy shirt, which actually belonged to great-grandmother, Mimi. *Enjoying being formal, are we?* I laugh now inside, thinking about the version of Candice that wore overalls and played outside in the summer. *My, how Candice can change!*

"I am going to throw up." Another classmate said.

I identified completely.

The paralysis of public speaking threatened to surface for me too, but I was more scared of losing fervency to propose a complete rewiring to the world through my controversial entertainment dilemma than to think about the physical repercussions of anxiety and foot pain. There we were, held outside the room where three judges sit waiting to trample on our little minds. Growth for us, of course. The bench and I were familiar with one another, with its sand wood finishing that reminded me of the wood at the preschool where I chased toddlers. And now it was here: a training ground for somewhere new, somewhere rather adult.

Truth did not need defending, I was reminded. But this was no cut-and-dry defense. Did any muddier topic exist?

"As unimaginable as the actions of Devin Moore were, the question I posed today has even greater ramifications. Let's be honest. Most teenagers simply aren't thinking about it. Entertainment is in one bucket, moral choices in another. But music is a mood enhancer, according to the *U.S. National Library of Medicine's National Institute of Health,* and imagery has the power to implement real-world actions, just as we saw with Devin Moore.

"According to a lecturer at Yale Medical School, both pleasure-triggers and spirituality are connected to the brain's reward circuits. There is an overwhelming amount of evidence supporting the connection between entertainment and its physical repercussions.

"In Romans 12, Paul writes for us to give our bodies to God because of all he has done, to not copy the behavior and customs of this world, but let God transform us into a new person by changing the way we think. Notice the word *think*. The power and problem is in our thoughts, just as Devin Moore's video game prompted thoughts that led to action.

"Paul writes later to the church in Philippi telling them to fix their thoughts on what is true, honorable, and right. I don't believe Paul would say anyone who plays a video game would want to commit murder, but it's obvious Paul has placed a premium on guarding what we allowed to fill our minds. You can choose to say, 'I want to bring as much of the world as possible to my walk with Christ,' or you can say 'I want to bring as much of Christ as I can into the world.'

"Just as author Head Adamson writes, 'We are all one rational excuse away from leaving our inheritance in Christ in this life unclaimed. ... In the conversation that echoes into eternity, you will never hear the voice of regret for surrendering to Jesus too soon.' What comes into our eyes, ears, hearts, and minds will directly impact not only your days, but our destinies. So guard your hearts, for it determines the course of your life …"

The first judge asks, "What would you say to the person who says you are imposing your personal faith convictions?"

"Everyone is free to live their life. Just as the person who makes opposite decisions than I do might be imposing their lifestyle, I don't have to accept it. I think there's a fine line between living it and preaching it. I let my life be the main testimony." I respond.

"I know exactly where you're going in that." The judge says.

And he's ready to run over it with a bulldozer. I think, foot burning with pain. I try to stand like a flamingo to keep the pain down.

"I am recalling the Russian writer who once said that art is the only way to experience that which you have not experienced. What do you think about how we have more options to experience entertainment today?" The judge probes. "What about people who use filters to watch movies? I don't use those filters because whatever happens I think it's more authentic. But contrasting those views, what would be your position based on the research that you've done?"

"The ability to make more choices—period—leads to right choices and wrong choices in entertainment. So of course there are more opportunities to make wrong choices. However, I don't think just because we have more opportunities to make choices that it's all negative. I think there can be both positive and negative consequences for our generation having a lot of entertainment accessibility. You can't separate your spirituality from your entertainment, because they're both connected to the same reward circuits in the brain. It all comes down to a person's personal convictions. I have friends who will watch R-rated movies, movies with explicit content, and they don't feel concerned. That's not my place to judge. But looking at the research I've done of how what you put into your eyes with imagery factors into your character, I'm not going to consistently compromise my life with movies that have language that would get into my heart and soul. There is not even a desire in me to watch movies that break the heart of God. It really all depends on where you are with God on that." I respond.

A new judge says, "Do you feel that more things are allowable now in this age? Discuss what you see as a trend, and more importantly what you think can be done about it."

"The closer we get to eternity, the worse the world will get, so we have to expect that. You have to examine your own life. What have you allowed into your life that maybe doesn't align with your faith? Or maybe you've ignored conviction? The more you ignore God's Holy Spirit that speaks to you, the less and less you're going to hear His voice. And that's the scariest place to be."

"There's a book I read several years ago that talked about our physical environment and its association with colors and emotions. Where else should this be explored? What else in entertainment do we often not think is associated?" The judge offers.

As much as I want to launch into the effects of light and sound and texture as grasped through my education and personal experience on childhood, now illuminated in Candiceyland, I remember I am being timed—and graded—to answer specifically on my thesis.

"I would expound on point number three on indulgence and pleasure in entertainment. Many people excuse greed and pleasure and indulgence as it's 'cute' or 'fun.' I think there needs to be more moral guidance around that, so I would probably expound on that, in terms of further research in entertainment."

"I'm wondering why this subject, why you care?" The judge asks.

It's an expected question that catches me off guard (adrenaline, maybe?).

Why do I care? I bite my lip, tasting blood.

Don't forsake logic! Don't lose your credibility! I hold back tears.

It is all before me again, so real.

Carissa, the cheerleader from private school, seems to sit in a judge's seat.

"Get in the middle, Candice!"

Eyes. Music. Sweat. The strobe lights hueing my skin purple and red. A brush against my arm, my shawl falling. Me, falling into a spiritual hole.

This isn't about just music, I realize. *This is about the atmosphere of losing yourself, of turning away from God.*

Sleep paralysis. Falling into a black abyss. Demons. Darkness.

Dismissing the spiritual world as if it is all a game, that none of it matters ... the rescue of light.

These events hover in midair between me and the audience. This was it—a time to stand.

"It is a very personal issue to me," I say with tears in my eyes. "Last year I was invited to different parties at a private school and so many little moments of compromise happened. In one moment, someone led me by the arm and said, 'Come in the center and dance!' It's hard because in a moment you don't know if you're being too extreme because you've never been in that situation before, but it's in those moments that your faith is defined and you're able to rest and what the Holy Spirit tells you to do."

The room shifts uncomfortably as I cry, but I don't care.

I continue, "One girl almost committed suicide and said, 'If it weren't for you I wouldn't be here.' It's moments like that you really realize this is why you live the way you do. Sometimes it takes someone stepping out for them to realize, 'Maybe I should look like that,' or 'I see the benefits in her life, and I want that for myself.'"

A cough-issued silence follows.

The judge moves on to the next question.

"The fact that entertainment and spirituality share the same reward system in the brain is quite alarming to me. Consider how people would say that Christianity is literally just a form of entertainment and we just use that as a stimulus to shape our environment. What would you say about it?"

Suck it up, Candice. You're on a stage right now. I tell myself before my mouth opens.

Miraculously, the tears are replaced with an assured boldness. "Entertainment is definitely connected to spirituality because it's in the same circuit, but it's also separate. For instance, prayer uses the meditation and the language side of the brain as well. Your spirituality is in entertainment, but it's not limited to that. It's more of a holistic lifestyle approach, considering the meditation side of it, the entertainment part of it, the social aspect of it, and the sense that you're connected to something greater than yourself."

The third judge asks, "How can you be convinced that the Bible is just not some series of chapters in a book that you enjoy reading, but how do you know for yourself that it is real?"

"For me personally, it's because of my own experience. It comes through divine spiritual realization of what I'm reading is not written by a man, and then also you have to accept it by faith. I wrote a paper my freshman year about the biblical evidence behind the scientific evidence of scripture. Overall, it is through divine connection. How does something written 2,000-plus years ago apply to my life? And how can it relate to my heart and convict me? If you read and feel something and it promotes life change and you sense that there's something greater than you out there, and that it happened so many years ago and it pertains to me in this day, and specifically if you look at even the prophecies that have come true from the Bible, you realize it is no regular book. I've come to rest in the fact that the Bible is absolutely divinely inspired."

"So what do you have there? Like you said about video games, are they not spiritual?" The judge responds.

"I think it's a combination of the three things I mentioned in my thesis abstract, because it's a sound, it's a visual, and it's a pleasure. So you combine those things …"

"Are you saying video games should be illegal?" The judge interrupts me.

"Absolutely not. My point is we have to connect our entertainment choices to what we do. The reason I mentioned it in particular is because it mentions all three aspects of entertainment. It simultaneously affects three parts of the brain, which means it is highly influential. Are all video games bad? No. Should you let your kid play all video games? That's between you and God." I throw up my hands.

"I just think that it's such a hard road to try to seriously alter the entertainment world at all. How are you going to do anything about it?" A judge crosses his arms.

"That's what I'm hoping to study, and what I am going to do someday. I would love to, first of all, write books. I'm in the process of publishing a book. Then I would love to turn books into movies. I love the film industry." I surprise myself saying this and smile as a result.

The judge takes a sip of water, and I drink in a few deep breaths from crying.

It's happening so fast and I fear I sound overly pious and underdeveloped. All I want to do is crawl back into infancy in the womb, snug and warm without a care, but there is no room for fear or flight on this stage. I make eye contact with my parents who slipped in for this momentous emotional blunder. *Focus, Candice.*

Another judge offhandedly asks, "What would you say to my daughters who are going to a concert by a very popular singer right now whose songs are not always, say, clean? They've bought their tickets, and I, their father, am letting them go."

Who am I to say anything about this? I think, watching Adrianna and Will sitting a little straighter in their chairs. *Is that Kelly Grace in the back of the room, too?*

"That is between you and God." I acknowledge. "But if you are saying you don't agree with this singer's lifestyle choices, why support them?" I walk to the right side of the room now, speaking directly to my classmates. "We have to ask ourselves, are we going to sing profanity but just not say it? Are we going to laugh at promiscuity but then just not do it ourselves? Where is the line?"

"So you're saying we should return the tickets?" The judge is visibly stunned.

"Unless you plan to live out the lyrics, yes, I would return them."

The room fills with murmurs. All eyes scream one thing: polarization.

I did not care to recant!

A feathered lady approaches me after my never-ending thesis.

"My daughter has been listening to this *very* controversial artist. Of course *all* the teenagers listen to her nowadays."

A line of people have waited to ask questions. I nearly cried from exhaustion on my way to my seat, feet so swollen they were turning numb. The room had gotten quite full, I noticed towards the end, with younger grades and their teachers eager to listen in on the senior speeches. A fifteen-minute interlude now commenced with opportunity for refreshments and off-the-record discussions. Two of the three judges had already cut right to me with more questions.

"*Anyways,*" the woman continued, taking me by the hand. "I just wanted to say what an uncomfortable topic *that* was." She leans in with the heavy scent of Florentine and Thymes. "But this generation *needs* to hear about it."

"What kind of books do you read?" I ask lightly.

The lady blushes. "Nothing *children* should read. Precious few things entertain me these days, and my girlfriends agree with me. So we started our own little, eh, book club *of the scandalous kind* …" she whispers.

"Sounds spicy," I say with a strained smile, spotting some seasoned pretzels at the refreshments table. As much as I'd love to make her blush further, I don't know if my foot will ever come out of this heel, and I need to leave the school now to prepare for my internship.

It always amuses me how some adults put shame on younger generations for unfiltered entertainment, as if just because their brain is fully developed and they have experienced more life it does not matter what they endorse.

"Excuse me," one of the judges taps my shoulder. "I have a few more questions for you about your personal entertainment choices on behalf of my daughter, if you don't mind …"

"Candice! You did great!" Kelly cheers from the side.

"Candice—come get a picture before your dad has to leave." Mom says.

"Thank you … yes … excuse me …"

Finishing my civil duties, I finally get to Jerry the Jeep parked affectionately in my senior spot, only to realize with horror that I don't know if I can drive. Upon removing the heels that squished my little feet that now look disfigured, just a pat against the pedal sends a jolt of pain through my leg. I sit in the car ready to burst into tears again.

God, I am not qualified to speak or write or even drive a car. But You have helped me overcome so many fears! Can I at least drive home today?

I wait a few seconds, pain lessening—barely—then I suck it up and drive.

"You need to apply to at least one school even if you don't want to go to college." Mom tells me from the bottom of the stairs.

"Mom, I don't want to think about it. You and I both know I can't get in anywhere." I whine, leaning against my doorframe. "Besides, I already looked into UCLA's focused writing degree, but it's too far away and intangible."

"Oh! That's a strong program," Mom says. "You should go for it!"

But I don't like it. I think, slipping on my tennis shoes to go on a bike ride with Dad. Some places just don't feel like they were made for you.

Or am I limiting myself?

"What are your other options?" Dad asks outside. We pedal circles on the driveway before hitting the street, as is our warmup custom.

"I basically just Googled top writing schools in the world." I laugh incredulously. "UCLA was one of them. They offer just the kind of degree I am after, a focused writing diploma—something I can earn while still working in the office and writing my books. I should probably just branch out and apply. It would be such an honor to get in."

"What was the #1 university in the world?"

"Oxford, I think. Haha—it's not like I'd get in there!" I peddle onto the street.

CHAPTER 12
THE EXECUTIVE OFFICE

12TH GRADE SPRING, EDMOND, OKLAHOMA

I don't know what it's going to take for you to start seeing yourself differently, but you need to figure it out, or else you're going to squander a really great opportunity in your life. ... and I had been wasting that opportunity because of my own insecurity.
—Matt Keller

"Welcome to the office." The famous Stacy herself is before me, having freshly corrected me for calling her 'Mrs. Stacy'—what every Southern child does by default—and escorted me down the hall of the large, red and gold warehouse-like building with enormously high ceilings and unusual darkness that makes your voice sound chamber-worthy. The offices of the church are white-walled and carpeted, with a light scent of coffee and some sort of spice I can't quite pin. We first pass by a cluster of cubicle desks called Operations, where three middle-aged women named Cheryl, Emily, and Christine type busily. A pun calendar reads Serious Business behind the one named Christine, who I hear mutter faintly, "We've all died at some point." The crunch of a straw in Sonic ice fills the fluorescently lit room in the chill of the wintery day. A board behind Emily reads the quote: WE'RE IN A NEW ERA. I adopt it.

"Cheryl, this is Candice." Stacy turns to the tan woman in the immediate lefthand corner of the office, hair in glossy black curls.

"Hi," I say as a rush of people pass me with backpacks and leather satchels, keys jangling like the sound of twelve reindeer about to fly.

"Peanut butter is like a whole thing for me ..." I overhear Emily say to Christine.

"That's the OKC wing." Stacy points to a large room sectioned off by glass doors with silver handles. When the last person rushes through it, the door sounds like a broken xylophone. "Where all of the staff who run the Oklahoma City Campus—where we are—are based."

"Ah," I acknowledge, peering for anyone remotely my age (there are none, by the way).

Stacy continues explaining terms to me, like how CP stands for campus pastor, and how everyone is called by their initials here, so I would be CG, which gets confusing when she introduces a CP whose initials are also CP. Stacy, aka SD, continues talking, completely undeterred by a joyous laugh that floods from a private office with a covered window. "One of the things we value is humor," Stacy says.

I am still in awe that *the* Stacy's initials are SD, like a Secure Digital card used for transferring and storing memory data.

But really, can one laugh in such an adultish office, clueless at their job?

Kelly Grace successfully played a trick on me when she began her own internship months before at a real desk like a real 9-to-5er, sending me a picture of a small TV tray table and telling me it would be my new desk. Situated beside a life-sized printer at the focal point of the OKC wing, I was horrified at the picture, but knew no different, and so I was relieved to see Stacy point to a vacant cubicle across from Cheryl and tell me I would be allowed to occupy that space during the span of my internship. Operations seems much safer sort of a place.

"'Scuse me, 'scuse me." A man with a satchel squeezes past, opening the xylophone door to the OKC wing.

"That's CP who's the CP." Stacy laughs. "And this, is the executive wing." She carefully unlocks a door with a square of glass at the top. Inside are three main desks and three brown doors across from the desks. " ... where the executive assistants and pastors work."

"Ah," I say again.

Stacy motions to a gray chair next to a red Keurig machine and I sit, dull and quiet in the office blocked off from the noise and movement of Operations and the OKC wing. After a caution to me that confidentiality is a virtue and value in this office, she tells me how good this internship will be to practice writing, as there are several communications projects ahead. I tell her I am not really planning to go to college but thanks for thinking of my future anyway. *I should probably tell her I don't want to work for a church, either, just before she says anything else ...* But I don't think today is the day.

"We are in an exciting season as a church with lots of events in process. One of the main pieces carrying much of that momentum is written communication. You can practice writing some drafts for things we send out"

"Like for emails?" I ask hesitantly.

"Yes, and for notifications and social media. Are you familiar with Instagram?"

I blush. "I don't have it, but I've seen it." *Hope she knows Candice isn't normal.*

Stacy eyes me thoughtfully, hands clasped on a lined notebook covered in bold blue notes. "Why don't I ask if Reagan has availability to show you some things tomorrow."

"Okay!" I agree, as the choice really isn't mine. That is one of the first things I note about doing an unexpected internship: you have to be prepared for anything.

Like a maze, I am sent down a dark hallway backstage of the auditorium in search of this woman named Reagan, who I am told is the Social Media Coordinator—heart pounding, head coming up with all sorts of escape routes. Footlights guide my toe-revealing Birkenstocks past industrial racks piled high with gray bins and glass vases, past corners of instruments of every kind, a dozen miniature Christmas trees, and, alarmingly, a gigantic dinosaur head mounted on the wall. I am in a Mama Hamil's t-shirt stained with Mama Hamil's Mississippi fried chicken from the last family road trip, and my hair isn't even clean—it's in one of those side braids where the wrapped-around side has an obnoxious strand that keeps slipping. I would redo it, but it doesn't seem civil to redo your hair at an internship.

Narrow stairs, great. I tiptoe up the stairs that Stacy said would guide me to the Communications offices, where the creatives scheme.

My people! I thought earlier.

My word! I think now, slipping.

Green walls mark a very graphically animated space with lo-fi music humming to the smell of strong coffee and somebody's overheated lunch. Modern glass desks with tantalizingly large computer screens mark some clean, some quite messy desks. A twenty-something girl walks toward me with long, platinum hair and a wide, radiant smile.

"Hello, are you ... Candice?"

"Yes!"

"Cool. I'm Reagan. :)" This is spoken aloud, but I can just hear a text smiley face in her slightly country, upbeat voice, coming from the dazzling face of what I assume was a popular cheerleader in high school, being petite and athletic, like one of Carissa's friends.

"Hi!"

"Let's go to my office. I hear you are a writer? Stacy said you are about to be helping with some write-ups for social media. That's super cool!"

"Yes!" I say again. *Why in the world did I not dress nicer?*

"I am the Social Media Coordinator. I studied graphic design in college." She motions to a black leather office chair that is high enough to reach the standing desk in her little closet space of an office, dark and soundproof. "And this is the main page I manage."

"Oh?"

Reagan hesitates while I take it all in. "You have Instagram, right?"

I shake my head no.

Reagan's face lights up, first with shock, then awe. "Wow, so, okay. Um, this is the Instagram home page ..."

I am wide-eyed and spongy, taking in this new and formalized time to learn I had no idea was coming, nor even desired to step into, but giving it all to God.

"I'm back!" I wave to my track coaches, Coach Barnett and Robnett. They are in coach hats and navy coach shirts, almost in the exact positions in the inner field of the track where I said goodbye to them last year before foot surgery and lockdown.

Coach Barnett is college basketball kind of tall; Coach Robnett has a cheer coach build. I like both of them, but I have fond memories of Coach Robnett taking time to massage my foot on a particularly hard day. Plus, she gave me her very own foam roller.

"Has it already been a year?" Coach Robnett throws out her arms for a big hug.

"You look strong." Coach Barnett studies me.

"I've been strength training in the garage." I sit down to put on my spikes. "For the Olympics, of course."

"Haha! Well, we're glad you're back! We've put you on the 4x400-meter relay …" Coach Barnett says in a faraway voice before yelling to a boy rounding the curve of the track, "Christian! Speed up!"

"So you don't have screws anymore in your right foot?" Coach Robnett asks kindly.

"Yes, finally! Now I just have three screws in my left foot."

"Do they hurt?"

"Not yet," I massage the foot with the new scar, still tender.

"Let's keep it that way." Coach Robnett jumps up before helping me to my feet. "Okay, where are my long-distance runners?" She yells, then turning to me asks, "You ready to join us?"

"Not yet!" I laugh.

"Someday." She winks.

Today Mom asks me out of nowhere, "Have you chosen a college yet?"

"Not yet. I'm kind of paralyzed."

"No; you're procrastinating," Mom corrects.

I proceed to set my lunch box in the sink after a long interning day, thinking, *I would totally tell you if I did apply to a college, dear Mother. I am just too busy and disinterested to decide*! As I start to run upstairs, Mom follows me around the corner and offers the most surprising proposal I have ever been asked: "Hey, what could it hurt to apply to that top writing school you Googled—Oxford, wasn't it?"

"You've got to be kidding," I laugh from the twelfth stair. "That would hurt bad."

"All you would have to do is apply." She says from the open door to the pantry. The glow of the pantry lamp shines bright around her head, creating a hazy sort of halo.

I rub my eyes.

"Oxford is in England, isn't tha' right?" Her voice perks with a rough cockney accent.

"Yeah. Across the pond." I picture a vague outline of Europe. Of course, I haven't once thought about Oxford seriously. I, as a romantic idealist, can't even let myself think about the utter possibility ... it's not healthy to think of such fantasies.

"Apply, baby!" Mom claps her hands. "You've got nothing to lose!"

I think, *Sure I do, my reputation ... my self-esteem ... my confidence to apply to anything the rest of my life. I could go many days without seeing an Oxford rejection letter and be okay.*

"Fine, I'll apply." I blurt out to appease, rolling my eyes and smiling. Totally not going to think about the possibility of being accepted—ha! That's taking life a little cinematically too far.

I haven't told anyone yet I have officially clicked the orange "Apply" button except my immediate family and Mr. Tim, our family friend who studied law at Oxford and shared stories about his experience at the university. I applied to become a part-time hybrid student of the

Diploma in Creative Writing *programme*. Funny how the Brits have 'me' in their program. I am not even sure what a diploma is, but the blue and white alone of the university's website sang "Candice!" Not to mention the literal motto for the University of Oxford's crest is *Dominus Illuminatio Mea*, which translates to 'the Lord is my light.' But just because my name *Candice* means 'full of light,' I should not jump to ideal conclusions.

There's absolutely no way I will get accepted into the oldest university in the English-speaking world, so why worry about it being a possibility?

"There's no way she'll get in," I heard my dad say to Mr. Tim over the phone. "She hasn't trained for this her whole life. She hasn't had a tutor or anything. She isn't equipped."

"If she were accepted, it would change everything." Mr. Tim replied.

When I heard this, I wasn't discouraged; I was relieved. I have nothing to prove and no one to prove it to. My parents think it's impossible (my dad, at least), and it's not like I have any tutors shoving practice interviews down my throat. Even if there is a chance that I did get shortlisted for an interview, it will be a tremendous honor. But there are so many applicants, so many writerly geniuses out there. I must content myself with writing my book in the secret room. I must focus on my internship and on running track for the last time. I must focus on being a good daughter, sister, intern, and servant of God.

Lord, I trust You with everything. And, I do have faith that You can do anything. I pray and actually smile really big tonight, for the glow-in-the-dark stars above my bed do look irregularly bright.

Reagan's bright company makes my days at the office fly swiftly, so between school and work and the secret thrill of having applied to a certain UK college on a whim, I feel energized enough to take over the senior yearbook pages at school and lead the senior sweatshirt project in an effort to bring some fun to my very serious presence in class. I even reach out to a publishing company out in California about a chance to possibly work with them on *A Time to Trust*. Zero connections and very far-fetched for a high school senior, but why not?

Why not intern in an unexpected position that pushes me out of my comfort zone?

Why not branch out and lead activities at school?

Why not wake up early, write my book, and email a random publisher?

Why not apply to the number one university in the world?

Interning was a terrible decision. I just messed up the one project Stacy gave me on this temporary computer at this temporary desk across from Cheryl, who has no idea what I am working on, not that it's a big deal or she would even care, but because Stacy told me to practice confidentiality in little ways and just do my business. I'm freaking out so bad I can't even breathe, because Candice hit 'send' on the email and the damage is permanent.

Knocking on the door to the executive office, also called the *Exec Wing*, I rehearse an apology and plan to state my resignation, although this is merely an internship.

"Oh, that's okay," Stacy says, her face unreadable. "Bring it here."

I never want to show my face in the office again. But Stacy still likes me—she wants me back here at 3 p.m. tomorrow ... to do it all over again. I can't even look at myself in the mirror. But here I am, still breathing.

Just picture me crying my way through a meeting with my poor boss who didn't know what in the world to do with me. I slammed my finger in the bathroom stall where I ran to hide and cry post-meeting. My tire went flat this morning, so I hastily jumped in Dad's car only to realize it was running on empty. Not to mention a guy got angry at my slow driving today and demonstrated it. I know this is all rather silly, but a girl sometimes just needs to vent about the little things.

Why can't I just be unofficially dismissed from this internship commitment? No one wants to work at something they're not good at and be repeatedly corrected. Every time she puts an Excel spreadsheet in front of me, I nearly go cross-eyed. Does Stacy know I am barely surviving high school math? Does she know that my mind works in narrative form, in storytelling fashion—at best? Does she know I am in fight-or-flight mode 24/7—just an eighteen-year-old thinking about her Greek mythology assignment due tomorrow?

The irony is, Stacy does—and still lets me near her.

She repeats consistently. "Will you trust the process and embrace teachability?"

I know I should.

I have been teaching myself to trust God and embrace change since I was fifteen.

I've taught myself how to run with screws in my feet, be content without friends, study even when it is difficult to comprehend, and be optimistic through foot surgery and a pandemic.

But this is different. This is like putting a truck driver in a ballet teacher role. More specifically, it is like putting a ticking bomb in the hands of a writer and expecting her to solve it using math equations foreign to her knowledge. Incomprehensible.

No, I cannot learn data entry or event planning. And I don't want to stay in a seat of failure. Why in the world did I email a random publisher or think I had any right to apply to ...

Ugh, I can't even say it.

"Good morning, Cheryl." I pass her kind face on my way into the executive office. Another day begins, and here I am, commuting and aging like a 40-year-old, making the best of things.

"Good morning, Candice. How is your book coming along?"

"Long," I laugh from the doorway. "I am up to 90,000 words."

"Oh my goodness." Cheryl raises her eyebrows but doesn't smile, reminding me of my aunt Angela. Cheryl is calm and reassuring, a demeanor I gravitate towards. Things surprise her, but not too much, so she is never rattled. "Is that your targeted word count?"

"I just thought I'd write the story and wherever it ended, it ended."

"Who is your publisher?"

"Fingers crossed, a brand-new company in California. But I haven't heard back."

"Well, let me know. I was thinking about your book over the weekend. I was also thinking about our conversation on matcha tea …" she opens her drawer. "I found these KitKat bars that are matcha flavored."

"Oh, I've never heard of it!" I walk over to her desk.

"You'll have to tell me if you like it." Cheryl smiles, and then her phone rings.

"Thank you!" I mouth, walking into the exec wing.

At a quick glance, Stacy is at her computer zeroed in on seven different tabs. Lauren, who works across from Stacy, is talking rapidly into the phone, and Vanessa, another executive assistant, is quietly anonymous in a separate meeting space behind Lauren's desk. I take a temporary place at the desk facing Lauren, across from Stacy, and try to zero my own self into what we are working on today. But as people enter and leave meetings in one of the executives' offices, I can't help but catch how funny their conversations sound out of context.

"Not everyone is administratively inclined."

"My guess is usually right. I just can't tell you why."

"She doesn't let any grass grow under her feet."

"You're picking up what I'm putting down."

"You're catching what I'm throwing."

"You know me and my margins."

"It's clearly a high priority."

"They didn't live up to their slogan."

"We can't just not give them what they asked for!"

"I'm just a man with an awkward haircut."

"If there's one thing you can count on is Candice sitting at her desk really concentrated."

"Oh, I'm sorry!" I say with red cheeks, hastily ceasing typing. "Hi!" I smile to Reagan, standing curiously at my desk.

"You upgraded, I see." She smiles bright.

"Oh, someone needed my desk by Cheryl, so Stacy let me sit in the exec wing today. I feel so cool!" I turn in my swivel chair.

"I like your roses and stack of books." Reagan notes.

"Oh. Thanks!" I guiltily acknowledge the stack of grammar textbooks. "It's my temporary spot while I work on this …" I stammer, remembering it is confidential. "Er ... project. Oh, and I found these books in my dad's office at home and thought they looked studious."

"That's funny!" Reagan says. "Hey, I'm going to Smoothie King, want anything?"

"Oh, sure!"

"Vegan pineapple spinach?"

"You remembered my order!"

Reagan laughs. "I might even try it today."

She's so cool!

"Change is inevitable," Stacy tells me evenly. "To reach your full potential in life, you must be willing to embrace it. But change inevitably brings risk and its next-door neighbor, fear. And fear has the power to roadblock your teachability if you don't learn how to handle it." She reads to me in our meeting, which are called "1:1 Meetings" (or in office slang, "one-on-ones") from the book, *They Key to Everything*. "When we honestly don't believe we have the skills or talent to do what needs to be done, we tend to shut down." [1]

Stacy then turns to me and asks what my roadblocks are, which I explain in bullet points:

- My biggest teachability roadblock is insecurity, which I know is rooted in pride.
- I am absolutely way too judgmental: to myself, to others, to everything on earth.
- As an idealist, I see things like they're in a book or movie, not as they really are.

"It is good to identify these things," Stacy says in her northern no-nonsense tone, smoothing stray blond hairs with a naturally tan hand. "Then you at least have a starting point for improvement."

"But Stacy, what if I really *can't* ever learn how to call people without being nervous, or negotiating with event vendors on the spot?" I ask vulnerably, feeling quite close to her after all the tense moments and time-sensitive deadlines we've been through. "I just think I was wired differently. School is one thing, well, school is a whole thing, really. But the adult world is a completely different matter. I'm sorry. You have taught me so much and I hate to be a disappointment. I just don't think I was cut out for administrative work. It's so multi-faceted. Every day is different. I can't keep up with the rush of the office."

Stacy laughs. "You'd be surprised, Candice, at what I see in you."

I laugh and shake my head, still disbelieving.

"You got offered a *job*?" Mom exclaims.

I nod. "In the *executive office*! I am in shock."

"We all are," Bria sits down at the dinner table laid with noodles in Kelly's homemade fettuccini alfredo sauce with sweet peas and mandarin oranges in tiny glass bowls. "I mean ... you're so ... unconventional."

"Yeah ... er ... creative!" Allison throws out.

"Weird." Angel adds.

"What they mean is," Jordan, who is turning seven this year, joins the conversation, "you're still a kid at heart. Like me." He bobs his head with a closed-lip smile, something he does a lot these days. His hat is flipped backwards, and little blond freckles dot his happy face. He says such mature things, probably from having five older sisters.

"Thank you all for the votes of confidence."

"Don't worry Candice," Kelly touches my arm. "You do have the capacity to be an admin! I believe in you! You just think very imaginatively."

"Thanks. I'm with you all," I acknowledge the girls. "I never thought I would work in an administrative role. But here we are."

"Stacy must really believe in you." Dad offers, twisting a strand of cheesy noodles.

"I love Stacy. And I love the office. I am just intimidated and feel ill-equipped."

"Every job is intimidating. The important thing is that you stick with it." Mom illustrates with a lifted spoon of peas. She was a straight-A student with hopes of studying journalism after winning her pageant crown and writing her first book, all by age twenty-one. "You just hold your head high and work hard, then you can come home and cry to your *momzie*."

"Okay, *Momzie*." I hug her, feeling once again like my childhood self.

"You've had a lot of growth this month, little pea. Hmm ... I love peas. Did anyone know that?" She hums giddily. "Have you ever thought about how strange the word 'spoon' is? Spoon ... spoon ... *spoon*." She flips her now-empty spoon to the back side where your face looks like an egg and smiles meaningfully at her reflection, repeating the word that has us all now questioning what else we have gone along with as normal. Mom has certainly led me to a place of wonder and imagination, and I have no doubt God will continue to crack my hard shell of a head, if I continue to open myself up to learn.

If life could not get any more surreal ...

"Mom ..." I creep into her bathroom late at night.

"What." She stares seriously into my eyes.

"I got shortlisted to be interviewed at Oxford."

It happens like a gunshot, right at the start of track meet season: Oxford wants to interview me. I call both sets of grandparents—Annie and Papa, Gigi and Poppy—to officially announce Oxford University's invitation to do a video interview for the Undergraduate Diploma in Creative Writing.

"Oxford?" Annie and Papa's voices are muffled and breathless. "They want to *what*?"

"Oxford wants to interview me," I tell them over the phone. "I applied just for fun." I pace away from my teammates in our track team's tent at a meet in Stroud, Oklahoma, knee crisscrossed in therapy tape. "I didn't want to tell anyone until I found out if I was shortlisted for an interview."

One of my teammate's moms tells me, "You must be smart!" I laugh and file it away to journal, because, no, God just favored me despite my weakness.

Physically, it could be no more evident than me lining up to run the 4x200-meter relay.

Me, a runner, of all things. I stomp my feet on the black track, waiting for the gun to sound. My knee almost locks when I am handed the baton and take off running my half-lap around the track. I ice it and lay down afterward, and Coach Barnett almost pulls me from running the 4x400-meter relay, my personal favorite race.

"I'll be fine!" I beg her. "This is my first time running the 4x4 at a meet!"

"No," she snaps, redoing a kid's ankle compression wrap. "Get physical therapy for that."

But when my backup runner isn't available, I am thrown into the race at the last minute. It is a perfect handoff event, and I bond with my three teammates—McKenzie, Kimaya, and Elise—rejoicing at how God allows victories, big and small.

Oxford wants to interview *me*!

PT is awkward for anyone, let alone when your therapist is a young, single medical doctor athlete who asks you to do yoga positions on the ground to test your knee strength.

"You're pretty strong for a runner," he says.

"I do lift consistently," I say blushing. "Sometimes more than I run."

"Flip sides." The therapist instructs, standing over me.

It is at this moment, to my embarrassment and humility, a peppermint candy falls out of my pocket and onto the yoga mat. Everyone laughs.

It's an obvious sign of compromise. Little, but says a lot. Me: braced up, in workout leggings, about to run at a track meet—also eating candy.

It isn't funny, but I still laugh.

At the last track meet, I got dead-last, sealing the loss for our 4x4 team by the last thirty meters. Ticked off and discouraged, I can at least pinpoint that I know I have slacked on my training. I can't blame it on my knee being in a brace or my foot's three screws causing pain. No; I can run faster, train with more discipline.

Irritated by my lack of focus, I had a sour attitude on the drive home, complaining about feeling restrained during my final semester of high school track. In her grace, Mom stopped to get me chocolate milk from Braum's Ice Cream. Feeling undeserving, I cried and iced my knee and watched the sunset from the back seat.

Despite a little slack and compromise, life is fun, busy, and friendless—an orange and white color wheel of track meets, team banquets, and senior pictures; ice packs, physical therapy, and vegan pineapple spinach smoothies. I am too tired to spend as much time praying and journaling. It feels like all I do is study, work, email, and run. I avoid family dinners. I ignore texts from family in Missouri. I even snap at my siblings.

But I am submitting my book to a publisher! I am about to be interviewed for Oxford! God has helped me get to this point, and isn't this a season of blessing?

Maybe I *have* allowed myself to coast into a routine of skipping church services to sleep and helping less with dishes in the sink. But I am repeatedly changing out of work clothes in the bathroom of the YMCA to go straight to track from the office, hearing *Gratitude* by Brandon Lake on the radio down streets like Bryant and Danforth and 15th. I really am thankful to run again, and I also just won first place four times at a district fine arts competition for First-Person Essay, Book Chapter, Short Film, and an Urban Dance Troupe entry, which means I will be going to nationals one final time in Florida this summer. I can't wait for another road trip!

For my senior formal in downtown OKC at the Devon Tower, up on the 49th floor at a restaurant called Vast, I wore a plain, blue-and-silver dress and sat beside Adrianna from school. I studied the skyline of my city and felt proud and accomplished and lonely. All that was on my mind was my Oxford interview. Up, up, and away!

Oxford interview complete. Unauthorized to record it or have anyone else in the room, I don't remember much other than making the professors laugh when I accidentally emphasized how much I was looking forward to learning from my colleagues ... and 'even the professors.'

"Even the professors?" they repeated to my humiliation, "Why, we've never heard that one before. I suppose we do have something to offer."

Thus sealed any possibility of getting into the world's top university.

Haha, like I even had a chance!

"You could have seriously injured everyone," Mom hissed in my ear.

"I didn't see the car," I argued back, humiliated this happened in front of my friends. "It's not like I was trying to wreck, Mom."

Mom's hair is newly colored and styled shorter. Her eyes, still their radiant blue, are less weary than two years ago when we moved. She is resilient, healing quietly from things both known and hidden to me. She still continues to face a tremendous amount of change, and I continue to be the problem and the source of our arguments.

And then I almost wreck in Jerry the Jeep when the Bricks, my old all-girls friend group from Missouri, come to visit Oklahoma and I drive them to downtown Edmond, while Mom drives behind me, watching the whole thing.

It's a breaking point.

I feel numb and defiant, pushing against things and expecting results.

It's an arrogance that has come from getting awards and facing new pressure without relying on God, expecting to continue to win races while stuffing candy in my pockets. The worst part is, Adalie sees my inconsistency and calls it out, but I get defensive.

I guess I am scared of failing at my book, scared of graduating without college plans, scared of a national track meet our team is attending. I realize I am wrong, but it doesn't stop me from acting rudely to the Bricks, who invited me to graduate with them in Missouri, and I am disrespectful to my mom. My Oklahoma graduation has come and gone, but it is a bit painful to relive, for I walked down the aisle in what seemed to be opposition to all my friends and family, snapping back at well-meaning people out of stress.

Oh God, I messed up so bad this semester.

I decide on an all-black, long-sleeved shirt with black jeans and a curly bun for my first official day as a part-time employee. It may seem severe, but since my new best friends are 40-year-old moms, I only consider what clothes will make me think deeply and work like an executive. After Stacy surprised me with a staff-wide clapping ovation when I walked through the doors, I settle in a desk in the exec wing preparing for a greater level of responsibility. I am honored to work at a place where I feel loved and valued, even if I am terribly nervous and stretched out of my comfort zone every day (Reagan has taught me this is normal and a part of the process).

Perhaps the best part of working here is that humor is a value. I used to get irritated by it, but now I realize it is my own introverted fault for not valuing other people. I need to learn to place other people's feelings above my own projects and deadlines. As Stacy says, "find the balance."

Today's office conversations have me rolling in laughter. I promise I do more than capture out of context quotes—Stacy even just said I did my best job yet at five different drafts we were working on—but I can't help being a writer surrounded by some of the most hilarious people!

Stacy walks over to me and slams a stack of papers on my desk.

"*Wow*," I say as she stares down at my little rolling chair. "I can't believe I am an 18-year-old in a cubicle at a real desk with a boss that just slammed papers on my desk."

"I didn't slam them," Stacy laughs. "It just made that kind of sound. It's your next project. Yay!"

Lauren says from her desk, "Leave it to Candice to think cinematically." A queen of spreadsheets, Lauren's mind is probably deep in numbered columns. "When life gives you a number, I can fill it in" seems to be her motto, taken from one of the executives.

Vanessa soars past us, "I need to get my brain to focus and do some work." She holds a pile of envelopes and shakes her head at me. "Mailing day!"

Stacy notes my eyes delighted to see a manuscript to edit. "Feeling excited yet, Candice? Feast and enjoy." She looks at her Apple watch. "Oh, shoot. Breaking all the protocols for today …" Her voice trails. She grabs her computer and charger before running to one of the private offices.

Christine, an operations admin, swaggers into the room with a Sonic slushy. "I like to think of myself as a very guarded person. Candice, how would you rate me?"

"You do have some of the funniest quotes in the office," I offer.

"I hope they're not all written down."

Lauren mutters from her desk, "I don't know what the problem was. But there was one. Something in this data isn't adding up."

Vanessa flies through again. "Do we work backwards in this office? No!"

Christine throws up her hands. "I just don't play with it."

Lauren replies, "Well, I get paid to play with it." She stretches her arms. "How do you drink so much water, Candice?"

"Track." I turn the lid of my aqua tumbler with *Candice* engraved in cursive.

"There's no gray line for Candice, is there?" Lauren shakes her head. "Have you ever had soda in your life?"

"I can't tell you what Coke tastes like," I admit.

"They should watch their ads in silence to see if it makes sense," Christine says.

"I need to download a water drinking app," Lauren reflects.

"This sounds too convicting, I don't want to hear this." Christine starts to leave.

"You know me and my non-water-drinking self. See that?" Lauren holds up two-thirds of a water bottle. "I started that last week."

I stand and stretch. "I need an ice bath."

"And I," Stacy walks back into the room. "Don't need to send another email for a year."

Vanessa calls from around the corner, "Wow, you really knocked out the day's work."

"I'm not saying it's all done," Stacy clarifies. "I am saying this is where I'm leaving it."

Lauren stands with her laptop showing the puzzling spreadsheet. "Vanessa, you're a trustworthy person. What do you make of this?"

"I don't trust myself," Vanessa shakes her head. "I trust the formula!"

Lauren squints at the screen. "Something's not adding up. I got double sugar and double caffeine this morning. Hopefully one of them will work."

Stacy jumps in, "You want to know what I think? I think at this point we're going to be done. I'm tired of this sheet driving on." She clicks her computer shut. "That will be my spring break celebration: getting the new Nitro Cold Brew at Starbucks." She stands with her purse. "Anyone want anything?"

One of the first things I learned about Stacy was that she loved Starbucks, and you couldn't separate the two.

Lauren nods slowly, "That's my kind of celebration."

"What d'you want?" Stacy says from the door.

"Oh, I was talking about this," Lauren turns her computer screen to an Amazon item. "That's the kind of crinkle paper I like. Who knew I would have a preference in crinkle paper?"

"I mean, we have a preference for pens, so it makes sense," Stacy muses.

"When you work with crinkle paper enough, you realize you have a preference." Lauren justifies.

After all, we are admins. It's an overarching job title for multi-plated producers.

Stacy points at me. "Candice? Starbucks?"

"I've got a track meet in three days."

Lauren teases, "C'mon, Candice. Live a little."

"I'm sleep deprived and need to make sure I don't get sick." I shrug and wave to Stacy, who laughs at me. I'm also picturing the peppermint falling out of my pocket at physical therapy, and how irritable I was with my friends and family at graduation. Little things, little things.

"That's important," Vanessa backs me up. "Every little thing matters before race day."

Vanessa, tall and elegantly poised, is a retired police officer who has run several marathons herself. If I have time at the end of the day, I love to sit near her desk and share stories.

Jacqueline enters the room. "And ain't nobody got time to be sick! I know I don't!" She's the newest member of the executive admin team besides me.

"Jacqueline! I didn't know you were in office today!"

"Girl, I had papers to sign," she says in a rich Alabama accent, deeply familiar.

I listen as Jacqueline launches into a narrative of the events of the week schooling her two daughters as she curls her long brown hair behind her ear.

Lauren is about to get in the carpool pickup line.

Vanessa is about to become a grandmother.

And I am about to graduate from high school with the Bricks in Missouri and announce that I have no confirmed college plans.

Girls in heels danced under the disco ball with boys at Julia's graduation party in Missouri. As a member of the Bricks, we cliqued at a round table near the front of the dance floor. I clinked my punch glass with Adalie's and joined my friends for one last hurrah of line dancing before a formal dance commenced on a following night. It was a night of old memories, new songs, and a seemingly harmless dinner.

After a painful dance in high heels, Adalie recommended we get fresh air. We followed a trail into the woods behind the event center and talked in voices hushed by loud crickets, Ozark humidity, and stringed lights.

"When have you been the happiest?" I asked quietly.

She sighed long. "I see that you're happy again?"

"I prayed and got my heart right," I admitted. "I forgot how I can't do anything in my own strength, and I hurt the people closest around me in the process. I'm sorry."

"It's okay." She put her arm around me.

What was ahead? Where would we go?

We both already felt removed—that feeling of leaving all things high school. Adalie graduated a year early, and I was away from the daily life with the Bricks after moving to Oklahoma.

Still, it felt somehow wrong to imagine it had all just simply ... ended. No more making *Anomaly Hunters* videos on YouTube. No more protocol dinners and sleepovers. Our conversation brought a young adult sense, reigning heavily on my mind.

After another long dance, I slipped away to a back table and removed one heel, my face sweating and visibly reading that I was ready to return to the farm with Gigi and Poppy and slip away from every conversation that somehow routed to asking where I was going to college.

I had one shot, and that was it.

The public did not know. It couldn't go on my senior announcement—I wouldn't dare! The blue *O*-word could not be found anywhere (most *O*-words are blue in my mind, and I think *Oswald the Octopus* had something to do with it). Without Oxford, I had no idea where I would go or what would become of me.

My former tutor, Mrs. Hammond, walked towards me. I hid my shoe behind my dress.

"You're a good writer," she told me, "but I believe God is going to use your public speaking. Perhaps as a way to share your stories." After studying my bewildered face for a deep breath's length, she added, "Yes, public speaking is you."

That's strange, I thought. *Me, the girl who's afraid to speak? The girl who is an introvert? What would I have to speak about, anyway?*

I thought about my senior thesis. A rush of expectation and dedication swept over me, and before I knew it, I was standing there, hands trembling as they always do when I am in front of crowds, saying what God told me to say. It wasn't anything I did that resulted in a passing grade—rather, what I allowed God to do through me.

Whatever comes will have to be orchestrated by God, for surely, I will not seek it out.

"Thanks," I tell Mrs. Hammond. "It was really fun getting to be included in the Bricks' graduation ceremony here in Missouri." I had been offered a chance to read an excerpt of *A Time to Trust* to the audience at the ceremony. I chose the scene where we said goodbye to the Bricks before moving to Oklahoma. It was rather sad but reminded me of how hard I had to trust God in that season.

God, even when I still don't know the answer to things, I trust You.

CHAPTER 13
NEWS THAT STAYS NEWS

12th grade spring, Ozark, Missouri

It wasn't hard; it was impossible.
—Dad

May 4

Last Sunday, on the perfectly plain morning before Julia's graduation party, I walked through the pasture at Riverview Ranch, pausing every few feet to watch hay blow in the wind. *Think of the lilies,* I heard in my mind, *how God dresses them in yellow silk.* They looked like beautiful blossoms of friends, dancing without a care in the world.

Friends and dancing were affectionately on my mind after dancing at Julia's party, and I was also bound to another formal dance, programmed like a ball, on Tuesday night. Heels were the last thing my feet needed before an upcoming national track meet, yet there was something so appealing about dancing with friends one last time, and I was thankful.

And if God cares so wonderfully for wildflowers that are here today and thrown into the fire tomorrow, he will certainly take care of you.[1] I prayed for the ability to trust God with my feet and unknown future.

I returned from the field to my room at the farm, still the 'sparest of spare' rooms to me. I did not sleep but spent the next agonizing 30 hours under an unexpected allergy reaction and dreamed horrid nightmares of Queen Elizabeth and fantastical illusions. I felt as though God tested me through the night. I again submitted my entire life, all my dreams and ambitions.

The deep feeling of being unwell lingers on me even now, late Tuesday night, May 4, and I still cannot eat. Everything is hazed and blurred ever since the last pure moment of feeling well when I sat among the wildflowers, but the sunrise of today brought an unexpected surprise.

After throwing up, I took a hot shower to shake off the feeling.

Immediately upon emerging, I had a sudden inclination to check my email. I know that I never should check my phone at such an awkward time, but I was not thinking clearly.

And so it happened in this glistening transitional moment alone I read something that would change my life forever:

Dear Candice,

I am writing to let you know that the University considered that your application for the Undergraduate Diploma in Creative Writing … starting in Michaelmas (Autumn) Term … was of a commendable standard, and that we will shortly be sending you an Offer which will detail the conditions which you will need to meet to become a student of the University.

Our undergraduate admissions round is highly competitive, so please accept our warm congratulations on your achievement. …

"No," I sunk to my knees. Dizzy. Anxious. Stunned.
It was addressed from the University of Oxford.

"Mom." I called her from the floor where I had slid and not moved, still wrapped in a towel, hair wet and dripping. "I have something to tell you. Are you alone?"

"Hi, Canzie. Yes, I'm at Annie and Papa's house." Her voice was normal on the phone.

"Mom, I got an email from Oxford."

Silence.

"I got accepted."

I heard a nearly inaudible gasp, followed by a scream, then my sisters' and grandparents' voices on the other end calling her name: *"Casey, what is it? Are you okay?"*

"Candice got into Oxford! She's going to Oxford!!!"

I smiled for the first time in 30 hours.

It would have been fun to plan ways to announce it originally to various people, but I was too sick and too eager for people to help supplant my lack of celebration to do anything creative. Plus, this was all a dream, so it seemed. *I might as well see how far I can get …*

"Gigi," I said later from the couch in her hearth room—the very place where we watched *An American Aristocrat's Guide to Great Estates*. "I have something to tell you."

"What, darling?" She stopped short of the laundry room.

"Where is Kelly?"

"Coming!" She called from the kitchen.

I sighed and took in their faces once Kelly came close, "Well, hello." I wondered what would change after I uttered the life-changing words: "Guess who got accepted into Oxford?"

"What?" They both seemed to say at once, visibly more excited than me. "No way!"

"Way," I smiled wearily, opening up the official offer emailed after I responded my acceptance. I read it aloud, hoping it would offer better words:

> Dear Candice,
>
> I am delighted to inform you that your application for admission to the University of Oxford has been successful. ... This offer constitutes your formal offer of a place at the University of Oxford and when you accept it you will enter into a contract with the University. ...

My eyes slide down the six-page document with British spellings such as *programme* and *instalment* and *queries*. I skimmed through academic conditions and accommodations before reading the line, "We hope that you will accept this unconditional offer."

"Oh, Candice. This changes everything!" Gigi exclaimed with wide, beaming eyes.

"I know," I nodded vaguely.

Did I actually? There was no way to know.

Some of the biggest moments of life are lived in such a way that you feel as though you are watching it as a third person. In that moment, I became less and less aware of who I or what I was doing, staring out the window to the pasture of the wildflowers, and so watched Gigi and Kelly celebrate conversationally with a deflated Candice before she realized the hand on her watch, and it was time to dress for the ball. She walked back to her room and over to the corner where she had sunk to the floor and thanked God. Feeling sick again, she reminded herself that nothing mattered but to be right with God, and that she should not become preoccupied with attention. And so Candice dressed reluctantly for the ball, fogged and distantly amused.

Life always felt like a movie …

Whether or not my life was a French comedy (Kelly once told me mine was), tonight's ball was decent—as expected when you are the oldest one there, unable to eat from a nut allergy reaction, your heels throb in your shoes, and your dress feels boring compared to the rest. The shadow of the navy-blue *O*-word loomed over me and provided a little smirk to my otherwise unentertained face and presence. The only joy of the night was whispering to a few friends, such as an enthusiastic Meghan, a member of the Bricks, how I got into Oxford.

It didn't feel real. It couldn't be real.

"*No.*" Meghan doubled over in shock. "I have chills!"

Meghan was one of the core members of the Bricks. She herself was bound to Europe on theater business, and squealed to me, "Perhaps we could meet up in the UK!" before the Viennese waltz carried us to the floor with partners who eagerly took our trembling hands.

My official date, the boy who was seated beside me at dinner and presented my corsage, was a head shorter with a 2-guard buzz cut. I tried hard to be gracious and understanding. It must have been intimidating to escort a senior in severe black who looked positively ill. All the while I inwardly wondered who my preferred date would be someday at such a formal event …

One of my dance partners approached Bria between dances and asked, "What's wrong with that one sister?" The poor world had no idea why I was visibly disagreeable. Nauseated, disinterested, and in complete shock. Reluctantly Oxford-bound. Cruel to myself, not nearly as celebratory as I hoped I would be upon acceptance. Shocked or stressed, I suppose, unaware of how to process that this literally changes everything.

When the foxtrot began and I was issued a new partner, all I could do was flash a glamorous smile and talk as bubbly as I could for fear of leaving the school with the reputation of an evil stepmother. I could already envision the lore of the girl who was shipped-to-Oxford-and-disappeared.

Of all the places to find out about Oxford, there I was in Missouri with friends and family, enthralled in party after party, watching slideshows of high school life, and giving hugs to friends already bound to the East Coast. It is strange how God orchestrated sickness around my college acceptance. One year from now I will be in England, and who knows what's to become of me—for this is not a dream.

CHAPTER 14
FINISH, CANDICE!

12TH GRADE SPRING, EDMOND, OKLAHOMA

*Nobody ever casually drifted up
to the doorstep of their dream life.*
—Matt Keller

"I feel like every night we find out something else shocking about your life, Candice." Bria dips a piece of chicken in ketchup at the dinner table. "They offered you a book contract?"

"Did someone save me any macaroni?" Allison walks into the kitchen in a ballet leotard, having just arrived from a Russian Classical Ballet class.

"Not just one, but two! I'm getting published!" I am still in disbelief.

"Where's the macaroni?" Allison asks again, and the conversation shifts momentarily, as is custom. "I'm absolutely famished! After we finished a *battement barre* combination, which is so quick and easy, we moved onto *fondue relevè en pointe* and the whole three-minute song just kept going up and down and up and down. My calves thought that were going to *explode!*"

I almost exploded when I saw the California caller ID. A rush of nerves hit me, but I still had a boldness to answer it (per Stacy's training not to run from unknown calls). It was the publishing company to whom I had submitted two chapters of *A Time to Trust*.

I pick up the conversation, "They sent me an email, too," and reach for my phone. "It talks about how they are pleased to let me know that they are issuing a publishing contract to me today ..." I scan the lengthy message. "And they asked if I could speak by phone again this week to discuss details."

"Candice—this is huge!" Dad shakes his head.

"It is all because of God. It was all because we moved." I lock eyes with each family member, hoping they gather just how serious this is. "Remember when we used to sit at our old kitchen table and Dad told us to consider moving to another state? Remember the feeling of realizing it was actually going to happen? Remember when we all went to different schools and Dad was in the hospital? Obedience, sacrifice, and blessing. I just pulled notes from my journals. I thought it might help other girls see that following God is always worth it."

"And now you are blessed because of your obedience." Mom points out, making her dinner plate. "Just like Kelly blessed us with these homemade rolls."

"I just can't believe it. A new job, two publishing contracts, and I can run track again!" It all feels too good to be true.

"What do you mean two contracts?" Angel asks, always picking up the lost thread of the conversation. "Are you writing two books? Can you change my name in them? Please give me some big scene."

"My project manager recommended splitting *A Time to Trust*'s manuscript into two books. I'll need to figure out what to name the second one." I say.

"A Time to Party?" Bria throws out.

"A Time to Run?" Allison adds.

"It'll come to you," Dad smiles. "God will bring the right thing at the right time."

Timing indeed. I return from a national track meet with a few ribbons from placing in relay races with my 4x400-meter and 4x200-meter team, stiff, sore, sunburned, and scraped up after humorously falling upon handing the baton to the third leg runner in the 4x200-meter relay.

"*Oohh* ..." The audience of spectators murmured as my body slid on the track.

I quickly stood up without checking for blood or broken bones and escorted myself off the track. In the midst of the infield crowd, I felt stinging on my hand and arm.

"Are you okay?" Jake, a lightning speed boy from our team, fist bumped my good hand.

"Yeah," I said. "Just a scratch."

"I'll say!" He laughed.

With his eyes on my elbow, I stole a quick glance at it and decided I should search for someone with a little more knowledge of medical things than Jake.

McKenzie, tall, blonde, and built like a fit Nike Run Club model, gasped. "At least you didn't drop the baton!" She says good naturedly.

Coach Barnett soon found me and rushed me to the medical tent, though I was still sort of numb. Even when the nurse sprayed all sorts of ointments and alcohols on it that usually burn, I still felt nothing. Our relay team finished 5th place, but I shaved two seconds off my last relay time.

"Looks worse than it is," I told my family in the bleachers. "I can't feel anything."

My uncle, aunt, cousins, and grandparents were so kind to come support me. My uncle teared up hugging me, saying, "I'm so proud of you!" over and over. They knew my story, how the doctors told me I shouldn't risk running track, and yet there I was—sprinting! I have never seen my extended family members so proud of me. Yes, they were excited about Oxford, but they were most proud of my determination on the track.

But this track meet cut me deeply. Without the Lord, I would be overwhelmed in guilt and frustration.

It happened to be during the final race of my life in track and field.

I was nearly in tears before, during, and after the 4x400-meter relay. It was one thing not to break my record in the regular 400-meter race, my personal event. Though I despised it, I didn't expect a week of sickness and dancing and heels to result in a personal record. But the 4x400-meter relay was different; it was special, and I expected a miracle.

It was the final event of the night.

10:44 p.m. The track field lights were lit. A team's loudspeaker blared rap beats that made me feel like a football player doing warm-up drills on the field. The night air was spring-cold, and I dreaded stripping out of my already freezingly thin team sweatsuit to shorts. It was a weird sensation being sunburnt and fevered yet shivering from the bitter wind. I wasn't the only impatient runner; Kimaya, Elise, and McKenzie vigorously rubbed each other's arms and jumped up and down, dreading the moment we would run in the dark without our layers.

I have to admit, the setting was motivating. Moments before, it had been worse. Mom and I were in a heated argument in her heated car. I cried out that I wanted to be asleep three hours ago and I didn't know how in the world I would run another race.

"You can and you will," she told me.

Candice was tired and ready for a decent night's sleep in a thin-sheet hotel bed at 7 p.m., yet here she was, facing her last race with determination.

I lamented to McKenzie, "This is our final time to run together."

Amazingly, I didn't feel much nostalgia. Perhaps it was the cold, or the fatigue, or the very apparent realization how young and immature all the high schoolers looked and acted around me, mixed with the fact that I had been just accepted into Oxford.

Our 4x400-meter relay team was strong. We worked well together. I was a weaker link, but I wasn't terrible enough to be discounted as a second or third leg runner.

Everyone—from the boys' teams to the junior high girls to even our proud bleacher screamers—looked forward to the 4x400-meter. McKenzie was already bound to have her pick at running college level, and Elise was winning medals in a variety of events by the minute. We were sure ... almost sure ... to place proudly in this race. Mentally, I was just there to capture it all, and to smile pretty. It was an honor to be included. I didn't deserve any of it.

"Hey Candice," Coach Barnett spoke up.

"Yes, Coach?"

"We were talking, and since it's your senior year, we want you to run anchor in the mile relay!"

"The *mile* relay?"

"Yeah!"

"But ... er ... thanks? It's just ... I have never done the mile before."

Everyone in the tent laughed.

"Candice, it's the 4x400-meter relay. The one you always do!"

"Oh! Well, that's a relief!"

And so, the slowest runner on the relay was assigned the fastest, most critical leg in the race: anchor. Keep in mind everything that led to the vivid 10:44 p.m. atmosphere: two foot surgeries, having POTS, throwing up from a food allergy, dancing in heels. I was crazy to even think I could run my usual. And yet, I was convinced I would run my best.

Finally, we were called to the starting line. A brown-haired runner stood beside me in lane three, still in sweatpants. We talked some while watching the first leg run.

McKenzie got us in the lead by a good 50-meters, and the team was screaming wildly.

Elise grabbed the baton and ran with all her might, keeping us in the top three and a sure shot of winning at least bronze, if Kimaya and I could hold our spots.

My heart was beating loud like an ultrasound monitor. As cold as the night was, now that we had stripped down to our tanks and shorts, I didn't notice.

I saw Kimaya holding third place wearily, approaching the line.

Stepping up in my lane, I extended my hand for the baton.

God, if there was ever a time I needed to run fast, it's now.

Running the fastest seven seconds of my life, I zoomed past

cheering crowds, feeling the adrenaline. Parents, teammates, and even random patrons are cheering my name.

"Run, Candice!"

I hugged the corner of the first 100-meters, still in third place. I could not feel anyone close behind me. I ran on the balls of my feet, but I knew as soon as I switched to running on my full foot, my pace would slow. I stayed running light past the 200-meter mark.

"Keep pace! Hold third!" Mckenzie's blurry face screamed from the sidelines.

My breath was heaving and feet were slowing.

100-meters left and you are off the track. I told myself.

50-meter mark and no shadows behind me.

"RUN ON YOUR TOES!" Coach Barnett roared.

But … I don't. I *can't*. It's either slow down or pass out.

I slow.

Out of the black of the night, the sweatpants girl I had been so friendly with zoomed past me, fighting even harder than my endurance level. And I couldn't do anything about it.

The bleachers went crazy. My team was in dismay. The race was over.

Final track meet of my life, and I failed. I thought. A gut-feeling hit that it was due to mental endurance that I had slowed, a compromise to not give my all, to not train fully, to sell myself in small ways overtime.

Would I ever run again, do it right? No, this chapter had closed.

So I end my track season, beat in the final race by a girl in sweatpants.

Oxford's Michaelmas Term does not begin until September. While my classmates are most likely indulging in the classics in preparation for the start of the term, I am still eighteen with an innate nature to avoid academia, and so spend the last month of summer watching movies, drafting *A Time to Trust*, and preparing to ride barefoot on the fourth family road trip to New Orleans, Louisiana. Authorially, I feel unworthily honored to be in contract with an editor, so I savor everything from choosing text styles to finalizing the cover design. Feeling adultish in this lens, I hold a starry-eyed confidence that I am growing up and can at least do one thing right.

I can't even think about running. I can think about movies, though. The romance of the Italian language has enthralled me in a new way when I watch *Life is Beautiful* twice before leaving for Louisiana. Guido's enduring imagination continued to convict me to consider my own role in children's lives. Even as I have retired from being a childcare worker, I am still fascinated with childhood. I continue reading the four-book series *Taylor & Rose* by Katherine Woodfine, for it is just that sort of crisp young prose I need while my college books ship from Blackwell's Bookshop in Oxford.

Now on the road trip, I began with *Peril in Paris,* feeling much like its heroine, Lilian Rose, elegantly disguised in the Grand Continental Hotel Paris while feasting on pastries and sun-warmed peaches. I am driving to the French Quarter preparing to dine at Café du Monde on powdered beignets to the rhythm of street dancers. *'Tis the summer before college …*

The lobby at the Crown Plaza hotel in the French Quarter in New Orleans is fragrant and humid, eerily old but beautiful, with blushing rose walls and checkered marble floor. Bourbon House's seafood and oyster bar is joined to the lobby brandishing a painting of a lady with a distorted face and cotton candy hair. We arrive and settle by 3 a.m., and so the brass luggage cart is ushered over by no bellman other than us, snapped awake by activity.

A man screams to us on the street, "Come get on the party bus!"

He walks alongside a metal bus stripped of paint blasting club music and moving slowly down the curb with disco lights raying through shattered windows. There has to be a driver, but I do not see one.

It reminds me of when I was a twelve-year-old clinging to Poppy's arm as we toured New Orleans by white carriage, gripping my eyes tight when shady eyes laying on sidewalks narrowed on me and my sister.

The spiritual darkness of the city is still as thick and suffocating as its southern humidity. I used to feel hopeless and vulnerable, but on the road trip as an eighteen-year-old, I feel full of light and peace. It is a relief to know whatever happens, no amount of darkness can swallow light. I pray over the city and over Oxford too.

When you are filled with the spirit of Christ, you never have to worry about your surroundings. The light in you is greater than any darkness around you.

Our trip is full of rich experience and stimulating conversation, ranging from the ratings of southern buffets to the history of space exploration in Houston. We caught the Summer Olympics' 4x4 track and field teams on screens at one of the seafood bars.

Did it make me miss running? So much so that I lost my appetite.

But running was over.

I don't have a team and I never made friends who ran, anyway. I do not run consistently and with duration enough to count, which makes whatever runs I did execute rather difficult. Training in the heat of the garage is dually unappealing, and so I have slacked physically, not good considering I am on my way into academic rigidity. Whatever.

Unfortunately, after three private circumstances occurred that quickly change our carefree temperament to a state of grief, our trip is cut short, and I am eager to return home to comfort friends and family and settle into academic routine. Sobered. Focused. Compelled.

It is up to the discipline of Candiceyland to keep everything crisp and in order until I go to my in-person Oxford classes for my summer residency. If I am going to be an at-home student with online assignments, it will require the severest form of discipline in my life.

And so it begins …

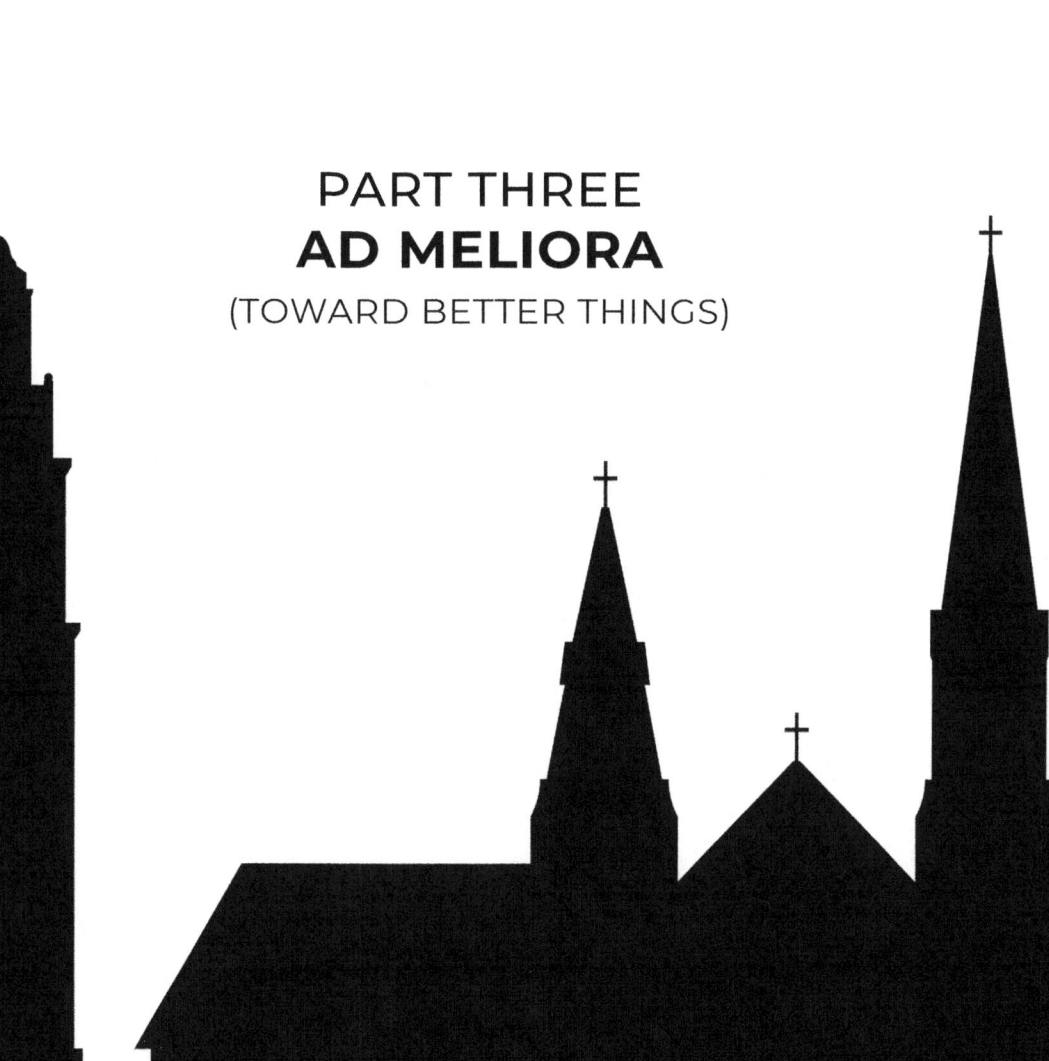

PART THREE
AD MELIORA
(TOWARD BETTER THINGS)

This is the strangeness of the uncanny, a flickering moment of embroilment in the experience of something at once strange and familiar.
—*Nicholas Royle*

CHAPTER 15
MICHAELMAS BEGINS

Michaelmas Term, Edmond, Oklahoma

You better get used to seeing things differently from most.
—Surprised by Oxford (2011)

I feel rather awkward closing my bedroom door for privacy on one of the biggest days of my life, as if it were another day of Shakespeare, not like I am about to be in live forums with eighteen colleagues from around the world. Or perhaps this is how it is meant to be.

A simple life prepares us to take the unexpected adventures ahead. I had written inside these walls. In a way, Candiceyland is perfect, for it took a reluctant studier in high school who did not imagine she would go to college to an eighteen-year-old Oxford student within one year.

Outwardly, I am composed in a turtleneck and warmed with a cup of Earl Grey. Inwardly, I am a kid clinging to a rapid carousel, hoping I don't fall.

It so happened that in this angst I just forcibly tried to move my desk, which turned into a shattered disaster before I had the chance to even type my first introduction to the class. Chessie, in his open fish's bowl, came crashing off the desk, clashing into a million pieces in the carpet, his little blue body lying motionless amidst green water and blue rocks.

"Oh, oh, I'm so sorry ..." I scooped him up and ran downstairs, slipping him in a bowl and doing my best to clean the mess. Amazingly, he survived.

Lord, please help me to make it to class in time that I do not look late or behind.

I open the blue link directing me to my Oxford Student Portal and immediately see five messages from classmates. Ignoring the thickening fish water and rubbles of rocks between my toes, I settle in and read the profiles of the people I will know for the next two years of my life. Dr. Ballam, the director of the *programme*, has already issued everyone into a time of introductions. My class is officially titled the Wolvercote Cohort.

I am a Wolvercote.

Whatever that means. I squint my eyes at the word.

I read the delightful list of names as each classmate adds their hello to the thread, smiling at beautiful names like Jackie and Katherine and Marianne.

A woman named Sarah who paints says, "I live at the highest point on Exmoor surrounded by sheep, wild ponies, adders, and, just last night, a whole bunch of bats in the bedroom ..." she is the first person I decide will be my friend.

Is it harsh to judge by the tiny circle profile pictures who I want to be my friends?

Well, considering I have two years with these people, I have time to figure it out. Another woman named Andrea, donning a pink blouse in her profile picture, tells how she likes to write about childhood, and I add her to my friend list, too, even if these women are twice my age.

"I work as an industrial radiographer," a lady named Ashley writes from the Lake District in England. "I mostly look at x-rays of things that go into space."

"I am from Mumbai, India: the land where cows race the streets with Audis. ... I worked as a screenwriter in Bollywood. ..." another reads.

James, the eldest of the Wolvercotes, introduces himself. "It follows that I am retired though we often wonder where the time goes, that is myself, Joan, and our three cats, Sand, Rousseau and Mirabelle. Too much drinking watching sunsets from the terrace, I guess."

Everyone introduced has such prominent characteristics: some medical physicians looking for a creative outlet, others seasoned writers with ambitions to strengthen their craft. And then there is me: the eighteen-year-old fresh out of high school and a barefoot vacation, glass and water crunching under my toes.

One Wolvercote member is a student of English and French at the University of Graz in Austria, another with "an abiding interest in psychoanalysis both in terms of theory and behaviour." One is from Guadalajara, Mexico, several others, Canadian.

There appear to be five main figures of high enthusiasm for the course, and I am one of them. Gradually, I realize I am the only American resident. And the youngest in the class.

Caught off guard by the age gap and cultural references, I massage my neck and forget I don't have my clear-rimmed glasses. I turn up Mozart's *Clarinet Concerto in A Major*, put a towel under my feet, and force myself not to overthink everything working against me.

Glass fragments, screen barriers, cultural references, downright ignorance.

"I am Irish Sicilian," another says, a lawyer *specialising* in discrimination.

"I used to work in fashion," a girl introduces. "I now work for a big media company that produces television shows."

I am endeared and confused by the world class writers on this screen; enchanted by their stories, the wit in the questions they write that show keen interest to get to know one another; the way they draw in the unexpected quote to a response, a silent lilt in the use of one quotation mark. Simply elegant.

"I write from tropical Kuala Lumpur, Malaysia," says a writer, surely within a decade of my age. *Whew, they're not all middle-aged lawyers.* I smile at her profile picture.

"I have come to realise that I would love for some creative element to compliment my theoretical knowledge about language and literature," says one of the scholars.

The course is broken down into units with forums for responses to the exercises and study, held within modules that each hold one assignment, the consistently large portion of the grade, apart from one end-of-year portfolio submission, a highly substantial piece of work, in one's chosen genre.

The school year is broken into three terms: Michaelmas Term (autumn), Hilary Term (winter), and Trinity Term (spring), followed by in-person summer classes that surround the completion of your Portfolio—finals—right when Michaelmas Term begins for year one. It is virtually year round, demanding of creative genius in or out of your writerly flow. Basically, you must submit your best writing under deadlines for all genres, else get kicked out of Oxford.

I learn to begin most forums with *somehow* or *perhaps* because you can't ever be dogmatic with the English at Oxford. Everything is a question, and if otherwise dared, a suggestion. Nothing is objective.

"I write animal horror fiction," a man with intense hair writes.

"I write contemporary romance ... the spicy kind." A woman in harsh makeup submits.

"Science fantasy stirs me to read," a scientist admits. "And I shall execute it, too."

Centered in a block of eighteen international geniuses, I am enamored by their wisdom and lore, the ideals of the customs of where they came from and what they have devoted themselves to believing. At first I think that I could write anything, enjoy any genre, taste it all—for wasn't that why I was here? Could I be a memoirist who wrote poetry and drama too?

Or was it that I really did have a strand of genius in one area, and all of life simply enhanced it? Could a life-writer get away from not writing about life if they tried?

Time will tell.

It is snowing in Oklahoma; voices below hoist ornaments on the live fir from Sorghum Mill Christmas Tree & Blackberry Farm. The smell of freshly ground coffee and apple cranberry pie lingered after being served to company tonight by the fire, but I dismissed myself after the roast dinner. Running upstairs in a black sweater with curls on my head, arms folded under tortoise glasses, I dragged open the secret bookshelf door, plugged in the Christmas lights, and crawled back to the plywood corner of the space dedicated to writing alone, alone.

I have 2,000 words of my best narrative fiction to turn in by midnight.

"I want to step into a *world*," the prose tutor explains. "Show me the colors, the textures, what type of grass is planted, and how it felt under your toes. I am thinking of Candice's memoirist mind when she wrote *Sunlit Tears* in our Life Writing Module."

That was so natural to write. I smile under the Christmas lights. *But very summery.*

"Some of you may feel inadequate. Perhaps you are a poet or playwright. Even our life-writers are about to be stretched. I want prized fiction! This course is not meant to simply praise your strand of genius but invite you to discover yourself as a different kind of writer. You were brought on this course because you are expected to perform prolifically. I expect nothing but the best from all of you, regardless your academic or literary background."

"I have an inclination that, being a life-writer as Candice, it is inevitable our minds will trace some kind of thread back to a memory or feeling to fuel our story. Is this necessarily a bad thing?" A fellow biographer asks.

"May I remind you of our last forum: lean into your genius. But do not mistake the prompt. I want rich fiction, the kind that a novel enthusiast will find satisfying, though it is inevitable you cannot write something completely original."

"You see," the tutor continues in a new paragraph on the forum page, I imagine sighing absently. "Allegories, character arcs, even the very concept of good and evil, are merely rhetorical devices. None of us will ever truly find our character arcs. These are simply concepts and tools we made up for ourselves to make sense of life. But we will never find complete satisfaction. That 'fairytale ending' is something we made up to make ourselves feel better."

Is it?

"Stories, like many things in life, are coping mechanisms." The tutor advises. "Since we cannot control the cosmos, we like to give ourselves meaning and order through narrative. Well, this is something I will expound on when you come to Oxford for in-person lectures. For now, please rest in the liberty that this is your story. You are the sole puppeteer, and there are no strings except the ones you create. Take full control. Bend the rules, if necessary."

That was one of the first things I learned about Oxford, and what surprised me even through the interview process. It was less that they, at least this course and my professors, wanted a straight-A rule follower, but someone who could think outside the box. They are the world's number-one university. They needed breakthroughs, not repeats. They wanted you to bend the rules of conventional storytelling to an effective measure.

But was the idea of good and evil as a mere rhetorical device taking it too far? Wasn't it a true representation of the Great Arc that preceded our existence? Surely this tutor understood that light and darkness is something we could not have made up ourselves.

This has me thinking about how real light, which is itself scary and impenetrable, had been severely closeted to mean safe religion, not a blinding ray of pure holiness and truth.

I bite my lip and shake my head.

What fictional narrative is on mind within this snow and ice?

Ah—yes. Christmas at the Cleveland's!

"*Christmas at the Cleveland's*," I write. "The words rang like a clinked glass on a tea tray. The Cleveland estate, a Victorian townhouse, curved at the cloverleaf of Classen and Corduroy. Of course it wasn't really an estate, stacked as the bookend of a street of gray two-levels, but as the Cleveland's were perceptibly wealthier than their neighbors, and as it was rumored they had once owned a grand winter estate, forests away, their townhouse was both humoredly and seriously referred to as the Cleveland estate."

Christmas at the Cleveland's was not a new or imaginary place. Fictional characters Billy and Diana, the respective ages of seven and nine, had existed in my mind since pre-adolescence, invented on one of those days of endless doctor appointments. But their fiction had been buried beneath 'real issues' like writing about moving and going to private school.

But suppose the realest issues are meant to be fictionalized in the same way fantasy provided not merely an escape, but an encapsulation that changes the way you think about ordinary life. Suppose my prose fiction era is coming back. Becoming a memoirist—a life-writing journaler—officially began at fourteen. But historical fiction was what twelve-year-old Candice wrote in scrolls upon scrolls on airplanes while others watched movies. Yes, I had created many worlds that have been untouched for some time, until now.

"Excellent work here, Candice," the tutor comments when my draft is posted. "It's great to see you mining the gap between your protagonist's innocent viewpoint and the reality of the adult world that has been so far kept at bay from her, but which we as the reader know will all too soon radically change her life. This tension is working well, but I'd love to see you exploit it even more. …"

"A rich and right royal Christmas piece!" Andrea types enthusiastically.

James observes, "Yes, a banquet on the eve of war offers enormous scope for conflicting points of view, some envisaging the grand scheme of things with possible disaster on the horizon, others more concerned with the here and now, even the apparently trivial, for how can an uncertain future compete with the sensuousness of the present. The reader can contemplate both however, either with relish that complacency and excess are about to be swept away or with genuine fear for the main protagonists, their worlds to be turned upside down."

"That's exactly what I was envisioning," I write. "The Cleveland's are a remarkable family in an unfortunate time. Diana has no idea how drastically life will change after the ball. It is a tensional contrast of childhood and adulthood, mirrored in feast and fire."

"Good work, realising the characters and becoming them," the tutor encourages.

"Oh, I haven't just now found them—they've always been with me!" I say aloud only to the ears of Charlie in the secret room, for I am alone, but in great well-drawn joy.

Pictures and mirrors are only reflections of real things ... I start to journal.

CHAPTER 16
A MODERN POET

Hilary Term, Edmond, Oklahoma

The artist is only the glass through which we see nature,
and the clearer and more absolutely pure that glass,
so much the more perfect picture we can see through it.
Never intrude yourself.
—Edith Philpotts

And the idea of us being placed in a position
to "examine our lives" … that is really something to think about.
—Andrea Campbell

It is January, the beginning of Hilary Term, the most dreaded portion of my creative writing education. Everyone knows poetry is centered on life's passions: love and death. Tangled and harsh, delicate and distilled, like the common British phrase, '*Hello love,*' the light words melt out of the beginning of our poetic exercise, tilting in causality. Words that sing together in that soft, melodic accent making hearts melt and flutter. Like frosted branches outside, clear and quiet and distilling. I could just see Sarah, the poet of the Wolvercotes, surrounded by her watercolors and wild ponies, clapping her hands: "Finally—we have reached poetry!"

James laments, "O, love, thou are discouraging me from reason. …"

All I could think was, *Oh great, poetry.* But this is a time to learn.

Is poetry in ignorance despised?

Perhaps, but I am at least vulnerable enough to recognize the deeper layer.

"You cannot be a poet without bleeding," our new tutor explains. "It is less about having solved the heart's crisis than it is recognizing there is a crisis in the first place. You would be surprised at how many writers ignore deep cuts and miss fleshing out their best writing. Think of the most prolific work you've seen. Think of the great poet you aspire to become."

Can't think of one poet I want to become, thank you. Apart from Ann Voskamp's Canadian free verse, I felt rather new to the idea, although Suzanne U. Rhodes' *The Roar on the Other Side* did surface in my brain once or twice.

"Each of us are keen poets, whether you believe it or not. For some, it is the lyrical assonance that elevates a poem off a page. For others, it is the sensual contrast, the colors and shape of words. For mature poets, all such aural qualities intertwine in one flowing ink. What color is your ink? Where did it originate?"

"I very much resonate with the naturalistic side of poetry," one Wolvercote identifies. "The polar bears are a keen interest for me. Ice with hibernation seem opposite to us humans who consider warmth with rest, and yet warmth is not hunted for polar bears. I don't know what begs me to discern it all. I think the ice of broken hearts has something to do with it, and my study of meteorologic effects on the brain."

"Very good," our tutor points out. "A cool-blue sleeping quest is ahead, I suspect. I wonder if you could write in a rather cool place?"

Ah—place is the effective nature of new clothes, or the right clothes, that is. I think. But I don't want to go up to the high ice clouds of poetry. The compression against my skull would snap me—thinking of Amelia in *The Aeronauts.*

"What is poetry without madness?" One Wolvercote exclaims.

"Or madness without poetry?" Another observes. "It would be chaos."

"Agreed. There is a demand for structure with an existence of chaos. Or are we back to the world being a spinning ball of fire?" Another says with an emoji, and I suspect, a laugh.

Radically engaged, our education takes on a drastic passion of execution in this module, ranging from Sarah's methodically exquisite prose to James' unsettling yet sophisticated verse. Villanelles, a nineteen-line poem with room for adequate composition, are of high interest to me, perhaps because of my love for the letter *l*. But it also sounds like *villain*. And that is what poetry is.

I see it all now: I am afraid to write poetry because I am afraid to write deep.

That is why my poems shared are labeled cheap, almost bouncing to depth only to shy away, leaving me hanging like a wet piece of embarrassing laundry. I realize ashamedly.

The tutor admonishes, "It is painful to write. But what in life isn't? Must we shy away just because we consider ourselves not worthy of being explicit? Do we demand honesty from others' work and not our own? I beg all of you to cut open those places too difficult for prose, too delicate for drama. Discern for yourself if poetry upholds the deepest form of human expression. But at all costs, do not neglect it for fear of failure."

Failure, I realize, is not the execution of a poem that breaks all the rules, but a dishonest one with perfect stanzas. In a mad scientist's rage, I flip open my old poetry notebook from high school to every dishonest haiku. *Didn't care about this one, still can't stand that one.* I cringe.

But then there is a section about how we see words, and I wrote about how I subconsciously read them in colors. Not one rainbow, but individual colors per letter. Strange, but entirely real. With nothing to lose, I post it on the forum thread. "'U' is gray, so mix that with 'r' which is purple, and 's,' yellow, and 't,' green, and 'a,' red, and 'e,' yellow, and 'd,' black … all those colors together make an unclear water." I explain. "In my mind, this poem seems contaminated and is therefore unappealing."

"Interesting view, Candice. The poem talks nothing of murky

seawater, and yet you've invoked feelings for distaste by dissecting it as such."

"It is an unfair criticism of a poem, I know, but this is how I evidently see poems." I realize. "Take the word *style*, for instance. In addition to the clarity of the letters 't' and 'l,' you have their colors: yellow (s), green (t), yellow (y), gray (l), and green (e). Therefore the word has a feeling of lemonade on a clouded summer day in a silk dress."

"Is that because silk has the 's' and 'l' too? A student jokes. "Yellow and grey?"

"Of course!" I smile behind the screen. "But the *k* offers a little clack of the heel."

"Is that not suffocating? Say someone sees *s* as magenta. Would that not ruin the picture?" A colleague observes.

"We don't want to entertain irrelevant barriers, but color can be used strategically for the subconscious. But why not consider the sounds and the feelings?" The tutor directs.

"And what if we were to read poems like paintings?" I propose. "What if poems have a musical assonance, also evoked color beyond a word's face value? What if it had the same effects as classical music that bleeds into how a person thinks …" I note, thoughts moving on as Vivaldi's *Violin Concerto in F Minor* plays behind me in Candiceyland.

Little snowflakes dot my window behind the sheer polka dot curtains. I tug the corner of my baby-blue cardigan and consider how my tea needs to be reheated, as always.

"Do expound," the tutor encourages. "How would you describe classical music?"

"I would almost describe it as a 'listening' aspect of life; a flicker of tinsels and letter headers and excellent time, a lifestyle unlimited yet defined. It is all an exploration, one vaguely identified in a poem, but still so vague to its writer that I have yet to express it clearly. It was instilled in me as a teenager and brushed off, ignored, like too-ripe fruit or too pink of a flower, but is now ripping itself open for interrogation and excavation." I write with adrenaline. "It is the lift of the spirit to a higher class. An invisible, melodic clock and alertness of the mind, marking the shine of the morning with the glow of a sunset. Icy hot, searingly feminine, bursting with testosterone. A reminder there is order in a world of chaos. The kaleidoscope reflection of a greater Light."

"Classical music indeed!" A Wolvercote rejoices.

" … clean, pink, and purple," I affirm. "In Candice's mind, at least."

"Listen to what you wrote. You used words to create sounds that are all very similar to your favorite letter list you previously shared (c, l, m, etc.)." Sarah keenly observes.

"Be careful, for you are becoming a poet," the tutor sends with a smiling face.

Odes. Elegies. Sonnets. Acrostics. Free verse. Villanelles. It is the musical art of the poem which draws me to see words not as part of sentences but sounds and colors. Poetry is fiercely powerful, often a bar between battle cry and laugh. Discussing these qualities with colleagues, I mention to fellow Wolvercote, Katherine, that just as music can be deep and effective without being the dooming kind of dark or explicit, perhaps villanelles could be written in both light and dim tones (or could they?). Narratives, as Sarah once mentioned, could perhaps be possible within a villanelle leading to the final couplet (two lines) of the quatrain (four lines).

"Or … what if it was reversed?" I add. "Could the story be told backwards, or leaning, even?"

Oxford has a way of challenging your own thoughts like this, even down to what you discern to be unchangeable, like my own poet status.

"Play with poems!" Our tutor admonishes.

"It wouldn't have to be structural form," I advise on a classmate's villanelle draft. "I am picturing art in poetry, the shape on the page, the shape of the letters, the 'shape' of the *tone*. It seems the villanelle is to serve as a lesson, or warning, or laugh, like it is something authorized to be remembered 'or else.'"

"If I have time, I will draft another version that meets more villanelle standards—and Candice's standards—it's rough but I'm endeared to keep pruning it!" A colleague jokes.

Soon in time, we each compile an anthology of poems that suit our taste. Unsurprisingly, mine revolve around autumn and life-writing. I guess you really can't be shocking in your selection, even if your whole concept of poetry is yet to be mastered.

In my own poems, I write in first person. Whether or not it is due to my two books being written in such or having been romanticized to commitment in the intense Life Writing Module, I cannot leave the voice that I had practiced year after year in my journal.

"One poem's use of the first person—such a skill. In your notes, you've really touched on some deep philosophical considerations in choosing these poems," The poetry tutor observes on my anthology. "Do you think that your empathy for autumn enhances the meanings of the poems, where you 'read' your own experience into them?"

"Yes," I acknowledge, reminded of the mysterious community surrounding my childhood house in the woods of Missouri, where lurid tones of carnelian and scarlet peak at the third week of October. ("But the days of gamboge are the most breathtaking, accenting stars of paradise that glide down like snow to the slopes of earth," I once shared with Andrea, my favorite life-writing colleague.) It is autumn where the sun sets and the dinner table is spread, and garlic bread slides out of the oven to dip in pasta sauce. ..."

"Themes are the hallmark of a great collection," my tutor remarks. "Autumn is a great choice of theme. When you put a collection together—I hope you will!—even though the poems are not written to a theme, you'll be surprised how your poems have themed themselves according to your own individual voice/meanings."

A collection! Could I really do that?

"As always you have the capacity for rich and sensuous language," a colleague further comments on my work, "which enhanced by American idiom, gives your poem both an exotic and comestible flavour. A homage in part to the oral phase of our existence? Perhaps not."

"You have truly refined and distilled your original work since the beginning," Andrea praises. "I relished that reduction, which in a few simple words contains so much complexity—a whole emotional climate, and the imagery to support it. The tangible and intangible of human relationships."

"Andrea, I agree. Even though Candice you did not blatantly write in first person this time, it's as though the woman herself is trying to justify her feelings to us." Someone else comments on another poem submission.

"Delightfully worded, Candice, written in your own inimitable style!" James commends.

"You give this scene such emotional ups and downs, that's gripping for the reader. You have sixteen lines—always good to have extra lines to play with as you polish and re-adjust. The rhyme scheme is striking at the end and the start. The title carries the almost-humour of the poem, with its witty cutting of the second part of this well-known phrase."

"It seemed necessary to detect what my bent was and detangle it to reform what it should be. Not relying on, 'this is how by nature I would write it' which would determinedly have to do with the colors and sounds of the words, but 'this is the way it should be.'" I explain.

"Detect, detangle, reform. The poetic process exactly!" The tutor praises.

"Poetry isn't all rigidity," the French scholar acknowledges. "It is a deeply sensual form of expression that requires simply feeling and letting loose—*fais ce qui te semble bien*. And yet there is a justification about it which must be settled."

The Frenchman offered a common theme across cultures: do what feels right to you.

"I disagree," another colleague suppresses. "Poetry is all feeling. No demand for reason. Just as truth is entirely subjective. There is no judgement of right or wrong here, just as all of our work is biased in some form or another. You cannot discern one of the other."

"Bad poetry is indeed discernable!"

"It is simply a case of dishonesty."

"But is there an absolute rightness about a poem? What about free verse?"

"Dishonesty with oneself is the highly capital affair."

"No poem whether observed by the poet or the tutor is free from biased examination."

"But anyone can detect dishonesty and would be a fool to say it is unrecognizable."

"Just because it is universally perceived as one thing it does not make it reality."

"Yes, bias is upon us, always …" They continue writing.

I smile at their words, thinking back to philosophy discussions in Mrs. Loose' classroom.

"True objectivity is absolutely unachievable, in my opinion," one writes. "It does not exist. The brain is a filter. It is not a direct experience of reality, if we could even agree on what reality is. Therefore creative activity a priori comes from a filtered perception of the world. Even journalism isn't free of this because it's undertaken by humans with their existing beliefs, assumptions, unconscious biases, fallible memory, etc."

So all of life is a lie. I frown, twisting my wrist to respond fairly. I don't run away from deep questions anymore.

"I agree the brain is a filter. We tend to embellish or denote what we choose, and it can seem hard to find 'truth' in writing. Everyone who writes has their own level of bias that will seep into their work, so it makes us wonder if there is even such a thing as truth. But that's why I have been able to rest in the ultimate reality of God's existence, and that's why it is so easy for me to write. I know I am flawed and human, my writing will be written in a biased way as everyone does, but in the scheme of life, it makes sense there would be true life objectivity and reality … it's not a cultural principle to 'feel good' or play a game. Writing is our interpretation of reality, but there's an overarching reality we can choose to believe in or not. (Thinking of C.S. Lewis in *Mere Christianity*: "The Law of Human Nature, or of Right and Wrong, must be something above and beyond the actual facts of human behaviour … you have something else - a real law which we did not invent and which we know we ought to obey."[1]) For me, there is comfort in knowing there is a true reality, in and yet beyond writing."

As people often get wet feet when creative forums turn spiritual, the conversation shifts to the theme of our introductions to an original anthology made by the Wolvercote class. Elated for a chance at prose after so many stanza crises, I write mine based on the idea of there to be a demand for light and darkness, and thus a demand for a higher law than human ethics.

> Wolvercotes: a rainbow of writers dripping color and clear, words curled in a 'noon-lit' filter against the deep of the day. Our graves are dug somewhere in the world. Choose today. *Seize* today: that is the tongue roll—unknowingly, yet purposefully, each poem is centered around space and sound. Light is mentioned seven times throughout. Water: five. Sea: three. The theme is heal. The urge is to drink. Salt. Melon. Glass. The centrality of us existing is measured and passed on to the next. Inescapable. We don't know where we're going; we know where we've been. We're not afraid of tinkering on the edge of eternity; we seek ascension, for *surely* light exists. The poems hence are ordered to fit our state: see, current, grip; reflect, grasp, sigh; strangle, gasp, decide. So lick the lemon among the salty dunes, then walk away. What if a 'loosening ... grip' of the mind allows one to become oneself, transparent and transcalent, for there is no darkness too deep to dirt-smell. Chase light and discern life, lest it slip through the hourglass of time.

My own poem in the anthology, titled *Riverview*, encapsulates three coming of age stages at Riverview Ranch in Missouri, and is *centralised* in the middle of the collection, right beside Andrea's *Afternoon French*.

"The long line really helps the drowsy aura." The tutor says in review of *Riverview*. "Assonance and alliteration all serve this poem well; sweet and suite, homophones—lovely. Also 'maiden' and 'mane' is clever, drawing out the sound with an extra syllable. Tiny point—you use nouns to end almost all the lines—like a bell chiming, very nice effect—so when you put 'and' at the end of two lines, this strikes the reader. You may want those lines to carry the reader on to the next line in a dream-like way and you might feel the bell shouldn't strike every line."

The bell shouldn't strike every line … now there was something to consider—in life!

At 5:30 a.m., a sound wakes me out of a deep sleep. It takes more than a second to recognize it isn't an alarm, but my tutorial feedback session, airing clear across the pond from London.

Throwing over my comforter, I flick on as many lights as I can in case they request a video call, which most tutors did, and I slip on a sweatshirt, unweaving my braid and hoping this tutor is like most Brits who shy away from excessive makeup.

Poetry—of all the assignments—and here I am, late and unprepared. This is a disaster.

"Hello, Candice," the tutor says without a camera on to my relief.

I stand at my standing desk trying not to expose how I am out of breath, wondering whatever happened to the 4:30 a.m. alarm?

"Hello, good day," I draw out calmly. "I do apologize I missed your first ring."

Jumping right into my three poems submitted for grading, the tutor tells me, "If you've not done poetry at all, it's quite interesting."

I rub my eyes, absolutely shocked. *Am I hearing right?*

"I can see you're quite a mature writer and you know how to look and how to work with poetry as much as with any other form. You probably know you've done this, but you have this narrative in this non-narrative piece. You don't use question marks," my tutor observes. "This can be finished and publishable because it does give the answer. I think it shows me, you absolutely have got an instinct."

"Really?" I slink to my habit of overusing 'really' adverbs. Genuine shock.

Writing of death and love in Christ's passion, my father's chronic pain, and the recent instance Kelly Grace flatlined due to a heart condition, I went there mentally and came out with words dripping in blood. It was uncomfortable, messy, explicit. Too painful to read, it was my best work.

"You have just the right amount of ecclesiastical reference, or spiritual reference, or biblical reference really. You could do a prose poem. You could do lineated poems as well. With a poem, people think it will be very abstract, floating on the clouds, so point them where you are going. What do they feel? What do they see? Talent you have there."

"I am realizing the absolute requirement for honesty in poetry—in life, for that matter." I thank her. To my surprise, we talk openly about God and the Holy Spirit, and of poetry in everyday life. Differing in certain views, we yet share a love for God and passion for emphasizing the ultimate Creator of beauty, summarized in one of my former draft poems:

> It seems not
> the beauty of waterfalls
> and cathedrals
> were meant to merely tempt us,
> as if beauty's purpose were to
> make a mockery of itself
> for its core to be a lie.
> The essence of pleasure demands
> that the acquittal of satisfaction be found,
> for sense would not have it
> that beauty would tempt us this way
> only for hope to die with ourselves.

CHAPTER 17
YOU THINK LIKE A CAMERA

Trinity Term, Edmond, Oklahoma

Movies are the ultimate storyteller.
—Forrest III

At the start of Trinity Term, which lasts well into the traditional American summer months, it is easy to throw off the internal undoing of stanzaic thinking. I am already in a daring mood after turning in a short story involving a dark carnival, high in contrast to light poems about classical music, and still, somewhere in the subconscious, I continue digging further into vulnerable topics, per poetry's influence. I dive explicitly into the extremity of the supernatural in writing.

The appeal of the carnival scene occurred long before Oxford. The short story was written in Frank Peretti style; short, severe, and dangerously set at the Finley River Park in Ozark, Missouri. When I think of screenplays, I hear screams. Is it because of the 'sc' and 'e' sounds that leave screeches, or that the screenplay is the scream of the world, as (subjectively) the highest form of engagement, more than the stage, even more than the page? A scarring visualization to the *spiritualis mundi* in fantastical horror? Can one watch a good film and not be scarred?

"Entertainment is just that—entertainment. Anyone who thinks it has anything to do with judging a person's character is …" a classmate once foully expressed. "When you write your script, it is for the indulgence of the audience, not the training of morales." But if we aren't going to discern entertainment, we might as well live the unexamined life in all areas. Arguably, entertainment is one of the highest formational modes of education. I know from high school that entertainment is too delicate a stage to dance wildly upon. Its foundation is generally subjective to a person's convictions. Yet there are moral laws that are clear and objective.

Still, I am about to be pitching my final assignment before the big end-of-year portfolio—worth thirty percent of my grade—to fellow classmates and a tutor who may disagree.

People may assume my ambassadorship of light and 'happy things,' whether by consistently smiling to coworkers in the executive office, writing children's fictions stories, or merely my love for a rainbow fruit salad, somehow point to an oblivion of evil. As my literal birth brought life to the name Candice meaning 'full of light,' some may assume I am immune to any sort of attraction to darkness. But consider the opposition against a word of the year (see 2020's *health* for me). It was evident that in some ways, to both my parents and myself, in some I was 'bent' toward evil in childhood (as we all are in one way or another) in a violent, darkened-mind sense. The jokes I told and movies I made were completely twisted and disturbing, but I relished having an audience with hand-covered mouths, and it was all entertainment, right?

Hardly. My little scheming director's mind was shocked when I was forced to delete a movie made with cousins at the farm that had scenes of slow-motion violence (staged, of course) and my company of child actors disbanded for a game of basketball. It happened again with friends when we filmed a rather immoral movie and proudly showed our parents, to which we were given a lecture on the effects of the lifestyle we promoted for fun. Other than temporary embarrassment, adolescent Candice wasn't at all fazed by these confrontations to glorify evil, until I realized, at sixteen, that there was no fellowship between light and darkness. Talking once with Mom reminded me of the dangers of fire, of thinking that some dark things can be good.

"This is the 'stage' I have long anticipated!" James, who has written and directed his own set of plays, excites our entire cohort for the drama module.

Reading *Into the Woods* by John Yorke provides an abundance of many underlined and added *yes*es and *ergo et sic*s that I transfer into text boxes in our screenwriting and stage play forums. Still intimidated by scripts, the core of the story plot is yet as natural as the recognition of how to breathe. I also know I can learn anything. I still laugh at the concept of being a poet.

Our new tutor announces, "Welcome to the most exciting form of the written word!" and throws out a list of films and plays to uncover. "For those who are scared of dramatic writing, it's time to immerse into your new favorite genre."

Announcing at the dinner table I had written a horror short story over the spring months and now had plans for an interdimensional stage play about a nightmare immediately froze forks.

"I thought you were into modern verse poetry?" Mom said.

"That was in Hilary Term. It is time to enter … the stage!" I threw up my hands dramatically. "All I need is my director's hat from childhood."

But not to glorify evil anymore, I reminded myself.

"But you're supposed to write children's stories!" Allison, who had beautiful new blond highlights in a trail of curls down her pink blouse, interjected.

"Candice rarely makes sense on paper," Angel mumbled quietly, a maturing twelve-year-old with braces and a new cat.

"Yeah, it's like that day Candice told us the story of Billy and Diana Cleveland in Dad's office …" Jordan remembered. "She said there was a …"

" … knock on the door. And when the maid went to answer, there was no one there …" I reenacted.

"And then I said, 'Candice! This is a children's story!'" Angel added.

" … There was a knock on the door. And when the maid went to answer, there *was* someone there! It was their friend, the mailman." I finished.

Perhaps scripts intimidate me more than poetry, from the literal length down to the idea of 'beating out a script,' as screenwriters call a form of outlining, but there is no marching up to my virtual Oxford teacher's desk demanding an opt-out of the next assignment.

Once you commit to becoming a writer, and I mean a *real* writer, you must embrace prose, poetry, and drama. As one tutor reflected, you must submit yourself to learning from all three, even if you *specialise* in one over another. Chances are, you might find that you like an unexpected genre by the end of the course. That certainly was the case with poetry. Scoring a Distinction—the highest award level at Oxford—in the Poetry 2 Assignment taught me to think outside the box, write in my pain, and bleed out authentic work. Being called a 'mature poet' was as surprising as receiving my first Pass—the lowest grade level before Fail—in a prose narrative review of my favorite teen book. What else would happen this year?

"I love children's fiction," I reflect at tonight's dinner table, full of Memorial Day flavors like seasoned hamburgers and fruit salad, heavy on patriotic berries. "I also love films that make people stunned, that are completely engulfing, that impact how people leave the theater."

"What about stage plays?" Dad asks, flipping patties on the skillet. "You've always loved performing. You used to do shows every night after dinner as a kid."

"Especially when we would have guests over," Mom smiles at me, lighting a summer-fragrant candle and opening the screen door, in usual hostess manner.

"Who's coming over?" Allison freezes in footed pink pajamas.

"*Cade*," Bria answers.

Kelly blushes.

"Honestly, I can't stand stage plays," I walk over to Dad after throwing away my plate.

"You didn't even get a burger. Would you like this one? It has Swiss cheese on it."

"I don't like burgers, either."

"Wow," his eyes widen. "Oxford really has changed you."

"I don't know, Dad. I do miss dance and the stage, I just don't know if I could write for it. I more like the idea of being in the wings. I've just never seen it done right. Every musical or play I have witnessed is ... well ... cheesy." I stare at the open Swiss package on the counter.

"What have you eaten your whole life on holiday weekends?" Dad's thoughts are still on the burger train.

"Fruit." I smile sheepishly.

"You need a good burger experience."

"And a trip to the West End show," I throw out lightly. "And a friend."

"But *horror*, Candice?" Kelly Grace passes us and whispers in my ear on her way to the door to greet Cade.

"It all comes down to the attraction of darkness." I say slowly. *Wait* ... "That's it!" I run upstairs to write down the idea—and read over seventy missed forum messages.

"I have never had a positive stage experience," I remarked today to Corbyn at the office in the bathroom, where we often meet up by accident. "I think I am insecure to write from the seat of a playwright because I have never been in a comfortable seat in the audience. All my experiences of productions are strictly dance related, otherwise, musicals and plays that evoked pure disgust."

"The stage is cringe unless you do it right," Corbyn told me. "Also, total side note, but I still remember how you taught me to get two paper towels at once by putting your hands at two dispensers." She added. "Now that has enhanced my life!"

As a new member of the Admins Anonymous group chat I created at work to create community amongst fellow admins in any capacity across the organization, Corbyn was a constant encouragement at work. She was also a talented opera singer who auditioned on Broadway. "You need a good stage experience to even see all the possibilities." She advised.

I thought back to that preparation for today's drama exercise, because no amount of research or study gave me the least bit of enthusiasm. The screen alone stresses me out, but I know it is out of insufficient knowledge. The stage is just dead unappealing.

Now that I think about it. when I picture something happening in life, it is with the freedom—and limitations—of the camera lens, not the sitting human eye.

"Imagine you are on the fifth row in a theatre, watching your play come to life." Our tutor stages enthusiastically, and yet I continue to wince, unimpressed. "Imagine the hush of the audience, the lights flicking on, the appearance of your main character center stage. Who are they? What is their quest?"

To take a nap, I yawn at the computer screen.

It is so strange going to school online. It is so intense, and yet my room is still and vacant. "I'm sorry," I apologize to the class for submitting the beating of a play with little effort. "I am learning to embrace this … er … stage."

James encourages, "Difficult, I imagine, to capture those fast-moving, stress-filled seconds whose perspective a director's eye must follow. I suppose it is a case of being both fully engaged with the moment as you would hope a member of the cinema audience would be, and yet sufficiently detached to have an overview … in other words how to achieve the cinematic effect you desire. But it can be done, if you try."

"Find your passion is what I always say!" The tutor admonishes. "Find that storyline that has you riled up and claim it with a passionate originality. Soon you may be on the street and glance to your buddy and say, 'I say, is that my play on the West End?'"

I am just dying to go to England and *actually experience it;* to put names with bigger faces than digital profile pictures and eat fish and chips and wear raincoats because of the dreary London drizzle. I was born to live in England!

Snap out of it. I rebuke wandering thoughts. An exercise critiquing the wirings of a particularly successful stage play is due, and I am not to be caught lazy.

"At … this … stage," I say aloud, typing monotonously like a boring lecturer as I write it in the forum text box, "there appears to be an overwhelming sense of thoughtfulness on mortality and humanity, the consequences of ideas and actions. By minimal character monologue and absence of props and bodily movement," I yawn again, "the characters' thoughts are spotlighted and people are able to focus on the matter at hand." I take a long sigh before indenting and thinking of ways to complete the word count answer requirements.

"It ... appears ... the ... overall tone is reflective in a mournful sense. The second character seems to shift the tone to one of humorous acceptance, as if she takes life as it comes rather than inwardly resisting it, like the first character implies. Perhaps location serves as the main source of dramatic tension, as their thoughts stream from their surroundings and overflow into emotion, yet when the setting shifts they may feel differently. One of the key themes appears to be the nature of human beings, be it fate or fury, concerning their life's duties and the finality of life itself, causing the reader to reflect on their own life and how they spend their days."

"You can always expect moral thoughts from Candice," a classmate comments.

You're welcome, I think. It's inevitable at this point. Even my past observations bulleted on an exercise where we were to discern a cartoonist's intent seem to point to ultimate issues:

1. We are the fool in the game of life, with apparent prosperity on a slope.
2. The cartoon makeup of religion and culture dilutes the spiritual world.
3. The powerful will always be tempted with pride.
4. Seduction comes in many forms.
5. There is pleasure in sin for a moment.
6. Behind all visible are intricate systems which govern the universe.
7. Without the distinction of Christ being Lord of all, the concept of 'good' itself takes on evil and malicious forms.

Rolling my eyes at the memory of such threads I felt I mishandled or was unworthy to respond to in the first place (it was impossible in that circumstance to go into detail about each very direct viewpoint), I start to question why I didn't decide to move to England instead of doing most of the school year online. It distracts and frustrates me to daydream, and I know this is unproductive. I haven't had time to really pray about any of this yet.

I continue to write character analyses for stage plays, tying up several simultaneous forum threads late into the night before turning off Candiceyland's year-round Christmas lights and preparing to close my computer in discouragement. *No summer break in this course,* I feel around for my charger in the dark, happening to see a new comment:

"This is just the sort of discussion I would hope to happen between writer, director and actors in a rehearsal or development session," the tutor praises my work. "Having such detailed knowledge of a character and their changing motivations is crucial to building both believable characters and coherent, compelling action that is driven by them. The prose is built on really strong and distinctive noun phrases, and there's some wonderful imagery. In terms of time management, your approach is very cinematic. It summons to mind the wobbly transition often used to show a retrospective shift in cinema. It can be hard to get away from cinematic approaches because we live in such a cinematic age. Keep in mind, however, this is for the stage, not the screen."

Cinema, cinema, go away, I mutter, bidding the world of Oxford goodnight.

And yes, I am wearing an Oxford sweatshirt.

"A little more sophistication and ambiguity would not go amiss and would not be lost on children who are becoming increasingly aware of delicate balances in the world and that the line between good and evil is a fine one, if indeed it exists at all."

I awake to this startling comment from one peer undirected at me. Immediately my heart begins to race. What is this again, the vague difference in light and darkness?

"*Caaaaanzieee,*" Mom calls from downstairs. "Want a gluten-free blueberry pancake?"

Passion must have a vice. I run downstairs, away from the controversial message.

Something's missing.

"I'll be down shortly, Mum." I run back up to kneel at my window seat and pray for God to forgive my ignorance, and to teach me how to think, for there are so many opinions and controversies, I never want to lose the objective causes that are worth pursuing. May there never be a confusion over the simplest of values.

God, please keep my heart in a good place!

"Good morning!" Jordan and Angel are at the countertop sipping orange juice when I finally descend. "Mom said one month from today you will be in Oxford!"

"That's right," I catch a glow in Mom's eyes, in love with English Cotswold villages.

"Are you nervous?" She pours a glass of chocolate milk for me.

"Only to get this screenplay turned in before I fly out. Critiques on my portfolio, the biggest project of the year, are going to be happening, in addition to daily lectures and afternoon exercises. If I can just figure out the bus system …"

"You genius, you." Mom sets a plate of hot pancakes before me.

"I'm not a genius, Mom."

"Well, you apply yourself."

"What is the fine line between good and evil?" I ask suddenly, a triangle of pancake on my lifted fork. A drop of syrup divinely lands on Charlie's little black nose.

"It can seem hard to discern between good and evil. But no, they are separate things. A thing is either drawing you toward God or away from Him. It is either hot or cold." Mom says seriously. "How terrible it will be for people who call good things bad and bad things good, who think darkness is light and light is darkness, who think sour is sweet and sweet is sour."[1]

"But then why the attraction? I mean, I know it is sin nature that we all gravitate to evil, but why do good people still laugh at horrific things, why the disconnect?"

"It's just like your studies in entertainment," Mom continues. "You can't play with fire and expect not to be burned."

"But people don't *know* it's fire. It hasn't burned them yet. ..." my thoughts trail.

"Spell it out then, Candice." Mom squeezes my hand.

I do spell it out, writing the opening scenes for the horror screenplay *How to Disappear Completely* and post on the public screenwriting forum:

"Baz Luhrmann's opening sequence in *Elvis* was a strong inspiration, along with his film trademarks of serious comedy leading to final tragedy. I imagine that kind of directing for *How to Disappear Completely*: vibrant colors, multi-filters, and excessive reality pushes. ... It was hard not to play 'director' with edits and transitions, and to this end I may have overstepped boundaries. ... but I am ready to enter the film world, at least, creatively enthused to do so."

"Basically and overall, well done, Candice," the tutor comments. "It's always nice to work with good work! When did the wheels turn for you to say, 'I am a screenwriter'?"

"I had this stark revelation my sentences were not concise," I share. "My thoughts were scattered. But I am realizing the flexibility of the script writer. The rules are to be utilized as tools, not handcuffs. My style reserves the right to grow smarter, but it is not formless. It is my responsibility as a writer to reel people into another world. And since drama brings the power of production with the curation of film, I am curious if some of my stories would have a larger appeal as a stage play ..."

I still don't know if I am capable of capturing the stage, but I dare to admit, "If I could learn to incorporate the landscapes in my mind to drama, painting the characters with poetic aural sensations and prose detail, I think I would have something. I have never written a stage play I truly believed in or liked. I am ready to change that."

CHAPTER 18
THE LONDON STAGE

KEBLE COLLEGE, OXFORD, ENGLAND

*But very quickly they all became grave again: for, as you know,
there is a kind of happiness and wonder that makes you serious.
It is too good to waste on jokes.*
—C.S. Lewis

Here I am, headed to the blue airport gate calling my name with my lopsided, overstuffed carry-on luggage, stomach fluttering just to hear an accent. If not for this insane amount of adultish adrenaline upon me that I am about to be in a foreign country alone, I could easily crawl back in bed and sleep two days straight. *You're flying to London, and that's that*, I told myself, having felt severely anxious for nights leading up to this day.

Sometimes the wisest thing you can do is not think too deeply.

Mom is graciously flying with me to Oxford, helping her college kid seamlessly move to an unknown city to live alone for a few weeks. She ordered smoothies for us before we rushed to the gate, now the mood is set to eat light and sleep hard once we connect in Dallas. With my high school backpack sporting an athletic brand, I am not sure the crumbs got taken out since pretzels were crushed under track spikes. Still, it isn't screaming too loudly "I am an American Athlete!" in neon, being mostly black nylon and generic, and I look serious faced enough to be, hopefully, beyond condescension. Except the airport desk lady is looking at me funny, almost pre-accusatory, as if she couldn't quite put her finger on what she didn't like about me. The problem isn't her obvious judgement, but the fact that I cannot get to London without passing her.

Here goes, I think, offering my most glamorous smile as she scans my boarding pass.

She stops me with her hand. "Hold." She points to the luggage allowance measurer.

Oh, great. My tiny carry-on suitcase holding a month's worth of clothes is too full.

I have no choice but to pop down the handle and wrestle it into the measuring rack. I know from the way she shakes her head as I meet her gaze to please just let us pass that she cannot be put under a spell. *Beauty has its limits ...*

"Step aside, please," she tells us, and the irked passengers behind do not even so much as give a sympathy sigh.

We cannot travel. Worse, we do not have time to think of an alternative plan. If we miss our flight to London, I am in jeopardy of classes beginning without me.

Here I am—so close to Oxford, overstuffed.

"Try fitting some in my suitcase," Mom offers. We haphazardly rolled and shoved and stuffed my carefully selected blue and white and black garments into side pockets and purses. At this point I do not care about the wrinkles. *Just to make it on the plane ...*

"Nope. Back out of line."

"Stuff it down your shirt! Do anything!" Mom hastens. Soon clothes are everywhere—clothes I meticulously sat out and folded for weeks, clothes that had been steamed and pre-selected and drenched in Badgley Mischka's *Petunia* because I couldn't take the bottle. Undone.

Just before we are officially too late, the lady finally excuses us on, frazzled and sweating, to squish beside a large Texan grandfather who is sympathetic to our story.

"She's going to Oxford, you know," Mom says between us. I am thankful to have pre-selected the window seat.

Breathe, I think. *You made it on the plane.*

Coldness.

A stream of purple trickled at my feet from my backpack to my ankle.

"*Oh no. My smoothie's leaking.*" I murmur to Mom.

Mom immediately rises to collect paper towels. *Such a loving Mom. Thank goodness I am not doing this alone*, I think gratefully. *I should probably text Dad that we finally made it.*

But as I reach for my phone and watch my mom disappear down the long aisle, excusing herself past the remaining people still fighting for luggage space, my heart sinks.

My phone isn't there.

"On behalf of the staff and crew at American Airlines, we'd like to welcome you aboard to today's flight ..." The speaker ruffles.

"Excuse me," I squeeze past our friend the Texan to wave in the direction of my blond mother, beret-hatted for Britain, and shout her name. "Casey! Casey!"

It seems my voice pushes her onward.

"Please fasten your seatbelts and stow away any loose articles ..."

"Ma'am," a flight attendant approaches, "you're going to need to take your seat."

"I need that lady!" I press unashamedly, smoothie cup dripping in hand, thumb poorly plugging the crack. "That one there!"

Understandingly, the attendant brings Mom over beholding paper towels with a smile, only to be replaced with my own helpless anguish as I explain the real trouble.

"She left her phone at the gate!" Mom is much better at handling public relations than I may ever be. "She is going to Oxford!" She presses in her signature exclamation-mark voice. "*She needs her phone before she is left alone in a foreign country!!!*"

No one needs to tell me to sit down and bury my face under paper towels. Through all of this, the Texan finds great humor at our expense. I drip with sweat.

It was all the Lord's timing: Mom was ushered off the plane and returned triumphantly with my pacific blue phone, held high above head like a trophy. A few people even clap.

What an adventure!

We officially landed in London Heathrow Airport (LHR), and I met an Oxford graduate on the plane named Lily. "Candice, if you ever need anything, just let me know," said Lily in a young British accent, definitely upper class. She was exactly the sort of blond English girl I'd be friends with, a history student, and I should have asked for her number, but instead I blushed and fumbled something about studying writing and turned my attention out the window to look for castles.

Mom pats my shoulder after the long nine hours of half-sleep. "Look out the window,"

"It feels like home," I whisper, feeling like Mia in *Princess Diaries*.

Coming on to the continent, in a way, truly does feel like I am going home. Not that this is my home, but as if something or someone is waiting on me here. Like I am being expected.

All these expectations have brought me here. I feel like saying, "Here I am!" which I told God this morning. I am not a tourist and would not be here if it weren't for school.

Upon landing I realize that London is hotter than expected, but raining as expected—tourists everywhere, people running into you as you walk on the right ride only to realize it is the left that is correct. Signs in the airport and on street billboards read Pret a Manger (a sandwich shop chain named after the French *prêt à manger*, meaning 'ready to eat'), Marks & Spencer (M&S), known for quality freshness and luxury modern food, and other various designer stores familiar to America, mimicking any large city. The airport itself smells like Louis Vuitton's *Stellar Times* perfume drenched over tall, cool women in beige trench coats carrying those small purses so fashionable in the UK. I breathe deep, taking it all in. The cobblestone streets, cockney accent of our driver, the 'hello loves' and 'oh thank yous' and 'no worries' that consume greetings and exchanges. The very fact I am present! Girls pass me with disregard mixed with mild curiosity at my printed luggage and American accent calling to mom that we must walk on the left.

Mr. Tim, our lawyer friend, escorted us to Paddington Station before we loaded in a little yellow taxi and drove to Central London, seeing Westminster Abbey, Big Ben, Buckingham Palace, and official governmental buildings near Kensington Palace, where the Prince of Wales currently lives. The Queen herself was at Buckingham Palace when we passed, as noted by the raised Royal Standard flag. While driving down The Mall, the front street where parades happen in front of Buckingham Palace, I was in awe.

I can't believe it. This is what I saw on TV that summer I spent at the farm, I thought.

What had brought me to the UK? A cultivated love for learning.

"This would be a lot better if I had a sandwich," Mom said out of the blue.

"What—what do you mean? This is *the* Buckingham Palace!" I stammered.

"Oh yes, that's great." She laughed, realizing the contrast. "I'm also just hungry!"

I love my mom.

London seemed grayscale and humdrum, elegant and iconic, quiet, yet crawling with tourists and traffic and businesses. A hint of New Orleans. But I was awfully tired while I was analyzing it and still feel quite sick, and I do not have any connections to London other than liking *L*-words more than *O*-words because of the way they lilt off the tongue with light elegance. I *am* excited to be here. I just feel physically sick and exhausted. In a week when I am alone and settled, I am sure I will feel much better.

Now looking out of the rainy window on the double-decker bus to Oxford, I am enchanted. All I see are sheep in green summer pastureland, broccoli-like trees planted on private farms. I have a glaze of "I don't care," a happy glaze, a content stare. I feel this rightness that I am where I am supposed to be. Tired and in need of a shower, I still have an overwhelming peace, like Jesus' arm is wrapped around my shoulder. It brings me back to when our family lived in Rochester, Minnesota for a month and rode the bus routinely to the Mayo Clinic. I recall the hotel stops, billboards, country music, coldness, dreaming about owning my own beagle and clubhouse. I had no idea at nineteen I'd be riding a similar looking bus to Oxford for college. Those bus moments literally felt secluded for a special purpose, one I have held onto until now.

And then it hits me: Oxford has waited for me my whole life.

"May I help you?" The receptionist at Keble College is a student around my age and strikes me like a young Juliet Holland-Rose whose white name tag ironically reads *Juliet*. She sounds distinctly upper class, or at least exposed to high society.

Working at the desk in the porter's lodge, she must be bound to a summer job ... I analyze as I watch the girl arch her slim eyebrows at Mom, who explains how I am an overseas student here for my portfolio tutorials, *blah, blah, blah.*

I wander over to a bulletin board and see an advertisement for a classical concert at Christ Church College, one of the more famous of the Oxford colleges, called *Instruments on Time & Truth*. Now that is rather nice sounding.

"Humphrey will escort you to your room," Juliet sighs dismissively, suspending a key with a fob above my hand for a moment before finally dropping it. "Welcome to Oxford."

"Oh, thank you," I say, surprising myself at how British I already sound.

"Hey, let's take a picture!" Mom poses me in front of the entrance to the college. Sweating from the walk across town dragging luggage after a nine-and-a-half-hour overnight flight, my smile is forcibly peeved. I hope Mom is happy.

Keble College is much smaller than the pictures. It is situated on the street opposite of Keble Road bus stop, where I will take the bus into Summertown, a suburb of Oxford, to Ewert Place, where lectures and afternoon classes will be held. The air is hot and the grass on the quad is dead-looking. Humphrey is walking too fast for me to have a chance to note anything else. I do know you cannot walk on the quad grass unless you are a professor.

After lugging my suitcase up stair after stair, Humphrey teaches me to use my key fob to open a second door from the staircase with glass windows that lead into a hushed carpeted hallway with brown numbered doors.

"And these are the girls' dormitories, I suppose?" Mom volumes to Humphrey.

"No," Humphrey says firmly with a shake of his head.

Embarrassed and alarmed at this coed discovery (I would have never asked), I cough and jiggle my keys fervently until the door to my quad-facing ensuite gives way.

"Very nice," I offer in a high voice that sounds like Juliet.

"Equipped with all modern amenities, apa' from air conditioning." Humphrey draws open the curtains to the quad, and I see a boy in the window across with a book in hand.

"But it's so hot in England!" Mom says astonished. "I would think that ..."

"Record heat wave," Humphrey says in thick cockney. "Fans sellin' out in ev'ry store."

"I see," I press and lift the window for a breeze. There is none.

"Electricity runs smooth if y'knock on wood. Towels on request. Housekeeping ev'ry three days. Breakfast in the dining 'oll there." He points out toward a stained glass hall, winged to the college.

"Very pleasant," I set my track backpack in the chair beside the window, taking in the vacant bookshelves and opposite desk. *I'll have to visit Blackwell's Bookshop and stock up.*

"Can you show me to my room? I am only staying a couple days before I leave for America, I just came to drop my daughter off. It's her first time alone in a foreign country." Mom explains, and I feel heat rush to my cheeks again.

"Right then, luv." Humphrey closes the door, leaving me to stare at the boy out the window. But then the boy sees me and whisks his curtains shut, and so I laugh and fall onto my bed.

After hopelessly getting lost in Oxford's City Centre with pounds of groceries bags hanging off our arms, Mom and I decide on fish and chips at a pink pub called The King's Arms, supposedly the oldest pub in Oxford, dating back to 1607. It is bustling with old professors and animated groups of students in more casual dress than I expected, but then I realize the official Michaelmas Term had not yet begun for them, and many are still on Long Vacation (the break between Trinity Term and the next school year's Michaelmas Term).

"Ello luvs," the bartender comes to our table with two glass bottles of distilled water, two large plates of cod and fries, and two little green bowls next to tartar sauces.

"Sir, what is that?" Mom points to her green bowl.

"Why, it's mashed peas, of course!" The bartender laughs.

"Mashed peas?" Mom looks at me funnily. "Who would have guessed!"

"I can't believe you leave tomorrow." I dip my chips (think American steak fries) in the peas. It has a surprising taste that blends smooth veggie on fried veggie, filling and comforting.

"If we can survive wandering down cobblestone streets for miles upon end with groceries on our arms," Mom laughs, "you'll be fine. Besides, I got you those new shoes, so you won't twist your ankle anymore. *Mmm.* I like peas! Do you feel ready to live here for a few weeks?"

"I feel tired and jetlagged." I cut into my fish. Like a ding-dong, I wore heels all day through the airport and into Oxford. (I just shuddered while packing, thinking about how I had worn a greased t-shirt as a new intern in the executive office. It was time to pull myself together!) My heels looked sleek and professional. They were also a recipe for broken bones on the rickety cobblestones that surrounded the most famous Oxford structure, the Radcliff Camera. "But knowing I'm not truly alone, I feel perfectly safe." I admit to Mom.

"I'm so happy you walk with God. It gives me peace. I hope you take it all in. Don't forget to explore the Bodleian Library with your student ID. I can't even get into that building! So crazy to think you're a student. Live it up, Canzie, and write me all about it."

"Thanks Mom. It's inevitable," I say. "Once you become a memoirist, you can't really 'turn off' during lifechanging moments. One of my tutors explained it's like an antenna; you have to train yourself to turn it off. I stopped journaling in June to give myself a break before Oxford, because I knew it would turn on automatically. I think I am going to fill a whole journal here."

"That's so interesting," Mom's ponders. "I never thought about that. You're going to be studying writing in your classes, while also living a completely separate story."

"So goes my life," I say, looking past Mom to an anciently smart-looking group of professors in a heated discussion on what sounds like theological matters. *Where is my husband?*

I wake early to have a nice run in the cool of the day at University Park, right across from the street at Keble, so to *familiarise* myself with the trail before I am alone and on my own. Laying in Room 3010 with my window open, breathing in the still air while listening to students get drunk below me, I kept wondering whether Keble College was indeed near a hospital, or perhaps there really were nearly fourteen-thousand cyclists injured or killed in England a year. There was an insane amount of ambulance sirens throughout the night, and the chimes of ancient clock towers did not help Candice enter dreamland any sooner, so after a cold shower and a hot towel thanks to a towel warmer, which is considered a standard feature in UK bathrooms, I lace my Asics and cross the street, not bothering to text my *mum* because I am absolutely a grown woman.

Sirens again? I hear them above Sight & Sound's *David*, a newly released musical whose lyrics have marked this entire trip and kept my head on straight. Even if I feel like my husband is in England, I can't lead myself on like that by listening to music that will stir up facades of romance. I need *David* and its musical repetition of scripture to keep me focused on God's goodness, faithfulness, and protection to even get me here. I mean, I'm an *Oxford* student!

I keep on running down the path in my raincoat, past many other young runners and dogs. I love the culture of England.

Alarmingly, the sirens grow louder, even as I distance myself from the street.

Lord, help whoever is hurt or in danger, I pray, thinking I should loop back to say goodbye to Mom before she leaves for the airport.

What in the world? I squint my contactless eyes at the entrance to Keble College.

A figure is waving at me wildly from the street—a figure that looks a lot like my mom in her pajamas, holding her blanket.

"*Mom?*" I laugh from the sidewalk.

"Where have you been? Come! Come! Cross the street!!!" She calls back.

Two firetrucks begin unloading beside the entrance to Keble.

"Some room above me is on *fire!*" Mom clutches my arm. "They won't let me get my passport or anything, but my plane flies out in three hours!"

"Oh no," I follow her to the quad. To my amazement, a crowd of people is standing on the forbidden lawn. We walk onto the sacred grass; Mom muttering things about how she had banged on my door forever and wanted to know why I would not answer my phone, and me feeling very much illegal for trespassing on the lawn and inwardly excited about a drama.

Humphrey is standing beside a composed Juliet reading from a list of names. "Right then," he flips a page on his clipboard. "Anyone seen a Richard Lexington? Richard, anyone?"

The crowd of guests is quite a sight: students with towels on their heads murmuring complaints about having little time to prepare for their upcoming award ceremonies, international visitors talking rapidly in their languages with crossed arms, a few graying couples in town for alumni events staring blankly at Humphrey with inevitable British reserve.

"Right," Humphrey notes Richard's absence. "Someone best fetch 'em." He flips to the next page, and no one moves, other than Juliet, who crosses her arms and sighs.

Mom and I stare at each other. "Er ... I hope Richard makes it," she whispers, and we laugh.

The firefighters themselves are strangely composed, walking blithely with the water hose toward the smoke with cool, "A lil' more 'ose, Reg!" "Right then!" They wave to each other.

After the peculiar roll call is completed to the satisfaction of the staff, we are dismissed to the dining hall for breakfast as usual, while flames and smoke rise from the windows above my mom's room. They would still not let her retrieve her passport, so we sit in the magnificent dining hall in pajamas and running clothes beside the students with towels on their heads being frowned upon by iconic historical figures in portraits hanging above us. What an ill-fitting contrast, but I don't call this an adventure for nothing!

Miraculously, Mom was able to retrieve her passport and board the bus at Queen's Lane bus stop to LHR, barely making it on her flight back to the United States, and I met up with fellow Wolvercotes on the upper level of the bus headed to Ewert Place, enjoying the presence of Sarah and Andrea and others in person for the first time since we virtually met last fall.

I feel at home in Summertown. Away from the tourism of Oxford, its quiet suburb of Summertown Cycles, Gail's Bakery, and Columbia Coffee Shop, seems a proper sort of place to raise a family, with mums pushing their babies in carriages to the floristry or *JoJo Maman Bébé*, and schoolgirls in uniforms on scooters or walking with friends.

Morning lectures are followed by independent study where I usually follow classmates to Gail's Bakery for a small glass of sparkling mint tea. Gail's, along with many other restaurants in Summertown, have 'secret gardens,' hidden patios surrounded by shrubbery and fences, where you can quietly dine and talk of high matters.

Oxford is just that: quiet, secret, profound.

On one occasion I joined students from another cohort, most twice my age, including Johnny from Italy, who carries his backpack by hand and who corrected me when I pronounced his name in the American version (think Italian *Gianni*), and Judith from Scotland. This was the time I learned that the way of culture—even with people from various European countries, had not quite the same way of saying things like some do in America.

"We should all go discuss this morning's lecture." I overheard Judith say to her cohort.

All *I* could recall was a comment the lecturer said while sitting on his desk, chatting with a millennial on drinking shots: "Oxford marches on food and alcohol."

"Would you care to join us at Gail's?" Judith turned slowly to me in an obligatory way.

"Oh, I don't mean to impose," I said, unsure.

"Not at all," someone from their cohort said rather shortly.

"Alright, I'd love to!" I sprang up from my front row seat. But on the short walk from Ewert Place to Gail's Bakery, I had a feeling that I was indeed imposing.

You have to give and expect double the courtesy of Americans and learn think that way, too. I make a mental note that if someone says, "not at all," it very well could mean you are a complete imposter and should run for your life.

Extreme? I had fun playing the game.

The first week of school passes by effortlessly. Daily, I write hundreds of words during in-class exercises, and tutors call on me often.

"Excellent. Prime example. Exemplary." The tutor says these things in front of the entire class. "This is a role model for you all."

Everyone seems surprised I am only nineteen, and some seem to harbor resentment. But I have nothing to prove, so I ignore them, focusing intently on all assignments and my life-writing portfolio submission. I add four books to my room's library collection:

- *Eat, Run, Enjoy*
- *C.S. Lewis: A Life*
- *The Queen*
- *The Cost of Discipleship*

Life in England: bursting with promise.

"It's funny to think we all end up there," I point to a graveyard as I walk home from class with a boy from Peru, who writes natural and animal horror. I relish the chance to learn and discuss topics as death and eternity with fellow colleagues on bus rides or walks home from school.

"Yes, yes indeed," he says.

"It seems that beauty was not meant to be elusive, nor life to end hopelessly," I offer.

"Death is but a doorway," he says in slow English. "There does always seem to be more."

We continue to talk about the spiritual world, and I was again reminded of my poem:

It seems not
the beauty of waterfalls
and cathedrals
were meant to merely tempt us,
as if beauty's purpose were to
make a mockery of itself
for its core to be a lie.
The essence of pleasure demands
that the acquittal of satisfaction be found,
for sense would not have it
that beauty would tempt us this way
only for hope to die with ourselves.

We later eat fish and chips with our Wolvercote colleagues at The King's Arms pub, laughing about films we watched in drama class and the rather difficult timed poetry exercises all of us seemed to fail but Sarah, being the prolific poet she is. I get used to ordering sparkling spring water in a glass bottle, hearing conflicting but eye-opening perspectives on eternity and childhood, and contributing to conversations without being afraid of failing in my response, for it is Christ who is in me, and I do not speak out of my own strength or understanding. I mean, who would have thought fifteen-year-old Candice, who was disinterested in even going to college, would be sitting in an Oxford pub as an Oxford student with friends from around the world?

James sits down in one of the hard booths with a pint. "I say now, I want all of you to describe to me all such invented characters from today's class."

"My character is average but doesn't want to be," a Wolvercote remarks stoutly.

"Ooh! Average but doesn't want to be? Too apparently perfect, you say, like she's ticking every box. Feminism, climate change, soil erosion …" Sarah engages.

"Mine is impossible to live with," remarks another Wolvercote. "She hates her life but defends it."

Andrea dips a chip in mashed peas. "When you said in class that she was self-aware, I actually think she's a little not self-aware, but she likes to depict herself as being self-aware."

"That's kind of the crux that's going on," the colleague observes. "She's not terribly self-aware and that's causing issues in her second marriage."

"A rather unkind portrait of somebody with actually admirable qualities."

"She thinks like, you know, 'I panic! I panic that I make coffee, then I reply to the abuse, I mean *emails*, and then I, you know, put vodka in my coffee.' That type."

"What role did her childhood play into this?" I propose.

"She would say, 'A childhood was for children, do we have to talk about it?'" My colleague wipes fish grease off her fingers.

Sarah nods respectfully. "She's blocked it, perhaps."

"She just remembers her dad holding a gun, pointed at mum, the sound, the blood ..." my colleague's voice trails off.

"Ah, but as they say, you can't disconnect the author from the protagonist." Andrea points to the ceiling. "Just as the fine line between fiction and life is so spare."

"Can't you? It's just a ..." the colleague shoots back explicitly, caught by her own tale.

What have we each blocked from our own childhoods? I think soberly.

"What do you propose on writing and childhood?" Andrea turns to me.

"Don't ask Candice; she's still in hers," someone says, and the whole table laughs.

I clear my throat, daring myself not to overthink. "Well, everyone's childhood seeps into their writing. For some, it is blatant, others, it is nearly an invisible trace. It is most usually in the internal dialogue and can also be obvious in the description of the world: cynical, deprived, unforgiving ... of these two outlooks, one can surely sense how childhood drew blood."

"So you're saying good childhoods are often the most obviously connected, but authors with comparatively negative memories still seep parts of their childhood into their writing?"

"Even the very fact they block off certain memories indicates something," I reason. "You cannot call a happy childhood author ignorant. Perhaps have taken renewed individualism and aggression on what they agree or do not agree with, as based on their experience. They remember and frame what they want to. All of childhood is involved in the author's works."

"I disagree strongly," the colleague with the troubled character says, and I imagine it laid out on a surgical table and we are all doctors deciding where to cut and with what scalpel.

Thin ice, Candice. I caution myself.

"We've talked about this before. Too much bias is in authors' work who had happy childhoods. It is some sloppy, massive disastrous work, full of hypocrisy. Really, it all goes back to religion. You'll find most people believe in God who had good childhoods ..."

Too much to say in response to that, I think with compassion of Mr.

Drake. *Bias works in both directions. You have people on one hand who think there is a God, because of childhood or otherwise, and you have people who don't for the very opposite reason. This does not negate the reality that there may be a God who stands on His own ...*

"No religion here, please," A man yells from the bar counter with a spilling beer in hand.

"At the very least, you cannot say it is dishonest," I say, back on topic to childhoods. "The person on the opposite end is guilty of the same thing. If they deem the world to be bad, neutral, or otherwise, it does not make the good side excusable just because it is fairytale-like."

James turns back to the troubled character with renewed interest. "Suppose your character *were* to share her spiritual views. What would she say?"

"I would say she spiritually drives a Ferrari, but it looks like a Mazda right now," my colleague says through pursed lips.

"She lying to herself." Sarah shakes her head.

"Ah, jolly good. Anyone want to join for *Instruments on Time and Truth* tonight?" James asks, and we all stand earnestly in the causality of the climax.

On my first weekend alone in Oxford, Andrea and I enjoy a picnic at University Park, where she introduces me to Australian delicacies, and we share experiences and perspectives of God, light, and eternity. Then I got a high fever and had to take the bus into Summertown to shakily search for the British version of Tylenol (it is Paracetamol, by the way). I missed having a hairdryer so bought one instinctively, then realized because of its Type G electrical plug-in cord that will never work in the United States. I also missed many classes but added pages upon pages to my journal, which already had 78 pages written just within the first week of living in Oxford. I can't even fully grasp yet all God is teaching me. This life-writer lifestyle is incessant!

After a particularly long day of writing, I am in the mood for an evening concert, and I shrug my shoulders down the hallway of Ewert House to board the bus, alone, tired, dismissive.

"Is that Candice Gibbons?" A familiar voice calls from an open classroom.

I wince.

There is no way that is who I think it is. It can't be!

I had just had a Zoom call with the American Harvard and Oxford tutor the day before.

"Dr. McKetta?" I see it is indeed her. "You're in England! I can't believe it!"

"Yes, haha! I am teaching another class." She smiles, and so my whole day brightens as we share the bus back to Oxford's City Centre, talking about childhood and motherhood and winter writing retreats. Seeing my favorite tutor feels surreal and becomes the highlight of my second week in Oxford, and I write twenty letters to friends and family back in the United States.

I happen to read the corner of my purple muesli cereal box in gold:

Why not take a wander somewhere new today?

Who knows who you'll meet along the way.

"You really should try long distance running," fellow Wolvercote Katherine tells me on our way to Columbia Coffee after a morning lecture. "I believe you would like it."

"I have always wanted to run long distance," I share. "I am just nervous after two foot surgeries. Running 400-meter races is one thing, but three miles—a 5k? No way!"

Katherine laughs. "It is a learned discipline."

"Learned disciplines I am familiar with," I order a hot chocolate warily, thinking of compromise during my track days. "Unnecessary torture is a completely different matter."

"Someday it'll hit," Katherine motions to a table where Dr. McKetta sits with Sarah and a few other colleagues, "and you'll be glad you went for it."

I do feel this is not only true academically, but in all facets of life. You cannot separate physical and spiritual just as you cannot underestimate the influence of academia and social interactions. Sitting at this table of geniuses, I feel unworthy yet at home in Summertown's suburb, young, alive, and ready to learn.

It happened. The London stage made itself known to me. Seeing my first West End production completely changed my view of the stage.

"I'm ready." I told Mr. Tim, who escorted me to a weekend in London for fun.

"Ready for what?"

"To go to the stage!" I looked out the taxi window at the contrast of luxury stores with homeless people sleeping beneath their lighted signs. "It all makes sense now. The music, the transitions, the limitlessness to what can be done with a platform and people. Seeing what happened tonight changes everything,"

"The stage is a very dark place," Mr. Tim tells me.

"Perfect." I smile in remembrance of my name's meaning: *full of light*.

CHAPTER 19
YOU'RE LIKE A JOURNALIST, CANDICE

Year of Travel, London, Nairobi, D.C., NYC

*... and now it's 'get to work' in a very exciting sense
of running into darkness.*
—*Journal #19, 19 years old*

I may never meet friends in Oklahoma, and I may not even get married, so I have decided to detach from Oklahoma in general. There is no use in dreaming about things God has yet to reveal, and I want to guard my heart from falling for the wrong friendships or relationship, just because someone is available. I must keep my standards high, but also remain humble and open.

Friendless yet busy, halfway through my two-year degree at Oxford, and based in Oklahoma for the flexible portion of my studies, there is nothing left to do but to hone my craft: reading wide, writing long, and living with impenetrable focus on all God has before me, like flying right now to Nairobi, Kenya, with an international non-profit to visit various humanitarian work projects. In love with international missions and travel in general, I have decided to call this a Year of Travel, and to practice life-writing in real-time.

I can't help but think that Candice, the girl who used to be reluctant just driving from Missouri to Oklahoma, is currently flying over

France, undaunted by over sixty days of traveling ahead this year, along with manuscript writing, Oxford studies, and executive administrative office work somewhere in there. How God has expanded my capacity!

Before this moment, my British-loving mum, seventeen-year-old sister Bria ('Brother' is really growing up), and I visited Mr. Tim, our family lawyer friend, in the city of Oxford for a little stop in England to break up the twenty-two hours of travel from Oklahoma to Kenya … and what a journey it was getting to this moment on the plane!

Last night, I was reading the Oxford student paper around 12:15 a.m. in the Shelley Suite at University College after explaining to Bria how Oxford is a *city* in England, but it is also the home of the *University of Oxford*, which is comprised of over forty individual colleges. Just as Keble College (where I stayed during my in-person classes last summer), is an Oxford college, University College, where Mr. Tim studied, and where we were staying, is part of Oxford, too.

"So you see," I finished telling Bria in a British accent, "Oxford is really a family of colleges, in its own city." I crossed my legs and leaned back in my chair like a professor.

With a courteous 'ah' Bria, the rising actress that she was, resorted to her personal strand of genius, memorizing lines for an upcoming audition, hoping I would not make her finish the movie *Joan of Arc*, during which she had fallen asleep the previous night. Mr. Tim was at the desk working on our visas as Mom paced up and down, asking lively questions like whether a real fire could be lit and whether she should stay awake until 5 a.m. (I had a fireplace in the Shelley Suite—it was my very own lodging on this trip). We had to be at Queens Lane bus stop on High Street by 5:30 a.m. to catch the airport bus to LHR to fly to Nairobi. I set my alarm for 4:45 a.m.

As Mr. Tim left for his suite, and Mom and Bria left for their hotel, I journaled my last page and read the last verse in Psalm 4 to ponder. I probably distinguished the lights around 1:15 a.m. I do not remember falling asleep; I was exhausted from our day in London. My throat felt sick throughout the day as the wind was colder than the actual 3 degrees Celsius temperature and we did not bring coats. I had read briefly in the Bodleian Library, savoring my student ID card, and after a hot breakfast of beans on toast and much walking, we caught the bus to London and were soon in the dark fog of downtown. The West End production we saw was well executed and gave me ideas for one of my stage plays. We got hot lattes afterward and walked the lighted cobblestone streets in fatigued happiness as if it were a dream (England always feels like a dream, honestly), ordering fish and chips at a rowdy bar. By the time we had returned to Oxford, frat boys were stumbling on the quad of University College, daring each other to race and grabbing each other hastily before one fell on the forbidden quad lawn.

You can imagine the stillness of my body as I lay in my king bed with fluffy white pillows and starched sheets, the quiet tick of the decades-old room heaters, the strike of the clock tower below and the laugh of a drunken scholar, add in the occasional ambulance siren. It was all more than familiar; it felt like home, comforting sounds of adulthood cloaked in God's purpose for my life, completely spelled out yet remaining a mystery to its main character…

Knock-knock.

In my dream I heard a noise, but it was so quiet, I just stared at the nothingness of the air.

Knock-knock.

This time I heard my name.

Oh no. I felt for the light and hit it several times—one of those frustrating touch ones they have in the UK. Sure enough, the clock read 5:20 a.m.

"Mr. Tim, I'm so sorry. I will need some time to pack." I apologized on the other side of the door in my blue ankle-length nightgown, hair in a bun I had been planning to wash.

I had not packed! I was going to shower! Today we were flying to Kenya! Why did my alarm not sound? I panicked, shoving clothes in bags and doing everything I could not to overthink my lateness with similar feelings to the missed lecture call with my poetry tutor.

Miraculously, I opened the door at 5:30 a.m., immediately hit by the coldest rush of winter on the exposed wooden stairs. Oxford's staircases are rarely enclosed at the colleges, so one step outside your room, you're outside. I did not cough but felt an ache creep in very deep.

We met Mom and Bria at the still and eerie entrance of the Mercure Hotel where five men were smoking and huddled at the entrance. Other than an earnest cycler peddling a path to greatness, Oxford was utterly empty and silent.

The moment our troupe of four arrived at Queen's Lane's bus stop, we did not realize the torture that was to come. Poor Mother did not have a coat or anything, and it did not take long for the fridged temperature to set in.

"I'm very cold," Mom said quietly. I did not realize how truly cold she was until she kindly asked Mr. Tim if she could wait inside until the Airline Bus arrived.

"No," he said, his own hands pocketed from the frost. "It's 5:36 a.m. The bus will be here at 6:06 a.m. Well, it should be."

30 minutes! I was cold, and I had been blessed with a new maroon coat! Mom would surely catch cold or lose a toe. What were we to do?

Bria was in good spirits, insisting we make a movie scene of the moment, but my hands were now around my mother's exposed arms, and we were breathing heavily against each other.

Don't move, I told myself, for any movement sent an ache through your bones. It felt colder than snow, colder than ice. This was like holding cubes in your hands while air like the slit of a knife sliced through your clothes. Invisible as it was, it crept up on you like someone's long-fingered hand around your neck.

"We've got to do something!" Bria pleaded with me. While the fog hovered over the dreaming spires and I admitted this was indeed cinematic, my brain could not think; not since I had heard the knock on my door sixteen minutes earlier.

"Ask Mr. Tim," I whispered.

I advised Mom to take out her blanket and wrap herself in it, but the energy she exerted seemed to have been a mistake; the blanket felt useless at that point and did nothing for my mom. Ten minutes later, I was utterly awake—so much so that I felt as if I had slept very well! I thanked the Lord for sleep and for favor as I had packed my belongings so feverishly unaware.

The bus was warm like a sauna, but not at all overbearing. The simple shield of walls and windows was a comfort on the drive into London. We were not allowed to board the plane for some time because of our failed visas to enter Kenya, and we prayed fervently.

Finally the man moved on, asked us about various personal issues, and we got in! Praise God!

At this point the adrenaline of the morning was slowing down, and I was grateful to rest after a long walk, train ride, and security queue for hot oats, a banana, and orange juice. Elizabeth, the international non-profit's host, who had graciously offered this invitation to experience Kenya, met us at the airport, and we all eagerly boarded the plane, ready for the next surprise—for we don't call this an adventure for nothing!

Now on the ten hour flight to Nairobi, the smell of African chicken and human odors mixed with heavy perfume fill the crammed flight of various ethnicities. We taxied for at least a good hour due to the frosted London runways. Bria and I slept wearily on top of each other during the first few restless hours, as one typically does on restless international flights. My head felt like a bowling ball hanging by a rope with nowhere to brace itself. What a joy it was for everyone when the plane's food cart pushed through with hot rice, broccoli, and African chicken with a side of bread and cheese and crackers! I felt full and cluttered. We all were. But the plane was back in good spirits, and by *back* I assume these people are usually more pleasant.

I still have yet to remove my coat or do my hair or makeup. We still do not have the proper paperwork to enter. But it really is exciting to leave everything behind—and by this, I mean all distractions of school and England and the longing for a relationship, as many girls feel when they are about to enter their twenty-first year. Until God brings him, I will be patient.

If I had to smile at anything, it would be because no 'thing' has me. Nothing ails me, and no*thing* can be added or taken away from this place of mine because peace is from the Lord. I have left Oklahoma's icy roads and cubicle hours, and I worked ahead on my Hilary Term assignment so I can focus on documenting travel. To be in the African sun will be good for me.

Much happened upon our arrival in Kenya after flying over Egypt and landing in the darkness of Nairobi. At first we saw only a pitch black jungle mystery outside with dispersed lights. I imagined landing in the middle of nowhere. But the plane finally neared a bundle of dim lights as we approached the airport around 10 p.m., Kenya time. A warm wind met us like the kind you feel on a Florida vacation, refreshing coming from England's dense fog, but it was countered with sick coughs and sneezes and odors of our full plane. I didn't know whether I wanted to stay in the security of the plane or rush to the unknown of our Kenyan hotel.

Immediately upon landing, we were shifted into an enclosed ramp and led down a staircase where the airport was staffed with a weary crew. At the end of our disheveled queue was a door leading outside to the quiet airport parking lot where we boarded a bus, and I held on to one of those ceiling loops as we rattled around the circular airport exterior. Elizabeth, our host, was knowledgeable and prepared but flustered. Her physical demeanor was calm except for her face, and in the moments of being bounced along the airport fields I began to be thankful I was not her, on whom our success hinged.

When it came time to officially be admitted into Kenya, we were 'played' in the customs and visa entry process, and paid an unnecessary fee for falling for it. In the past I would have taken this personally and demanded justice, but when you've flown across the world to bring light to a dark place, you have bigger things to think about than ethical procedures in airports. I expected opposition, like a wind blowing at my candle to see how long my flame would last. I wasn't named 'full of light' for nothing!

Waiting in the midnight Kenyan breeze of the airport's basement room, as one wall was completely exposed to the outside air, it granted us time to hear from Elizabeth about the international non-profit's various projects, which sounded increasingly complicated the more I heard words like *government affiliations* and *sponsor funding* and just how much was needed to bring and establish things as simple as clean water to a remote village. There much to be done. But I did not let myself get overwhelmed because a) Stacy taught me better, b) I am not the answer to everyone's problems, and c) the best I can do is focus on my own work and serve.

Tulia (which means 'relax') is an oasis at the base of Mt. Kilimanjaro (I journal it as 'Kili'). I see its dark cloak stretched high above the dry planes where two elephants and a giraffe are at a watering hole. A barbed wire fence around our tents with spider web ends blowing in the wind are spiked off to block the 'big five,' the most dangerously hunted animals: the lion, leopard, elephant, buffalo, and rhino.

After what seemed a 4-hour drive to the middle of the earth where ostriches and zebras are the only thing you see on the side of the road, we were led down a trail of stone lined with sweet smelling African botany to a tinted lobby resembling the unconventional craftsmanship of Disney's *Swiss Family Robinson* treehouse, built on the ground however, and held by a singular tree in the center, overlooking a far distance of flowers, elephants, and Kili. Our team was each handed a cold towel and then a glass of papaya and mango juice. One could feel so calm and sensitive to the Lord's Spirit on those rural plains of yellow, orange, black, and white.

Before this we stayed in the city, where guard dogs had to enter our vehicle and sniff for drugs every day. We passed by men with guns at security checkpoints more times than I can count. Yet overall, Kenya is friendly and welcoming, and people have a common love for music, dancing, and taking their time. We flew to Kisumu one day and enjoyed trying new foods like *fufu*, *jollof rice*, *bobotie*, and *egusi soup*. They have an excellent rice bread that's thick and moist. I toast it and pour beans atop, just like I do in England. I love how they have beans and toast here! They also have decent porridge and delicious pineapple mint puree.

As a journalist, I have such a desire to write peoples' stories. I am in love with Kenya's culture of dance and hospitality, and people's sincere hearts to hear and experience Jesus' love. It has given hope to so many mothers and fathers and teenagers and children. Windows are often bare but for flowing curtains and iron bars; wildlife roams free and peaceful. I watch the women tie kanga cloths around their waists as beautiful skirt-like aprons. I watch hostesses after meals make masala chai, which quickly becomes my favorite post-dinner tea, a creamy spiced drink served in orange mugs, and talk about how the love of Jesus has changed their village and community. Many also share about the sacrifices that come with being a Christian. Mine are of no comparison, and I have a deep layer of admiration for these people of high faith under great risk.

Bria and I laughed the day we ate cooked goat—to the sound of goats bleating behind a fence. We laughed even harder the night we were served such fine African dishes we did not even know what they were. It was a formal rooftop dinner, and to my surprise, I was seated next to the American president of the large international humanitarian organization.

I promised myself I would behave. I wore a black and white fitted skirt with a white blouse, my hair in a loose curl against bright African blue beads, feeling like a real journalist. As he spoke, I tried hard to eat the little fish circle things on my plate on the little wooden boat in front of me, but I could not swallow it.

Just be gracious about it, I told inner Candice, who was ready to laugh and make a scene. *You are twenty years old now, you can't just laugh in inappropriate moments.*

"Would you care to try one?" I mischievously offered one of the little circles to Bria.

Unable to swallow her own meal, Bria shook her head, and we both poked at our food.

"And how are your meals?" The president leaned over to me.

"Oh, just delicious." I smiled, taking a large bite to cover my guilt.

I could not swallow. I didn't dare.

Bria, on the other hand, was a natural actress, and somehow her plate looked as though she had eaten half of it.

Good grief, Candice. Swallow and don't make a scene. I coached myself.

"Jambo!" A Kenyan dignitary got the attention of everyone from the opposite end of the table, and I had to drop my fork out of respect. With a glob of whatever was in my mouth—fish?—sickening me by the second, I had to act fast, so I discreetly folded it in my lap napkin.

"Greetings from the United States." The president was now saying beside me, and my napkin slipped cooly under the table once again. "It's a privilege to be here with you today. I want to thank and honor all the ministers and community leaders. Blessings to all of you."

"Blessings to all of you," many said unanimously.

"Blessings to all of you," Bria and I said, delayed.

"We have worked now over 30 years on the continent of Africa ..." the president talked on, and a warm nighttime breeze blew my hair. I thought about all we had witnessed in the last seven days: slums and refugee homes and meetings with medical doctors and dignitaries, driving up mountain edges and dancing with fatherless children. I felt so many thoughts bursts and was agitated at myself for not writing all of them down, but a part of my twenty-year-old resolution had also been to prioritize truly *living* life first, then writing it down.

"We welcome you to help us in this project." The Kenyan dignitary spoke again, and I zoned in. "We are in the process of continuing our development of laboratories and maternity services, in addition to providing over four million people with clean water, thanks to your partnership."

"Blessings," everyone said.

"Blessings," Bria and I followed.

"We are honored to send high-tech, good quality medical equipment and other resources that are necessary for clinics and birthing centers." The president acknowledged. "In partnership with our doctors from the United States and health care workers from Kenya, we're hoping to build a wonderful first-class birthing center that is going to make childbirth a much safer process. And we believe in giving Africa our best. Yes, this is just the beginning."

"Amen."

"Amen."

Suddenly, everyone stood and clapped. I stood proudly too, forgetting my napkin was in my lap with the lump of fish inside. Slipping under the table, I felt for the corner of the napkin while my head went back up, for the president was now asking me questions.

"Yes, honored to be here … blessings …" I answered calmly, folding the napkin against me, only to realize the fish was gone. " … delighted …" I stalled, eyes searching for a sign of it somewhere, thinking I could hide it under my shoe. I did not see it anywhere.

Oh no. It's under his shoe! My face burned red.

Never getting asked back here again!

Finally, after what seemed an agonizing ten minutes, the president left, and I guiltily sat back down in my chair. "Jambo," I said to Bria, for we were alone.

"Jambo …" she said slowly, staring down at the ground. "I think I found your fish."

Standing in a safari bus for hours with the wind in your face and sun on your skin as you race at the base of Kili alongside hyenas and giraffes is exhilarating. Our team, which includes married couple Andrew and Dr. Roberta ('Bobbi'), Mom, Bria, Elizabeth our host, and I have laughed so hard together, I had to start a quote list:

"This is on my shower playlist," Andrew had said of a song. "I have a sleep playlist too, but I never listen to it."

"You have to experience the African massage," one of our guides told us. It is a phrase used to describe the impossible pain of unexpected potholes on an African road.

"I'm not bougie but I really like things that are effective," Bobbi said.

"I will never forget this, Anthony," Mom said to Andrew, seriously thinking that was his name. We called him 'Tony' moving forward.

"Everyone had a good night? No one got eaten by a lion?" A local once asked us one morning. He wasn't being funny.

"I heard you snoring," He joked to Bobbi.

"No, I was fighting a lion," Bobbi said.

"Did you win?"

"No," Bobbi replied.

Our most common quote was: "Make good choices." This applied in the most unconventional senses: 'Make good choices' could be spoken as a warning when someone was getting a little too close to a giraffe, and inevitably about to be licked by a thick, slimy-silver tongue, or simply when someone had to leave the group to go to the bathroom.

And then there were the one-liners:

"Look! It's three hyenas!"

"He doesn't want to shame you, but that's a rock."

"That's exactly what every YouTuber says."

"Are those penguins?"

"Oh ok, those raisins have legs."

"Every time you sing, they leave."

"I'm out of money. You give me a dollar." Tony told a group of women shoving beaded necklaces and feathered sculptures in our arms in exchange for money.

Perhaps the most awe-inspiring moment was when our guides took us to the remote dusty plains away from tourists to a parade of elephants. There were big daddies and little babies, all with noiseless stomps.

"This is very dangerous," our guides told us. "We've got to make sure they do not surround us, or we will die."

"What do you mean?" I whispered back intrigued.

"They will surround the van, rock it back and forth, and tip or crush us."

Fair, not ready to die out here in the alpine desert. I thought.

So when the elephants came close, our voices hushed to silence, shocked, scared, and quite literally speechless. It was surreal, a once in a lifetime moment that I lived almost in third person, hazed by the desert dust. Taking in that real moment, I resolved not to feel guilty about refraining from capturing the majesty in words or picture.

Must guard the writer's antenna. I recalled my Oxford tutor's advice.

The impact of international humanitarian work is so deep to my heart, very new and weighty. As Bobbi said, "We're not *not* going to do it. Sure, it's overwhelming, but we're not stopping."

We visited the heart of the slums on Tuesday. Even our host, Elizabeth, said she had never been in such a high-trafficked place. We parked outside of a prostitution center, and a man kept knocking on

Bria's window, her bright blond hair like a glowing magnet. But there were men stationed around our troupe to guard, and I will never forget how a man with no arm came and shoed the guy away from Bria protectively.

In the streets were corners and curves of smoke and salmonella; flies on fish skins, bare feet and bald heads, many children and scary eyes of men on us. No friendly waives, but no real hostility. All the village girls had been gathered in a tin roof building held up by two posts and mud. We were quickly ushered off the streets and led down a tight alley where the stench of lentils and human feces mixed in the warm breeze and caked your shoes. We climbed a staircase of a slanted aqua-blue building with a view of the slum roofs like a sea; uneven floor tiles and tin slats, an elevated ground against the sky. I stopped and promised never to forget that heavy barrier, suffocating freedom like the darkness of a grave. It reminded me of the top of a blockade of soldiers with shields above them as they marched toward the enemy. It seemed no one could rise above this tin canvas, this sea of poverty. To the people in the slums, there was no blue sky.

But there was a man in a bright white shirt, a long silver necklace, and a curious smile that didn't seem humanly possible. In his care were sixty-one children in this blue home he runs, and he lives on pure faith.

This was Kenya's *George Mueller*.

"This is my territory," George told our anxious faces after he gathered us in the tiny, bright blue room. He said he could not be happier, even after losing his mother to cancer, facing constant poverty, and expected anger towards certain powers. "This is home. I am happy. Life couldn't be better." Even through all the tragedies, his hope was in the same Lord as mine.

One woman shared how she grew up at the edge of the garbage dump piles. They were huge. They looked like small mountains. I saw them from a clear distance and thought they were indeed mountains at first. Birds like unearthly dinosaurs swarmed overhead tiny shadows of parents and children sifting through waste in the mountain's smoke. Everyone talked about how this was outrageously sad and infuriating. One teen mom came and stood bravely before our entire team and asked for any kind of job to provide for her toddler. She looked fifteen.

Oh Lord, I cry for these people.

It is summer now, and I am soaring through Tennessee, the Smokeys and Appalachian Mountains, on my way to Washington, D.C., and New York City for the fifth bi-annual summer road trip with Poppy and Gigi. Virginia is hilly, rainy with cold warmth and crickets, and I love it. How excited I am to turn in my life-writing Portfolio—my final Oxford assignment—read *Nightfall in New York* on Times Square, and tour monuments and museums!

Washington D.C. is fairly calm and businesslike. The culture is diverse and economical, with dog walkers and coffee shops more common than billboards and gas stations. Our car is beige, the seats uncomfortable but propelling, like how Candiceyland makes me want to sit up straight and stay clean.

I officially turned in my final Oxford assignment at The Morrow Hotel, which smells like a luxurious lobby of a Las Vegas resort, with 1930s atrium pillars, low furniture, and pastel blues. To celebrate my final Oxford assignment's submission, we ate at Hamilton's in the heart of D.C., a jazzy, patriotic pub with toucan wallpaper, luscious booths, and the best of service. Poppy, Gigi, my cousin Brooklyn, and I enjoyed laughing over shrimp linguini and a tart key lime pie with blueberry sauce. We read our road trip quote list and I shared a summary of vision for the future, which is basically that I will be writing and traveling until any major interruption.

It was in that moment I looked through the window and saw towering stone walls across the street, thinking about where I would be next year, or the next.

Who am I? Where am I going? Why am I here?

Oxford felt like a dream.

Kenya felt like an awakening.

D.C. felt like a climax. I finished college.

I sank back in my airline-stewardess-looking dress and thought about all the mysteries and adventures ahead. *Who would I meet? Where would I go?*

Later, to the rumbling of Union Station, the Lord reminded me about the endless possibilities of props in stage productions when I visited a museum that had a display of diagonal white ropes slashing in two walls of rope-sea, along with a tunnel of white that reminded me of those studios in old music videos that sometimes have large alphabet letters, a dimension of paper and space in bad dreams. But rather than one rainbow hue coloring the air, there was an ombre, slow-moving gaze that silently shifted hue to hue. I thought about the colors, textures, words, and shapes that had all swarmed through my head since Oxford, or really since being a preschool teacher—a season marked by deep writing, and loneliness. But there wasn't time to mourn over *that* ever changing.

Crickets and moonlight at an August bonfire. Middle school girls running, swinging, singing, on the porch, all friends of Angel, in that final stage you still get excited over popsicle handouts.

I am home for once, still in the Year of Travel, restless and unofficially graduated (my Oxford award ceremony will not commence until March of next year).

"What's on your mind?" Dad asks me, adjusting the wood in the fire pit.

"Oh, them." I watch a beautiful pre-teen with crimped blond hair and braces named Aylie tag my sister Angel, squealing.

It's a surprise, coming from the 'uninvolved' sister; the girl who was hardly at home, off writing thousands of book words, portfolio lines, journal words, practically going insane.

"I miss being around the girls I write for." I watch them distantly. I start to remember their names—wise Lydia and talented Shylah, laughing Evie and listening Suellen who quietly asks deep questions—all Angel's friends. Memories of being that age come closer. The feeling of being fourteen. Despite the prose, poetry, and drama I have written,

A TIME TO LEARN

I know my heart just simply wants to write for girls, to share inspiration —just like the 'Rachels' did for me.

Is it enough to just write to them?

"I miss having friends, too." I say even quieter to Dad, who frowns.

I think of the Bricks, of all our middle and high school memories, of how influential they were in shaping who I became. *Was now the time to be with people again?*

"I think I should become a youth leader or something," I throw out to Dad. "Because I don't want to just write for teenage girls, I want to live in their world."

"Wow! I was not expecting that," Dad says. It's too dark to see his face until he turns toward the fire, and I see he's smiling, too.

What I'm getting myself into! Like when I threw out the idea of running track to Dad, now that I have verbalized it, it seems there's no turning back.

"I have this feeling like I am supposed to be with these teenagers, like there's something for me to do here in Oklahoma." I think back to when I was in New York City a couple weeks ago and God put a name on my heart, but at first I really did not know why.

It is making sense now why I felt led to pray for this mysterious girl, whose name is Riley, newly-married and new to working at our church as the youth pastor's wife. When I first began to pray for Riley, I blocked out putting any sort of action behind my prayers, i.e. actually *helping* her: I never got involved with youth at our church. I worked in the executive office; I was busy and in too many adult worlds. Disclaimer after disclaimer filled my mind, but I could not deny that I felt like God wanted me to not just pray for her, but serve under her leadership.

Still, Riley is intimidating. Distinctly beautiful and evidently popular, she seems to have all the world as her friend. Riley is one of those naturally pretty girls who could go without makeup and people would never notice. I have seen pictures upon pictures of her friends, family, and unfiltered moments of hilarity, and I sense she is lighthearted and authentic—highly compelling traits to a friendless life-writer—but there is no way we could be friends.

"I don't know if Riley will consider me an asset at all," I admit to

Dad, "but at least I can be another volunteer. I will tell her I can be a youth leader."

It is inexplainable—this feeling of nudging towards a completely random opportunity. I am stepping out to do something out of sheer obedience to God, whether any of the other youth leaders or girls like me (thank God I'm used to doing life alone). I have absolutely no friends!

God, I'll step out and do this out of obedience and with joy.

CHAPTER 20
SURPRISED BY RILEY

Post-Oxford Months, Edmond, Oklahoma

… that changes right now.
—Riley Rentz

It is September now, and as the golden month promises, clean-aired and divinely simple. October is a complicated sort of beauty, leaves adrift, a new age for me, air blushing from color to ice, promising riches and rest, but September is the bland scent of apple, a waying whisper of harvest before hearth. Except today I add the spice of entering the real world of teenage girls by becoming a youth leader. Startlingly, feelings of inferiority which I have not felt since private school wash over me like a bucket of little centipedes.

"There are two rules," Elijah, Riley's husband, says to me and other volunteers arriving at his house where we gather for our first youth leaders' meeting.

I have been working in the executive office all day, head in spreadsheets, and even now numbers seem follow me. *September. Month #9. Nine has always been yellow in my mind …*

"Number one—have fun. Number two—read the sign on the door." Elijah says this with a decisive smile, as if he has rehearsed this with great joy. I expect 'remove shoes' on the door or something of that nature, but no, it is something I have to understand by moving closer … a curious runners bib is flipped to its blank side, taped on their glass door reading three words, all capped. I stop and study it, wondering what it'd be like to wear a runner's bib.

Riley must be a real runner, I think, climbing the concrete stairs and, voluntarily, preparing to take off my shoes. The door reads:

WELCOME TO HISTORY

Like September, the Rentz home is bright, clean, and orderly—endearing in small ways, like the blue-and-white China plate on their white countertop next to a wine bottle of roses. Flora is everywhere, from vines curling down on the sink to vases grounded with that deliciously honest smell of soil. There is a meticulous attention to life in the *now*, from gold-framed wedding photos to raw vegetables drying on the counter. I am scared I will mess everything up. Not the vibes (although I do feel quite like a dead leaf in comparison, wearing all-black and thinking about how much Candiceyland capitalizes on the past) but that I will expose the invisible, isolated air around me of knowing no one and nothing at all on how to act.

You've been the new girl before, I console, but it does nothing.

In a certain hue, this is more frightening than Oxford. I have no screen to hide behind, and, like the shining glints of sun in this white kitchen, everything in me is exposed. Good.

"Which one are you?" A voice says to my left.

My eyes meet a strikingly beautiful girl with glossy black hair, perhaps a year or two older, tall and effortlessly tan, with gold rings stacked on her fingers.

"Hello, I'm Candice." I blush embarrassedly.

"Like, which sister are you?" She asks with a disarming smile. "Don't you all do different things?"

I open my mouth to answer, but I am distracted as *the* Riley enters the kitchen flipping a pink hand towel over her shoulder, waving at someone in the living room.

"In your white guestroom bedspread?" A lady's voice apologizes. "No, I'm so sorry. Blueberry muffin crumbs are all in it now! I shouldn't have let my kids eat in there."

"Oh please," Riley shrugs with true dismissal, "I don't mind at all! They're fine in there."

Wow, she is gracious, I think admiringly, only to realize the dark-haired girl, who reminds me of glamorous actress and heroine Lilian Rose in *The Sinclair's Mysteries*, is waiting on a complete answer from me.

I fumble, "I'm the oldest … the writer." *Is that what she wanted to hear?*

"Ahh," she says, adding a sincere smile, "I'm Emilee!"

I see on Riley's calendar behind where she is standing that Emilee is spelled with two *E*s, for there is a 'BESTIE YOGA/ERRANDS DAY' with an 'Emilee,' and pieces click.

"That's such a lovely way to spell it," I remark, reminded that my mother almost named me Emily—and humorously, Elijah, if I had been born a boy—as documented in her pregnancy journal. Foreshadowing? Who knows!

Emilee and I put nuggets on plates and walk into the living room to talk about youth, the common interest of the night, but all I can think is how remarkably youthful and hospitable Riley is, and how those children eating muffins really ought to move somewhere else, and studying this mysterious Emilee with two *E*s. *Does Riley really have a guestroom with a white bedspread? Now* that *is hospitality!*

"Candice! You made it." Riley gives a light hug before flitting to the porch to welcome a late guest with effortless enthusiasm. When she enters again, she confirms, "Emilee is my best friend," Riley explains. "I told her all about your family. Also, I will show you my guestroom library after our meeting."

"Yes, we're besties," says Emilee merrily, who I have observed is in running clothes—the really cool and expensive kind—and sipping water from a large pink bottle with a rubber straw. "I came to help Riley with the youth group."

"Fun season!" Riley squeezes Emilee's hand.

"That's wonderful!" I smile big, enamored by how they both are so at ease and carefree, really self-assured. It seems there is no need for me here, but that's okay. Like everything else that has happened over the last five years, I am here to learn, not find friends.

Still, it makes it hard to stand on this philosophy completely when Riley invites me into the third room in the small house designated as a guest room, with floor-to-ceiling brown library shelving, and says, "I thought you would appreciate this." She walks me through her book categorization process. I barely know her, and she hardly knows me, so it amazes me when she says, "C.S. Lewis' collection," and motions to a synthetically spined shelf of cream-and-rainbow covers, "amongst others." She waves dramatically.

She reads Lewis! I literally named my dog after him. I can't help smiling.

Emilee follows in behind while twirling a strand of hair with hot-pink nails. "Remember that time we went hunting for books in St. Petersburg to take to the beach?"

"It's right here!" Riley retrieves the thick spine of a neon blue hardcover. "I hate hardcovers."

"What are your books about, Candice?" Emilee asks lightly.

I wish it were an optional question. Save all the world's icons and authorities, here I was, massively intimidated by two twenty-three-year-olds. Suddenly Oxford forums seemed like a safe place. This is real—they are real.

What in the world is happening?

I am almost too stunned to speak. For the first time, I sense a level of artificiality about me. I suddenly wish I had authored hot-pink book with 3-D lettering and a dazzling headshot with a shocking bio. Of course that would be artificial, but it would certainly seem more appealing than me in the present: glistening from the evening sun, frizzing uncontrollably, wearing an outfit too large to hold myself together and too exposing to wrap inside. I should have known better than to wear my mom's clothes. This is so eerily similar to my first day of private school when I wore my dad's oversized black shirt. Do clothes really foreshadow historic introductions such as this?

"It's a story of a teenage girl who lives in Missouri …" I cringe.

Every time I preface my books for someone, it comes out a different way. This is all wrong.

Before I can say any worse, Emilee taps her black-on-black phone to the exact page of my first book online. "Found it. So cool. I want to read it!"

"Oh, thanks!" I say skeptically. Most people may say they like to read, but it takes a special person to call spiritually topical YA non-fiction enjoyable. I neither expected nor fully wanted the world to embrace fifteen-year-old Candice unfiltered. Too narrow a road. *Why haven't I already written another book?*

"What do you like to do for fun?" I offer.

"We both read!" Riley speaks up, adjusting the stem of a rose in a vase beside the guest room window and dusting muffin crumbs off the bedspread. "And run! And travel!"

"Oh, that's amazing," is all I can say without sounding strange, for all I can think is, *Did they just read off everything I like to do?*

I doubt my hearing even more as Emilee adds, "We are training for a half-marathon." She's now reached my second book description online, eyes flicking through the summary with careful precision. "Two books? Wow."

"A half-marathon? Wow. I am nowhere near that," I redirect.

"Oh! Do you run too?" Emilee's face lights up.

Yes! I've trained my whole life to run with friends! I'll join you tomorrow. I want to blurt out. On the other hand …

Never ran in my life. Never even heard of running. I realize comparatively.

"Yes," I finally say. "Though I am nowhere close to thirteen miles. That is remarkable."

"I wasn't, either, a few months ago," Emilee reflects, as we make our way to the meeting room where Riley has begun addressing the room. "I started running in March."

"And you are already preparing to run thirteen miles?"

"I just ran four today." She laughs.

Remarkable!

The Rentz' are extraordinarily optimistic and generous hosts, with all the grace in the world. Riley showed me everything—as personal as the inside of her closet to her photo board, as well as the back story behind various artwork—and I could not help but feel shocked and honored.

They say what flows out is reveal what is within, and so I try to hold my breath so nothing comes out. All that's in me are time-sensitive emails and book manuscript deadlines, a vocabulary that ranges from 40-year-old coworkers to 60-year-old international colleagues. I have never seen anyone like Riley, a girl nearly my age and married, live in such openness and honesty to this welcoming degree; it is an unveiling of my own rigid temperament. Because of this, I try soaking in the real things everyone is saying. I've gotten rather good at asking questions. I think this is out of insecurity—me knowing everyone loves to talk about themselves. Just being talked to is so weird for me, it doesn't take much for my tank to be filled socially. Look at all this plastic rigidity inside me! Was Oxford really the culprit of turning me 40 after 18? I have so much social catching up to do. But again, it seems I was wrong when I told Dad Riley needed me. She has friends. I am here for the students, and Emilee is here for Riley.

September 13

I work late in the executive office and drive home in my gray suit jacket, not bothering to change. I need to run, but I also have our second youth leaders' meeting to attend. My stiff hips and hard-drive-of-a-brain are overheated and emotionally tight. I wish my initials were SD—like Stacy, like an SD card—and not CG, which seem to stand for Constantly Guilty.

Unthinkingly, instead of going into the house, I take off down the road, fully dressed, because runners run. It is an impulsive decision, running in work clothes, but I need a mental win.

I get back in the car and realize I'll be showing up sweating to the meeting. It can't be helped. I didn't even put my hair up. Already late.

I have this vague image of everyone sitting in the living room that night of WELCOME TO HISTORY, and so I have an idea of the faces that would be there, but it doesn't make this any less daunting, especially as I nearly ride the entire curb in sweat and nerves while turning into Starbucks, clear in view of everyone at the outdoor table. Now it's not just the remarkable Riley Rentz who is intimidating, but her beautiful best friend, who is there for the very reason I am … with clout.

Two minutes late and I don't even look like I came from work because no one sweats this much at an office. I look like I had just finished a soccer game in office clothes. My UK sneakers are sweaty, and my hands are now shaking from embarrassment. I park on the hidden side of the building so I can take the first seven steps without being seen, although some have already spotted me arriving in Jerry the 2006 Jeep.

Don't think about it, I tell myself. *Just act normal.*

Or did I need to explain myself?

There is no time to think deeply. *Be real … be real …*

"Candice is here, welcome." Elijah waves.

Ordering our coffees, we settle in for small talk. Our team tonight is larger than on that historic night and uniquely covers most demographics of age and background. One woman is involved in mental health for children and teenagers; others are parents, and several are out-of-college athletes willing to invest. I fumble where to sit and land where Emilee is opposite; Riley is beside.

I nervously sit.

"Everyone go around and share why you are here." Elijah says.

Why? Because it is time!

Why? God told me to join!

Why? This is where it's at! Oh, what isn't there to love and hate in teenagerhood?

Nerves make my heart throb fast—also this caffeine!

This is such a weighty role—being a mentor for formidable and unsure minds of sixteen-year-olds, the ones who just dyed their own hair and don't like it; the ones who got roped in to the wrong crowd and can't get out. As Riley said, I consider it a burden and responsibility.

As I hear their own journeys, I recognize Riley and Emilee are clearly self-motivated. They have their eyes on what actually matters, with distinct drive and individualism in a non-conformist way, and so I have a ground layer of admiration. It is rare to find girls of one mind and purpose like this similar to me, especially for such critical causes like mentoring teenagers.

I don't know what they really think of me. I don't know what I even think of myself. I am not used to being around people my age like this.

The meeting ends, and I find myself lingering under the outside lights, around 8:30 p.m.

"So, what does community look like for you?" Riley asks me.

Oh no. What does she mean? My heart races.

If I say I don't have community, would she judge my lack of intention to pursue proper friends at this stage? But I can't say I had a good community; that would be lying. My community is a little around the world. I have not done life with people since Missouri since the beginning of high school.

In one giant flash, I think of leaving my old friend group, the Bricks, missing out on doing school with them because of moving to Oklahoma. I think of the cheerleaders at private school inviting me to join their clique, and then me leaving the school to be homeschooled. I think of the football games I never went to, the lunch outings and girls' trips and parties and homecomings and everything exciting associated with high school and college. My mouth gets dry, and I think about how college is over. I am an adult. All that's left is to work and die.

But you were obedient. I remind myself. *Obedience led to the blessing of Oxford.*

I explain this to Riley and Emilee in a short version. My whole life is now laid out before two beautiful strangers, and I have no idea how they will respond. All I can think about are past situations of rejection from girls in junior high and high school, of supposed 'covenant friendships' that turned to ice. This is, without a doubt, scarier than Oxford.

"Well, that changes right now," Riley says instantly. "Consider yourself part of our friend group."

What in the world? Does she say this to everyone?

As if reading my thoughts, Riley proceeds to say, "We don't say this to everyone."

"You don't even know me," I say quietly.

And I don't know you ... I think. But I admire what I do know about you.

"Props to you for writing two books," Emilee adds. "It shows the discipline and character that you cultivated in your life when no one was watching."

"Thank you," I breathe softly. Hearing this from someone my age, not a family member or tutor who expects it from me—makes me, for the first time in what feels like years, feel seen.

"Also, you're turning 21, right?" Riley asks.

How does she know that?

"What are your plans?"

"Oh, um ..." I fumble, embarrassed. "Nothing has really been planned yet."

"Oh!" Riley claps her hands. "We should throw Candice a party!"

"Yes!" Emilee exclaims. "We should have everyone speak in a British accent!"

"I ... I don't know what to say," I stutter.

"Candice, don't you worry," Riley puts an arm around me. "You are officially in our friend group."

The rest is, in fact, history.

It feels like a lifetime ago Riley uttered the life-changing words that I was unconditionally going to become her friend. Disbelieving, just like my reluctance to become a poet, that the cultivation of a kindred spirit friendship was impossible to ascertain. When one has been rejected, the idea of love again is always cautious.

But if there is one thing Riley does not bow to, it is timidity.

Perceptively, Riley is extroverted and intimidating; intimately, she is down-to-earth and profound. You can't see her and not get excited. Deeply transparent, she often says, "My life is an open book," but with a clear gift for discernment and a mind that could easily suit an FBI Forensic Analyst, I recognize she is coded with many mysteries no one may ever unlock.

Naturally curious and intuitive, Riley has streetwise approachability and knows cultural cues so well that she has the status of passing classes easily, leading friend circles effortlessly, and conquering defining feats such as climbing mountains, running marathons, or initiating confrontational conversations. That last one is especially attractive to me, a non-conformist who has long yearned to be with people who think deeply and aren't afraid to express those deep things, even if it proves to be controversial. Riley does this all while possessing an inner tenderness, a mature appreciation for hidden and seen expressions of truth and beauty.

Half-Hispanic and Mexican, Riley has deep green eyes, beautiful tan skin, and wavy brown hair glistening with blond highlights. Her favorite colors are pink, orange, and white—mentally, I think of flora in this color scheme being tossed from her arms to the world. She likes fizzy sodas and scary movies, Oreos accompanied with milk, and, like me, she has a strong conviction against ill-fitted things and seeks perfection, whether aligning pictures in a scrapbook, arranging books by spine colors, or doing a vibe check in a struggling social dynamic.

Like most people when watching a confident and articulate stranger from afar, I found it at first rather daunting talking to her. She seemed as though she was looking right through me! Not one for assuming I have a mask on per se, I realized I do, when my face reddens, and she says something about what I feel that I thought was hidden within the caverns of my soul.

Deep poetry, deep friendships.

Unpretentious and unassuming, just what a girl dreams to become.

When I see Riley through the executive office window wildly erasing a white board in a French smock, hair in a messy bun with straying wisps in her eyes, it reminds me of my own rigidity—buttons fastened up to my collar, hair slicked in a braid, nose red from denting glasses after hours of copywriting. Through elements like her subtle style, I notice just how rosy she sees life, and yet it is not at all through a lens of fake ideals, for she is an objective stater of reality and decidedly calls things like they are, but this is where the genius comes in: she has a keen sense of recognizing stagnant potential and chooses to see beyond what might have been or what is and looks into what *could be*. It could be no more evident than her taking a chance on me.

Not only did Riley and her friend Emilee throw me an elegant surprise party for my twenty-first birthday, they invited me into their intimate core circle of friends without even fully knowing me. Ashamedly, I did not believe them when they mentioned a party on the night of September 13. I had absolutely no reason to believe that two absolute strangers would throw another absolute stranger a party within a month of time. Having not really heard anything firm from them within that window of time relating to a party, I assumed they forgot, but all the while they were planning a cake-and-tea affair at Emilee's sea glass house with a coral door.

"Surprise!"

There my friend Riley stood smiling, in a blue-and-white fitted sundress, barefoot with messy curls, beside a dazzling Emilee with a silk ribbon in her glossy black hair. They did it all: Sparkling pink bottles. A rainbow fruit charcuterie. Cucumber cream cheese sandwiches. Iced scones. Blueberry jam and cheese. Pumpkin squares. Porcelain cream and gold teacups and a boiling wood kettle. Personally arranged pink and purple flowers in a large blue and white vase, with another overflowing vase of tiny petals ... I could not take it all in.

Genuinely, I felt as if I was observing it in third person. Yet as surreal as it was, I do remember they had a white cake with blueberries, and I blew out candles. How kind they all are! Riley and Emilee gave a birthday card with a pink yoga mat.

"For Friday yoga class! You really must go!" They grinned.

Emilee explained from a blue chair, her dress draped over her feet in white heels, "I thought, *What kind of music would Candice like?* Well, I decided on classy jazz ... seemed to fit."

It was then the iconic song *New York, New York* played, which had left its mark on my summer road trip to New York City, and it was as if the Lord was tying together my moment of obedience to step out and be a youth leader.

All I could think about was how true it was that when you follow the Lord, you can expect three things: *obedience* on your part, which inevitably leads to *sacrifice*, but then certainly follows inconceivable amount of *blessing*.

Many may only witness the blessing when they pass through their earthly life and become fully themselves at the reconciliation of going home and existing eternally in spirit, and oh the joy of those who follow God without having experienced blessings on earth! Yet He still chooses to give us tastes of heaven, undeservingly.

Thank you, Lord, for friends!

Riley and Emilee bring the depth of the light things out of me, and so, in the last four months of knowing them, they have completely unraveled me. It would take a whole book to cover their hilarious quotes, the lessons they have taught me, and the memories we have shared *(I do plan to share them with the world someday)*.

"What do you *mean* you've never had pepperoni pizza or drank Coke?" Riley's eyes widened as her head turned to the backseat of Emilee's car to stare at me.

"I've never really thought about it," I laughed.

"Well, you're about to," Riley said emphatically.

"I have no doubt about that. You've already exposed me to Oreos and milk."

Riley grinned, "You just wait, Candice. We'll teach you to have fun again."

"Get this—she's never seen *Spirit*. That's core childhood," Emilee said from the driver's seat to low-humming pop music. "Hey, you should run the marathon with us next spring!"

"I still can't run four miles!" I admitted.

"Don't give me that," Emilee held up a finger. "I told you I could barely run at the beginning of this year, and you came to witness the day I crossed the half-marathon finish line. Anything is possible."

"Come on, Candice. You've got to learn to live a little!" Riley playfully slapped my arm.

I guess I am signed up to run 13.1 miles with two people I met four months ago.

CHAPTER 21
RUN CLUB

Post-Oxford months, Edmond, Oklahoma

*Live as if you were to die tomorrow;
learn as if you were to live forever.*
—Mahatma Gandhi

It is the year of the Paris Olympics. Sydney McLaughlin-Levrone's picture has been taped in my secret room alongside the other three USA 4x4 Olympic champions holding an American flag from the broadcasted night I watched them win gold in the New Orleans seafood bar. Now, Sydney is running for gold again, and I am offered a chance to train with real marathoners for Oklahoma City's largest race in remembrance of the Oklahoma City Bombing in 1995. Maybe I am crazy for signing up to run 13.1 miles with only four months of training. But this year is already purple in my mind, thanks to something deep in childhood that showed me 'four' in a shade of violet, so seeing Paris' purple Olympic track seems to yet confirm I may have been preparing for this long distance race my entire life.

You really shouldn't wake up one morning and decide to run thirteen miles (or twenty-six, as far as that goes, which Riley and Emilee are training to do). You must give up everything you've ever valued—

sleep, snacks, time, and energy—to profit one gain: winning gold. Just like you can't graduate from Oxford overnight, it will take sacrifice, discipline, and a collection of insignificant moments to prepare to win.

In my case, gold is crossing the finish line without dying. I don't even care if I am last. *Just finish, and don't lose your new friends in the process,* is all I can ever hope to obtain.

My introduction to Riley and Emilee's infamous Run Club happens upstairs on a snowy January night in downtown Oklahoma City's Peret's Dessert and Coffee Bar. I find it, apprehensively, up an elevator of an obscured building, after cluelessly wandering the exceptionally busy lounge before seeing Riley and Emilee's animated tan faces at a faraway table.

Thank goodness I am not with cheerleaders. I think back to high school nerves of meeting scary popular girls at downtown social events.

"It's time to initiate Candice into Run Club." Emilee pulls up a chair.

"Are you ready for this, Candice?" Riley asks a final time. "You've been entered into the most active group chat of your life."

"There's no turning back now." I laugh.

My first text is from an unknown guy named Justin:

> Welcome to run club. have you been informed of the very real very serious rules?

Emilee responds in the group chat titled 'Run Club' with two emojis I have never used together in my life along with:

> not yet.

She adds:

> we wouldn't dare give them without u.

Justin, the unofficial bearded leader of this exclusive club, proceeds to list the rules, which I hold my breath while reading:

> rule number uno: running sucks. Rule numero two: do the pose after your next run. send us your run. we gas you up. (examples of said pose will be shared in a bit). rule 3: this chat is for bragging and hyping each other up. so brag whatever run you do! if you do anything at all ... a win is a win!

Several pictures are sent of people making the Run Club sign ('I love you' in sign language), sticking out their tongue. Justin adds:

> previously mentioned pose, with room for your personal variation and creativity if desired.
> excited to have ya candice!

"She's official!" Riley says aloud.

And with that, my initiation into long distance running is permanently irreversible.

It was one thing to try to learn the language of Run Club, the slang and jargon used to hype and vent while hyperventilating. It was another thing to show up at Lake Hefner to run six miles for the first time in a twenty-degree windchill. I wasn't letting myself think about it, not my inefficient layers, my old high school track tennis shoes, hair and headgear—no, I let myself agonize over it.

Who knew that fear controlled so much of my relationships, even running itself? Every text that came through in such an endearing, uncapitalized style sent me into panic. Would I, Candice, send a text back with no caps? Could somewhere in the metaverse my Oxford professors see my error and choose to reverse my merits and distinctions?

Deep down, their way of writing in casual abbreviations was so terribly intimidating, and even a bit admirable. It now seemed wrong to respond with normal grammar and punctuation. I would have to prove to myself that I could learn to speak like them and prove it to them I could endure the long and dreaded lake stretch in the cold come Saturday morning.

Riley and I have a youth event to attend on Saturday morning before the first group run, and she offers to drive me to Lake Hefner. This is during three weeks of early morning prayer we have as a church, one of my favorite times of the year, so we attended the prayer service together before the youth event and the run to follow. I am already praying for physical growth, so it seems fitting to throw in during my prayer this morning that I hope I don't die next to my new friend, who happens to be extremely fit. Funnily enough, I remember meeting Riley at a prayer service last August, but we did not hit it off. It shows how God is the one that brings friendships together at the right time. *For everything there is a season …*

"Oh! You're repping your high school track team shirt!" Riley exclaims as we change clothes in the bathroom. She is wearing her high school long sleeve shirt as well.

Off to a good start, I think as I slide into her white Ford, heart beating from nerves and the slicing air that froze us just walking to her car. *How in the world are we running in this?*

"What is your car's name?" I ask.

"It doesn't have a name." Riley looks at me strange.

"Oh, well we must name it then. Does it have any endearing qualities?"

"Well, it's faithful."

"Alright, he's a faithful one."

"*She*, Candice, it's most definitely a 'she.'"

"She's a faithful one, then." I laugh.

Faithful drives us to the vast Lake Hefner, with a white lighthouse and seaside restaurants, like Red Rock Canyon Grill. Cold knives invisibly cut into us as we emerge once again outside into the age of icicles. Snow still froze bits of grass and mud filling the cracks of lakeshore rocks while the waves tossed with a furious mist as gray clouds above darkened the sun. It is beautiful.

Is that Leanna, Christian, and Justin? I stare ahead at the three famous runners. They feel like celebrities. They *are* celebrities. Their names have popped up on my phone every day for the last two weeks in running selfies, commenting on each other's times, and congratulating newer runners on consistency in short runs. They are all young parents from different families, all highly successful in media and marketing careers. And here they are, having given up a slow Saturday morning drinking coffee with their dog and spouse, being a parent, sharing little moments. This is one of the first things I learn about them: they genuinely miss their kids, even though the run would take less than three hours. They value the cold, the pain, the strenuous exercise after a sleepless night, that betters them as a spouse and parent. That's commitment.

One mile in, Justin cracks jokes, and Christian gives disclaimers on why he was not meant to run in this kind of cold, being Puerto Rican. Leanna, who has long, silky hair tied with a white ribbon, runs gracefully beside me, sharing how she, too, is new to long distance running, but had an inkling to sign up for the half-marathon.

Riley keeps our pace up at the front of the pack, while Justin rounds up the end. Emilee couldn't make it this first day, but everyone talks so highly of her being the inspiration behind Run Club, and really, a core leader and motivator.

I can honestly say I feel no pain the first or even second mile. Breathing is excruciating just because of how cold it is, how much effort it takes for your lungs to rise up and down under so many thick layers that somehow still let wind pierce through the holes.

I have random moments where a needle of air slits down my neck as my jacket twists, stinging like a wasp. But it is exhilarating. Here I am, running with friends in an actual running club, hardly gasping any worse than everyone else. I slow down around mile three when the trail widens out from trees and the slate lake landscapes our view on the right. But not everyone reacts as I expect; it almost brings a relief of tension to a run that fell silent half a mile back.

"I needed that," Justin says, unscrewing the lid to a water bottle strapped in a glove.

I need that, I think, realizing I didn't bring any sort of hydration or fuel.

Everyone had a reason why they run, but it really all boils down to perseverance. Mental fortitude. Pushing yourself physically so you can endure everything else in life.

"It's about doing something hard in community," Justin explains as we reach mile four.

I have run this distance before, but definitely not recently. I start to sweat even while shaking with frosty red hands. It feels so victorious. So adrenalizing.

"It's about doing something you didn't think you could do thirty minutes ago," Christian emphasizes, quoting Philippians 4:13: "For I can do everything through Christ, who gives me strength."

"Have you ever thought about Philippians 4:12?" Riley sticks a glove in her mouth to pull out her phone and read us the passage of the lesser-known verse: "I know how to live on almost nothing or with everything. I have learned the secret of living in every situation, whether it is with a full stomach or empty, with plenty or little."

"Wow ... that's so good," Leanna says between breaths. "It does seem to hit different right now when you wish you had water. Looking at you, Justin."

"I sure could use a Chick-fil-A right now," Christian comments.

"Yeah. It's crazy to think ..." I gasp in between words, "Christ really is the secret to living anywhere or doing anything."

"Facts," Justin said, and we all put in music for the final mile.

As Riley leans in and we share music, she starts laughing. "If running with Candice, be prepared to listen to anything from Irish to afrobeats to Veggie Tales!"

"You never know with me!" I skip ahead of the group to do an Irish kick.

If only they knew the journey of my entertainment!

I can't imagine anyone running today. Even in March, ice slicks the roads and wind cuts your ears just by walking to the car. Like their summers, Oklahoma's winters can be oddly extreme. So are the texts I read in the

Run Club group chat. It is the most entertaining part of the day. I almost need Riley sitting next to me to culturally translate the words and phrases used. I love learning how to sound like a 'real' Run Club member:

> The wind was brutal. I was running at like 13:00 pace hardly moving and my heart rate was at 178. It was nuts. Definitely the toughest run.

> Like Candice says, lazy people have dreams too!!

> im jelly.

> zay self destructed. that was actually so hard to watch.

> This weather is so nice! My Achilles isn't strong enough to run yet, but strongly considering a good frolic in the sun.

> it got dark way earlier than i thought. i was supposed to do 6 miles but i just ran until the street lights ran out and then called my mom because i got scared.

> These excited and neutral vibes today are my spirit animal.

> This weather is amazing i could cry.

> Saturday slay.

> Who's in for a longgg run tomorrow at lake hefner??!

> 7:30 am? 16 miles (or however many u want)???

> I dedicate this run to Candice.

> yeahhh the next like 8 weeks are the really tough stretch for us. 15, 16, 9, 16, 19, 21, 9, 20 for our long runs.

> 8am lake hefner tomorrow. be there or be square.

> 15 miles on deck. it's on.

> CASUAL FRIDAY LETS GO.

> i'm sorry, so casual with 12?? Queen.
>
> When do we need to go get out stuff.
>
> Next Saturday.
>
> And then eat Texas Roadhouse.
>
> 6 miles of swollen hands.
>
> 9 works for me tomorrow !! probs gonna test out race day outfit just to make sure.
>
> DANCE THROUGH THE FINISH.

"Ah, this is the most ideal running weather." Riley and Emilee had stretched as we started our nine-mile trail run.

I still could not believe I was running with friends!

The previous night, my childhood best friend Anna came to Oklahoma for a sleepover, and we enjoyed a late night of movies, snacks, and girlhood stories. The next morning at brunch, I ordered an acai bowl, light and healthy since I would run after she left. Nine miles with Riley and Emilee in the middle of nowhere was on the agenda. I still could not believe I, Candice, the girl who had two foot surgeries and still had three screws in her left foot, was about to run *nine miles* like it was no big deal. But I felt very aggressive and invincible.

After bumping along gravel roads in Faithful, we stopped at a wooded campground welcome center that reminded me of my childhood days when we spent the month of June at a campground in Missouri: the crank of gravel, beetles and birds, the pure calm of rustling pines and water. It was a particularly summery day, and I was frustrated because I suddenly felt nauseated, especially with Riley and Emilee so happy in their neon blue and rainbow-colored crop tops and pink nails and new shoes. Whether or not my black-and-gray outfit foreshadowed a stormy run, there we were.

They were so good-natured as we set off on the first two miles. I felt dizzy, lightheaded, and positively ill, but I wasn't about to say, "Hold on, I have to throw up."

But eventually I did say that, multiple times. Nothing happened.

There was a simultaneous ultra-marathon happening on the trail we were on, and every runner that passed me looked just about how I felt: dying a slow death.

Lord, please take away this feeling, I prayed.

It was the strangest thing. Deep down, I felt God wanted to test me.

I ran the first two miles feeling this way. I laughed and kept pace and did my best to be good-natured, but God began to humble me when I couldn't hide it anymore. Riley and Emilee knew I'd run eleven miles before; I wasn't a new runner anymore, so nine wasn't the problem. My feet did not even hurt. I was just plain sick.

God, why can't I just throw up? I prayed, but by the middle point of the run, God brought to mind all the times I pushed boundaries with Him, justifying sin. Every step tested my trust in His sovereignty, my repentance from sin, and my literal physical stamina to endure being sick in the middle of the woods with no water.

While Riley and Emilee sang songs I did not know, I prayed.

When they had to stop and rest because of me, I thanked God for teaching me humility.

Eventually, their lighthearted conversation shifted to how good hot dogs and pretzels at gas stations were, and I finally swerved off the trail and threw up. Of all the times, this runner guy came up behind me and stopped to talk.

"Hey! How's it going? Are you okay?"

I wiped hairs out of my eyes and looked up at him like, *What do you think?*

"Oh ..." he said, realizing what was happening.

Talk about humiliation! There was nowhere to hide. I had no water or purse, no place of privacy or recovery. I just had to stand up, leave my dirty hair as it was, dust mud off my knees, and walk back to the glowing girls in the trees, feeling like I may as well be naked, too.

But despite the dismantlement of the next two miles that followed, I sensitively knew Jesus was with me. Had he not suffered more? Each time a terrible wave of pain came. I tried to think of that. I didn't know which was harder: the actual sickness or the social embarrassment and vulnerability.

This feels a lot like having a nut allergy reaction, I thought. There were times I had to smile. I had to be quiet even when I wanted to say something, due to being sick with nausea. I had to smile for pictures (hilarious to look back on now!). I had to leave be sick then come back and keep pace. I had to be dead to myself, not allowing it to bother me how Riley and Emilee had a great many reasons to leave me, to never invite me back on a run. There's nothing I did to deserve such good friends, and yet it hurt most watching them be friends to me.

Riley came into a bathroom where I had just thrown up again. "Candice? I brought your water for you. No pressure at all, but we are in the car ready to go when you are, only because we know you want to be home."

What friend would venture in? What friend would care?

Then I realized, that was what made Riley, *Riley*. She was that friend who walked with you into your darkest moments and stood by you unconditionally.

It was at this third stop I felt the most sick compared to every moment up to that point. I could only lift my head to the skylight and pray whatever the plague was to come out all the way.

"Poor Candice," Emilee sympathized through the rearview mirror where I cried. Tears streamed down my face, and I dry heaved and threw up all the way to Riley's house.

Delusional but not defeated, I then drove myself home, trying not to crash as I cried and threw up. It was not wise to drive, but I was disillusioned. I wanted to speed. I wanted to honk and pass the white truck taking its time, but God was teaching me patient endurance. *Couldn't you heal me now, Lord?* I asked, but no, I'd pushed and pushed for my own way so many times.

I was sick of all facades, of all the pride that came with feeling as though I had expectations to uphold, to look and act a certain way around friends. They had now not only seen me at my worst, but had to live it with me, and nothing could erase it from their memory.

I was sick of being sick.

Secretly, I knew the acai bowl had nuts in it. I also knew I had eaten it before and not been sick. Why would I risk it?

Because I was used to pushing the envelope.

Used to compromise.

Used to being stubborn and getting away with it.

Used to disregarding my body was God's temple.

It was a dramatic flash back to dyeing my hair, pushing for the 'unnatural.'

Alone on the floor in Candiceyland, everything turned still and white.

Flashes of Riley almost stepping on a snake and a tick crawling up my leg in the car played in my mind. I felt everything had come to a climax. I would either blackout or die.

I prayed. *I now understand Your complete sovereignty.*

Then I thought about how I wouldn't get to say goodbye to people.

At least the world has my journals ... I thought, and then my eyes closed.

A period of time passed, but I wasn't aware.

Then my eyes opened.

I felt beside me for my phone and barely had enough energy to call my mom.

"I need a hospital," was all I could think to say, knowing I would soon fall unconscious.

"Oh, hi Canzie!" Mom said. "You probably just need water, you runner you. Wow! Nine miles is a long time. And it's hot today!"

"Mom, I think I need an ambulance."

My throat felt like it was closing.

It was absolutely a nut reaction. I had never had one so severe.

"Oh, you'll be fine," Mom said. "I have to run downtown to drop off Bria, I'll be back soon. Drink some water and lay down."

"*Goodbye, Mom. ...*" My eyes closed again.

God must have known I had more books to write before I died. Miraculously, it passed. Mom apologized when she found out it was a nut allergy reaction (to her credit, she did not know), and best of all, Riley and Emilee are still my friends. I have no idea how that is possible.

I am the happiest I have been all spring because I no longer compromise in little areas, and because of Run Club, I have accountability in my runs. I have learned so much from each person on our team that I really could fill an entire book.

Watching the dynamic of Riley and Emilee's relationship is so refreshing and eye-opening, an exposure to what true friendship looks like when two girls are totally transparent, yet with a deep level of respect and understanding and grace for one another.

"Remember I started running one year ago," Emilee tells me on our run. "I couldn't run at all before then. Now I am about to run a full marathon."

And I thought I was disciplined!

As I really got to know Emilee, I soon couldn't imagine life without her, for we were literally doing life together, nearly every day—leading a high school girls small group, on our way to a run or yoga class or a simple Target run, or to watch movies at Riley's house.

Gracious and unassuming with effortless charm, Emilee is a real depiction of actress and heroine Lilian Rose, with glamorous unflappability that makes her easily approachable while remaining completely iconic. As an overthinker who never schemes, Emilee loves clarifying and deep questions, so we immediately click. Privately, she reads fantasy and is a digital journaler, publicly, she possesses an eloquent presence and could easily pass as royalty.

"What can I say, I am Italian!" Emilee often says, tying on an apron to cook homemade spaghetti. A relaxed hostess gifted with hospitality, she is by nature quieter than Riley, but still has strong opinions about everything from sports to politics, and having lived most of her childhood in Hawaii, she cares for many plants and often talks about how she belongs at the sea.

Emilee Catherine, as I sometimes use her middle name, knows the lyrics to every song that has ever played, every movie and its cast, and she herself sings the National Anthem at pickleball tournaments; a former show choir enthusiast, once traveling to Scotland in troupe. As easygoing as she is, she is, like Riley, full of complexities: pouring her milk before the cereal ("so the cereal stays crunchy"); her house is full of neutrals, but she herself is often dressed in hot pink or red. She may be in platforms one day and Air Force sneakers the next. She is stubborn and daring like me, and yet carries the gift of a peacemaker, like Kelly Grace.

"I can't believe I am just now meeting you at this stage in life," I tell Emilee on a run. "We live minutes from each other. We both moved to Oklahoma in high school. We both run at the same park …"

"God's timing is everything." She points a gold-ringed finger to the sky.

"Alsoooo," I drag out, suddenly thinking, "I can't believe you even live on the road that you do." I am realizing just how significant this is. "When I was fourteen and our family came to Oklahoma on casual road trips, we stayed at multiple Airbnb houses right down the road. It was in one of those homes I heard the story of Rachel Scott, which made me begin journaling and changed my life forever—in a way, leading me to Oxford."

"God really does orchestrate things in our lives we have no idea about!" Emilee smiles.

"He still is!" I laugh, for it seems our adventures together are just beginning …

Christian texts on race day:

> SHOUTOUT RUN CLUB FOR GETTING US THROUGH OUR FIRST MARATHON TRAINING EVER I'M SO THANKFUL FOR Y'ALL.

At 4:22 a.m., Riley sends Run Club the best type of motivation, reminding us that the physical and spiritual are connected:

> *Therefore, since we are surrounded by such a huge crowd of witnesses to the life of faith, let us strip off every weight that slows us down, especially the sin that so easily trips us up. And let us run with endurance the race God has set before us. We do this by keeping our eyes on Jesus, the champion who initiates and perfects our faith. Because of the joy awaiting him, he endured the cross, disregarding its shame. Now he is seated in the place of honor beside God's throne. Think of all the hostility he endured from sinful people; then you won't become weary and give up. After all, you have not yet given your lives in your struggle against sin.[1]*

It's dark and raining. I have been up since 3:30 a.m. After a breakfast of blueberry waffles and eggs, I drive to Riley's house where the smell of bacon fills the white kitchen. We paint glitter in our hair and tape up our feet and knees for the big day.

Riley's dog, Luna, digs in the trash.

"I say, describe to me your dogs," I later ask Riley and Emilee in Faithful the car, recalling how James in my Wolvercote cohort was so good at starting discussions in this manner.

I love learning new things about them; for they are both so individual and distinct! I could write a **RILEY AND EMILEE** dictionary —but would it fully do them justice? All their character qualities are so endearing and beautiful, and they bring out ten-year-old Candice who used to express herself through double-scooped ice cream and dance. *Is 'used to' even correct anymore?*

Hold the Line plays from Faithful's speakers, and as I watch blurry skyscraper outlines pass, I feel love for my city, forever surprised at the turn of events for having friends in Oklahoma—just like what I prayed on the night of my sixteenth birthday party!

"I'm pretty convinced my dog Luna is the runt of the litter," Riley says from the driver's seat. "She's just so tiny and funny; she loves trash and has the attitude of a teenage girl, dramatic and chill. A messy husky with bright blue eyes and a tumor. I treasure every day with her."

"My dog Moses, on the other hand, is an Australian shepherd," Emilee dabs glitter in her ponytail. "A very illegally bred backyard dog that doesn't have all the normal features; shorter paws and brown, he has a dot on his nose. You're gonna leave his house with a wound. A very big, extroverted people person. Spazz. Very active, loves to run.

Loves attention. Honestly, he could run the marathon with us. He's done all the training."

"True," Riley nods.

Unfortunately, Moses did not come, but we do meet up with Justin, Christian, and Leanna and put on ponchos because it is raining. I wish I could write down every Justin joke, Leanna reflection, Christian story, Emilee surprise, and Riley breaking-news announcement. I am adrenalized by the vibrant green city trees, the neon purples and blues on athletes, the frightening wind and foam shoes and .5 selfies. I think of all our runs when we didn't even run, but instead chose to skip, dance, laugh, groan, limp, stretch, and fist bump our way to the lighthouse finish line at Lake Hefner. Now, we run the victory lap.

I ran the half-marathon! I felt completely ready, prepared, and strong. All we can do is prepare ourselves. Victory belongs to the Lord.

Performance is perfected not merely in the hours before, nor even the days before, but in the weeks and months leading up to the race.

Although my coworker Vanessa let me borrow her cute pink running skirt (and I finally found a way to secure my phone on a run!), I knew appearance wasn't everything, it was the character and endurance that was built inside of me that mattered most of all.

Everything you sacrifice adds up. Everything you accept or refuse lifestyle-wise builds what you think and who you are. During the race, I passed people who weren't as disciplined in their training, but people passed me who are more disciplined than me, training year round; they certainly didn't make excuses. Discipline can always be increased.

The first part of the race was the most fun: standing in the dark corral under drizzly rain with Run Club in downtown Oklahoma City with thousands upon thousands of participants, counting down to the gunshot. Next was running up Gorilla Hill eating bananas at mile six, where we split off and I put on my headphones. I passed a lot of people at this point and focused on the race set before me. It rained again and was so cold, but I just ran eight, nine, ten miles … it felt so surreal! At the final stage I caught up with Leanna, and we ran with the joy of winning set before us. "I'm going to sprint to the finish," I told her sooner than I should have, for the finish line seemed to move away as I ran fast and hard to get my silver medal and chocolate milk. Everything burned, but what felt best was being victorious at the finish line. I wasn't even lightheaded! Poppy, Dad, Mom, Kelly Grace, and Jordan were all there, and I vaguely remember seeing other friends like Ashlyn, Kaitlyn, Jonathan, and Stoney cheering on Run Club, too.

How thankful I am for Run Club, for the sweat, tears, and pain!

CHAPTER 22
LOOK UP, THE SKY LIES OPEN

Sheldonian Theatre, Oxford, England

Then do the multitude cry out, "A miracle of genius!"
Yes; he IS a miracle of genius, because he is a miracle of labor.
—Sydney Smith

Four years after stepping into Candiceyland to do hidden work alone, I wear a blue dress and walk down the aisle of the Sheldonian Theatre at the University Oxford to receive an award of Distinction from the world's top university. Drinking it in, I can't help but think …

if I had not left Missouri on January 4 to begin a new life in Oklahoma,
if I had not learned what it meant to stand and be a light at private school,
if I had not left private school to pursue isolated study in anonymity,
if I had not applied myself in further study during the anonymous final years of school,
if I had not clicked the orange 'Apply' button to get into the University of Oxford,

if I had not prayed, journaled, and digitalized my journals into books,
I would not be here in the Sheldonian Theatre shaking the Vice-Chancellor's hand.

"I am delighted to recognise your success," the Vice-Chancellor addresses the room. "It is your determination and perseverance that has enabled you to be here today and I applaud you for this."

I smile and breathe deep, no longer held in mid-air, breath sucked in. I look over at Sarah in real life, my fellow Wolvercote friend, and up in the galleries at my family.

"The aim of the University of Oxford is to teach you not only knowledge in your chosen subject area, but just as importantly, lifelong skills in how to learn, how to engage constructively with differing opinions, how to be unyielding in your search for truth, and how to remain curious. This is the transformational power of education. I am certain you will find exciting and fulfilling ways of using your new-found knowledge and I wish you every success for the future." The Vice-Chancellor finishes, and to my surprise, the guest lecturer chosen to present at my award ceremony speaks on the value of 'play,' and how play is not just for children …

"QUEEN CANDICE." Emilee writes to me, and as I slip out of my blue dress after 1:00 a.m, and a long drinks reception in perfectly fitting heels, I can't help but think …

if I had not given my life to God,
if I had not started to journal and wrestle my faith at age 14,
if I had not committed to studying God's word throughout high school,

if I had chosen not to get up early and run in the dark,
if I had not refused the wrong friends even when I was lonely,
if I had not guarded my entertainment and influences,
I would not be here, pure in heart, healthy with the right friends, at peace with God.

Standing at the top of the Devon Tower in downtown Oklahoma City, up on the 49th floor inside Vast's elegant restaurant, next to Stacy, and my other admin friends from the executive office, I lean to her and whisper, "Thank you."

She is, quite literally, my mentor: her profile is pinned in my text messaging app, and her voice is in my head during big decisions. "Thank you for teaching me to embrace learning."

"Remember when I asked you, 'What's holding you back? What are you afraid to do on your own? What do you feel you don't have permission to lead?'" Stacy reflects.

I laugh, staring out the glass wall, down at the lights of the city. *My* city.

The last time I stood here, I did not have friends, or college assurance, or really anything but the trust that if I obeyed God, everything would work together for good—even if that good was different than what I had in mind.

"Thanks to you, Stacy, I don't fear phone calls, or driving to sketchy parts of the city, or even confrontational conversations …" I see Riley approach us. "You changed my life."

"*There* you are!" Riley runs toward me, and I find my glass almost spilling as she pulls me by the arm towards a group of youth leaders. "We can't have a picture without Candice!"

To the song *Dancing in the Fire* I run up the hill toward the yellow cottage in my old neighborhood in Missouri, reminded that the best kind of blessings are surprises that come from God, not the ones you force on yourself. And yet you can still track the connection of choices and consequences in things as little as what you eat, what you wear, and the songs you endorse.

I lower my posture and quicken my pace at the curve in the road, where the tire grip marks start. These tire marks weren't here when I was a child. We slid on ice.

"Are you going back to Oxford?"

"What about journalism—have you considered Harvard?"

"When is your time to love!!" Peoples' well-meaning questions fill my mind, too, for what twenty-one-year-old girl isn't already thinking about it?

Sometimes it is easier not admitting that there is a time for everything, but I dare not follow what is easy or expected. Something has brought me back home to Missouri. Something is left for me to do. Do I know all of it yet? Well, no great ending concludes all questions.

Goodbye, Oxford … for now.

*Let this be the ending of the book
but by no means the end of the searching.*
—*Thomas Merton*

ACKNOWLEDGMENTS

Tremendous thanks to the team behind *A Time to Learn*: in a split second of time, Allison photographed me as I walked into the Sheldonian Theatre; Lauren Short then executed such a timeless cover design; Kelly astutely proofread the manuscript as its very first reader; Ingrid Williams gifted hours of editing expertise and was a sincere answer to prayer, and Christopher Maselli's publishing knowledge was a true blessing. Stacy let me publish her quotes, which was a big ask (or rather, big risk, since it was without her consent). Thanks to her, I answer emails in a timely manner. Riley and Emilee, bringing the 'depth of the light things' as they do, would not settle for anything less than the perfect graduation dress—thanks to Riley, after a strenuous day of editing, I tasted pepperoni pizza and Coke for the first time, and Emilee volunteered to fly with me to London on a whim for an alumni conference while I wrote *A Time to Learn* ("I am just the sort of person who'd love standing in heels at an event with you!"). Thanks to my dear friends and family in Missouri and Oklahoma, supporting me even when I am an irritable nerd. Charlie, my little Ratatouille dog, has now been with me through three books, three foot surgeries, and three moves. Special thanks also to my Oxford friends and tutors, namely Andrea Campbell's letters of writing motivation; and all figures in history who formed parts of my character during my anonymous years: Dietrich Bonhoeffer, Elisabeth Elliot, Rachel Scott, and Christina Rosetti, to name a few. Finally, thank you Wildflowers—*Aylie, Angel, Anelia, Cora, Evie, Hazel, Ivey, Lizzy, Lydia, Lori, Maerin, Phoebe, Sarah N., Sarah W., Shylah, and Suellen*—for being fans of the *Times* Series, and to *all* readers who have enjoyed this series and decided to embark on the adventure of following God—it's not called an adventure for nothing!

Candice Gibbons is the author of *A Time to Trust* and *A Time to Stand* (Trilogy Christian Publishing, 2022). She graduated in 2023 from Oxford University with an Undergraduate Diploma in Creative Writing. Since the age of fourteen, Candice has compiled an estimate of over half a million journaled words. When not adding to this number by hand, she may be running or writing, traveling to document others' stories, or simply at the pool with friends. Candice mostly writes for teen girls, but readers of all ages can stay up to date by following her on Instagram, as there is *always* a book in the wings.

instagram.com/author_candicegibbons

BOOKS BY CANDICE GIBBONS

THE *TIMES* SERIES
A Time to Trust (**Book #1**)
A Time to Stand (**Book #2**)
A Time to Learn (**Book #3**)

A fast-paced series documenting one girl's coming-of-age through seasons of obedience, sacrifice, and blessings.
Order online at Amazon.com.

COMING SOON
Memories in Missouri: An Ozark Childhood

END NOTES

1. FEUX D'ARTIFICE

1. "Enneagram Type 1: The Reformer," *The Enneagram Institute*, 14 Feb. 2024, www.enneagraminstitute.com/type-1/
2. "ISFJ Personality (Defender)." *16Personalities*, www.16personalities.com/isfj-personality

2. DANCING IN THE FIRE

1. Psalm 119:143 (NLT)
2. Joshua 1:8 (NIV)
3. Joshua 1:9 (NIV)
4. Psalm 136:16 (NLT)
5. Proverbs 24:10 (NLT)
6. Ephesians 1:11 (MSG)

5. EXPLICITLY CHILDHOOD

1. Isaiah 40:31 (ESV)

7. JO WRITES

1. Romans 1:20 (NIV)
2. Gibbons, Candice. *Morality: The Nature of God*, Challenge III Philosophy Class. Presented 6 December 2019.

8. REBEL INTRO

1. 1 Corinthians 9:27 (NLT)
2. Longfellow, Henry Wadsworth, "The Rainy Day"

9. LOCKDOWN

1. "Declaration of Emergency" approved by Dan O'Neil, Mayor. Signed 18 March 2020. City of Edmond, OK, City Clerk's Office. Natalie Evans, City Clerk.
2. Daniel 10:19 (NLT)

11. IT'S JUST ENTERTAINMENT!

1. 1 Corinthians 8:9–13 (NIV)

12. THE EXECUTIVE OFFICE

1. Keller, Matt. *The Key to Everything* (Nelson Books, 2015), 28, 47.

13. NEWS THAT STAYS NEWS

1. Matthew 6:30 (NLT)

16. A MODERN POET

1. Lewis, C.S. *Mere Christianity*. (HarperCollins, 1952).

17. YOU THINK LIKE A CAMERA

1. Isaiah 5:20 (NCV)

21. RUN CLUB

1. Hebrews 12:1–4 (NLT)

Printed in Great Britain
by Amazon